FINDING OUR GROVE

FINDING OUR GROVE

A Story about Life, Family, and College Football

JAMES GARDNER

ISBN: 979-8-218-74039-9

The groves were God's first temples.

—William Cullen Bryant

All that is gold does not glitter,
Not all those who wander are lost;
The old that is strong does not wither,
Deep roots are not reached by the frost.

—J.R.R. Tolkien,
The Fellowship of the Ring

For Mom—my first teacher, and
For all the guys that came along on our wanders,
And for all the gals who encouraged us to go.

Welcome to Holland

When you're going to have a baby, it's like planning a fabulous vacation trip – to Italy. You buy a bunch of guidebooks and make your wonderful plans. The Coliseum. The Michelangelo David. The gondolas in Venice. You may learn some handy phrases in Italian. It's all very exciting.

After months of eager anticipation, the day finally arrives. You pack your bags and off you go. Several hours later, the plane lands. The flight attendant comes in and says, "Welcome to Holland."

"Holland?!?" you say. "What do you mean Holland?? I signed up for Italy! I'm supposed to be in Italy. All my life I've dreamed of going to Italy."

But there's been a change in the flight plan. They've landed in Holland and there you must stay.

The important thing is that they haven't taken you to a horrible, disgusting, filthy place, full of pestilence, famine and disease. It's just a different place.

So, you must go out and buy new guidebooks. And you must learn a whole new language. And you will meet a whole new group of people you would never have met.

It's just a different place. It's slower paced than Italy, less flashy than Italy. But after you've been there for a while and you catch your breath, you look around…and you begin to notice that Holland has windmills… and Holland has tulips. Holland even has Rembrandts.

But everyone you know is busy coming and going from Italy…and they're all bragging about what a wonderful time they had there. And for the rest of your life, you will say "Yes, that's where I was supposed to go. That's what I had planned."

And the plan of that will never, ever, ever, ever go away…because the loss of that dream is a very very significant loss.

But…if you spend your life mourning the fact that you didn't get to Italy, you may never be free to enjoy the very special, the very lovely things…about Holland.

Our Toughest Flight

"I'm not sure I can do this." My brother's text stared at me—unflinchingly. For a moment, I contemplated texting back words of encouragement. With hindsight, I sort of wish I had. Instead, I just thought, "I hope he makes his flight." Twenty minutes or so earlier, after what seemed like a five-minute cry in the airport bathroom, I had mumbled similar words to myself. As for my son, who sat next to me as we waited for our flight, he had initially shown only signs of excitement. Now, in the moments before we boarded, his early morning smile finally began to crack with an occasional quivering lower lip.

Although heavy-hearted, there was also much to be happy about. Neatly packed in our suitcase were four crimson and cream football jerseys—all bearing number 51. Three of them had the name *Kelleher* stitched across their backs and had been dropped off at our house the night before. The fourth, an earlier Christmas gift for my son, revealed Kelleher's first name as printed across the back was *Kasey K.* None of us had ever been to an Oklahoma football game before, and I was relatively certain none of us had ever set foot in the *Sooner State*. This year would undoubtedly be different from our past football pilgrimages, as we would be guests of an actual player on the team we were visiting. For the first time, we would also be joined by our uncle—Uncle Frank.

There were new wrinkles on this trip, but the plans, like the blueprints of a house, provided a familiar and well-worn guidebook. This was not "our first rodeo." In fact, this was our eighth such "guy trip," having largely conquered the *SEC* with trips to South Carolina, Arkansas, Ole Miss, LSU, Texas A&M, Georgia, Auburn, and Alabama. After nearly a decade of fall frolic southern style, we had finally set our sights on the *Big 12* Conference (Oklahoma has since moved to the *SEC*). With our heads hung low throughout the year, when we finally looked up, it seemed fitting to look outside the deep South towards something new and different. "Keep the tradition going, no matter how hard it might feel," was our shared battle cry and with our personal connection to Oklahoma, it seemed the perfect place to do just that.

The plans were as follows: Daniel and I would fly from Cleveland to Oklahoma City via St. Louis; my brother John would fly in from Virginia; and our uncle would fly in from Miami, Florida. Together, we would rendezvous at the airport sometime in the early afternoon, grab a rental car, and take it from there. Having fallen for old John Wayne movies again in my middle age and, knowing we had several hours before our dinner reservation in Norman, I had already decided to steer our party to the *National Country & Western Heritage Museum*. They just didn't know it yet and if anyone questioned my idea, I was prepared to remind them that Wayne had played football for the University of Southern California (USC). If time allowed, and if we could muster the courage, I had also contemplated a visit to the *Oklahoma City National Memorial and Museum*. Football might be king, but long ago, our trips had taken on a more total immersion in all things local. At some point, we would need to make the 20-mile drive south to Norman, Oklahoma, and check in at the *Sooner Legends Hotel,* where I had booked two adjoining rooms. Lastly, our annual Friday night dinner, always planned by my son and my mom, had us dining at *Charleston's* with a 6:30 reservation. My mother, known by her other grandchildren as *Granny* but called *Gee* by my son, had also been known to slip Daniel cash for the dinner, allowing him to "pick up the tab." This tradition would remain, as would my son's habit of forgetting to bring his wallet to the first night's meal.

Our Oklahoma trip first took shape at Christmastime, a year before, when Daniel's childhood friend Kasey Kelleher had returned home to Cuyahoga Falls, Ohio, for the holidays. The two had graduated together earlier in the spring from Woodridge High School. Kasey, like many of Dan's friends, had gone off to college while Dan remained in his special education classes. Although Daniel was genuinely excited about the adventures that awaited his friends, my wife and I noticed a discernible level of sorrow he experienced saying goodbye to so many. Thankfully, a few have remained connected with Daniel and do so to this day.

As for Kasey, his post-high school journey had led him to Oklahoma and the Oklahoma football team, where, although red-shirted his first year, he was in line to be the starting long snapper the following season. During the winter break, the two had made plans to meet up at a high school basketball game, but after Kasey's flight was hopelessly delayed, our family left the gymnasium disappointed. It did not help that the Woodridge *Bulldogs* had lost that night as well.

The following morning, on December 23rd, we were awakened by the sound of our doorbell. My first thought was, "Why would UPS ring the bell on a Saturday morning when they could just leave the package on our porch?" To my surprise, when I arrived at the front door, I spotted Kasey and his younger brother, both dressed in Oklahoma garb. They also carried a large, wrapped gift. Fresh off a 41-17 drubbing of TCU in the *Big 12* Championship game, Daniel was given an Oklahoma *Big 12* Championship T-shirt, and the second gift was over-the-top cool. Kasey had gotten an *Oklahoma Memorial Stadium* print signed by every player on the team. NFL players, including Baker Mayfield, CeeDee Lamb, Kyler Murray, and many others, signed the print. A uniquely beautiful gift made even more special by number 51's signature and knowing that he lugged it through an airport during the holidays—all for my son.

A week later, our entire family gathered around the television, with my son donning his new *Kasey K* jersey from Santa, to watch Oklahoma duke it out with Georgia in the college football playoff held at the Rose Bowl in Pasadena. The *Sooners*, to our chagrin, lost in overtime. As for our family, we would also face our own stinging loss in the coming months.

By the following summer, during the muggy-hazy days of late July, Daniel and I had decided our next college football game would be in Norman, Oklahoma. Dan and Kasey had stayed in touch, usually via text messaging, and when I called Kasey to confirm our decision, the wheels were put in motion for our next journey. Their excitement was contagious and after a flurry of calls with family to coordinate schedules, we set our sights on the Oklahoma-Baylor game on September 29th. When I initially divulged our plans to friends and family to visit the *Panhandle State*, I had inquired if we might meet Kasey's family before the game but soon learned that although they traveled to as many Oklahoma football games as possible, it was not possible for them to attend the Baylor game. To my surprise, we were invited to sit as guests of number 51, along with other friends and families of those suiting up for the Oklahoma football team. It was the first of many countless beautiful gestures.

In the final days leading up to the game, I had been in contact with Kasey and the Kelleher family. Not only had we packed matching jerseys loaned to us by his parents to wear to the game, but Kasey had also asked me to make sure Daniel was in the front row for the "*Walk of Champions*" as the Oklahoma team exited their team buses to walk into *Gaylord Family – Oklahoma Memorial Stadium* before the much-anticipated game. He wanted it to be a surprise for Daniel, so we agreed to stay in constant contact, which I did by texting him that our flight was leaving on time and that we would see him the next day. As father and son lifted off from a Cleveland runway, we were sad but did indeed have much to be excited about.

The following day—on game day—after receiving multiple texts from an unknown team hotel and later from an unknown seat on a team bus, the reunion between two old friends would be perfectly scripted. It also helped that the *RUF/NEKS*—those *Sooner* rally leaders that race the easily recognizable little covered wagon known as the *Sooner Schooner* onto the field after an Oklahoma score—also fire shots before the game to announce the location and ultimate arrival of the team buses. It was like I had my own GPS for the entire Oklahoma team, especially No. 51 and when the buses finally arrived, Oklahoma's long snapper was one of the first players to step off and make a beeline for Daniel and our crew. The embrace that followed was a much-needed family hug. I just wish my father had been there to see it.

Daniel

Decades before the trip to Oklahoma, on an unnaturally humid day in early April, our world was turned upside down. When my wife and I woke up on a Saturday morning in 1998, we had no idea how our lives were about to change forever. What we did know is that she was several days overdue, but we had been told this was not unusual, especially for a firstborn. Our plans, hatched the night before, were to have a relaxing weekend and wait it out. At some point in the late morning, our plans also came to include vegetable soup from a nearby takeout joint, and as I drove to appease my wife's latest craving, I noticed the sky was filled with puffy yellow clouds. I remember thinking that some atmospheric mischief was afoot, but I just figured we were heading for a downpour.

During lunch, my wife began having contractions. We still blame the soup and the quirky barometric pressure, as it never did rain. Thankfully, we had packed our suitcases the night before and stashed them in the trunk of our car, as I would have otherwise left without them. When we arrived at the hospital, after seeing a nurse, my wife was put in a small room where her contractions were being monitored. Another monitor was being used to measure the baby's heart rate, and this, in retrospect, gave us our first clue that a potential storm was brewing. I noticed that the heartbeat would dip down and, at times, seemed alarmingly low. Although we brought this to the attention of a nurse, she initially showed no concern. However, she did tell me it was probably a good idea to retrieve the suitcases from the car, as my wife was indeed in labor, and we would not be leaving anytime soon.

I remember singing to myself as I wheeled our suitcases through the nearby concrete parking deck. I was so excited that we were going to have a baby and, since we had decided to be surprised about the sex of the baby, we had no idea if it was going to be a girl or a boy. As I happily pondered whether I was about to meet my daughter or my son, I had no idea my car would remain parked there for the entire week.

When I got back to the hospital room, it was empty. My wife was gone. Where was she? Had she gone into full labor while I tap-danced outside? How could this happen? I had literally just gone out to grab our suitcases. Then, from the corner of my eye, I caught sight of her in another room, hoisted up on a delivery table of some sort. She seemed scared and in a great deal of pain, and as I approached the open door, I also noticed a pool of blood below her. It was then I knew something was wrong, and I sprinted towards the door, only to be joined by others. Voices were elevated, and I heard somebody say, "We might have a problem here. Does she have a husband?" The next thing I recall is being told that my wife was probably going to be all right, but they needed to do an emergency C-section and that they believed they could save the baby. "What? Save the baby?" I mouthed.

The doctors believed the umbilical cord was wrapped around the baby's neck and that our unborn child was literally being strangulated with every contraction. Throughout my wife's pregnancy, like all expecting parents, we enjoyed feeling our baby move. However, it had been a week or so, and we had not felt the baby kick. We had also learned that orange juice typically got things hopping, so I convinced my wife to chug a big glass of OJ to see if that would do the trick. A few minutes later, we both joked that it felt as if the baby was doing backflips, but in the hospital, I wondered if I had somehow caused this horrible situation by making her drink the orange juice. Funny how the mind works. In any event, within minutes of our discussion with the doctors, I was signing a stack of waivers and consent forms.

Our son was delivered by not just one doctor but by two. Although one of her OBGYN doctors was in the hospital, his pager was not working, so they called his partner and apprised him of the situation. In the end, they both arrived at the same time and performed the emergency C-section together, side by side. Daniel James entered our world around 6 p.m. that night. We had a 6-pound, 9-ounce baby boy and a can of blue paint seemingly in the very near future. Unfortunately, our rollercoaster day was just getting started. Our son was looking rather blue himself, especially around the neck and face. He also had a bowel movement sometime during the short labor, which caused some concern about his choking, and his breathing also seemed labored. After a few good coughs, he burst out crying, much to the relief and joy of everyone in the delivery room. Daniel was bundled up and put under a heating lamp. With things seemingly better, I snuck out to share the news with family. When I finally made it to the waiting room, I immediately saw my father and said, "Daniel James." Just as I said my son's name, I was approached by a nurse and asked to return to the delivery room.

Once there, I was informed Daniel was indeed having trouble breathing on his own, and they believed it would be best if he were taken to another part of the hospital where he could be given oxygen. Naturally, we agreed, and as my wife and I sat in a dark recovery room, we could barely speak. She was exhausted from having undergone major surgery, while I was simply numb from the whirlwind of events. None of this had gone as planned. Along with other young couples, we had taken Lamaze classes, where we learned special breathing techniques and other natural relaxation practices for a natural birthing process. It would be a team effort with soothing music and plenty of pillows. Now, all our planning had been thrown out the window in one chaotic afternoon. Together, in this darkened room, as we held each other's hands, both delivery doctors, again as a team, cautiously entered and told us they had additional news to share. Several nurses who had been caring for Daniel noticed a darting tongue and extra skin around his eyes. They also noticed the back of his head seemed flatter than normal. Without further conversation, they told us our son appeared to have Down syndrome.

We both started crying. It was all too much. How could this be happening to us? Why were we being robbed of our special day? Judi's entire pregnancy had gone without a hitch, and just several months before, we had celebrated a normal amniocentesis (AFP test) wherein we had been assured our baby did not have Down syndrome, cystic fibrosis, or other genetic disorders. In our minds, we had been promised a healthy child. Why else did we even do this dastardly test? None of it made sense, and despite this perceived unfairness, things were about to get even scarier.

After being left to process this avalanche of shocking information, I eventually ventured out to the waiting room to give the family an update, and I even managed to field a few incoming calls from those loved ones living out of state. Everyone cried. Some more than others, but *everyone* cried. Looking back on it, I suppose there was no good time for the hospital staff to tell us their opinion about our son, which is why, in turn, I relayed the news almost immediately as well.

Newborns with Down syndrome and other genetic disorders can face a plethora of medical issues, including, but by no means limited to, heart problems, lung problems, thyroid problems, neck problems, and feeding disorders. Daniel also had to contend with the umbilical cord wrapped around his neck and the bowel movement that was believed to have gotten into his lungs. We were given little time to cry about his potential diagnosis, as the doctors told us that Daniel's current condition was serious, if not critical. We were also told that some babies, regardless of a specific diagnosis, are unable to survive long outside of the womb. Now, we could barely breathe. They believed he should be moved to Akron Children's Hospital immediately, which just so happened to be across the street. We simply shook our heads in agreement as we had no idea what should or should not be done. It was all so mind-blowingly unexpected. My wife insisted she be given the opportunity to see her son before he was taken next door, and with the help of a nurse, I wheeled her bed across the hospital and into the room with our son.

Our little guy was in what can best be described as a "plastic bubble" and surrounded by a team of medical professionals reminiscent of a trauma team or, for those Marvel fans—*The Avengers*. Seriously, they were all business, and I'm glad this is how they rolled. Although we were told "time was of the essence," we were permitted to hurriedly reach into the bubble and touch his little fingers and tell him we loved him and would be with him as soon as possible. A moment later, he was whisked away. Alone again, we sobbed uncontrollably. Wheeling my wife back to the maternity ward—adorned in stork cutouts and pink and blue balloons and filled with happy laughter—was a surreal experience. That night, as we sat in a darkened room, the walls seemed especially thin. With saddened hearts, we were stuck right in the middle of an island of happiness. At some point during the night, presumably to alert an unsuspecting nurse, a "teardrop" tag was hung from the door of my wife's room.

Early the next morning, and at the urging of my wife, I bolted from her side to visit Daniel. The Neonatal Intensive Care Unit—commonly referred to as NICU—is a truly amazing place and getting to see it firsthand would be the first of many wonderful surprises in this unexpected journey. It is intense and the people who work there must be intense as well. The stakes are high as the margin for error is minuscule. First, getting into the NICU is like entering a prison. It is in a separate part of the hospital with additional security, and you must have permission to enter. Once you are buzzed in, you must walk through a room where you are given a gown, mask, and a package of soap with a plastic cuticle stick. A nearby sink, equipped with windows to facilitate observation, is provided for scrubbing your hands, including under your fingernails. Only then are you permitted to enter.

Inside, several large open rooms were filled with dozens of babies who were sick or born prematurely, with some only weighing a few ounces. Again, I was stunned, as I had no idea it would be so large. Later, I learned the hospital takes 600 babies a year in the Neonatal Intensive Care Unit. As for our baby, he was in a bubble crib immediately on the left side as you entered a second large room. Still unable to breathe on his own, he was resting peacefully, and when I asked about his prognosis, I was told by a doctor that the next few days would be critical. Every good moment seemed to be followed by a sucker punch, and I was glad those words had only fallen on my ears and not Judi's. After my visit, as I walked back toward the maternity ward in the neighboring hospital, I stopped at the hospital chapel along the way. It was a small space with a few oak pews, burnt red carpet, and a large wooden cross. Here, I had a frank and curt discussion, filled with tears and questions, but with only one specific prayer— "Please, God, let my son live."

The next major hurdle was finding a way to get my wife over to see our son. Although she had undergone major surgery, we obtained permission to take her over in a rigged-up wheelchair with extra padding. We could still not hold Daniel but were permitted to put our hands through several holes in his plastic bubble crib to touch his little fingers and toes. He clearly reacted to his mother's touch and to her voice. She stayed by his side, letting him grasp her fingers, talking to him about anything and everything, and softly singing lullabies until they made us leave for the night. I remain convinced her presence played a key role in his recovery.

Going back and forth between the hospitals soon became our routine, as did my stops at the hospital chapel. Although the tears had yielded, my questions continued to flow unabated. "Why did God do this to my son?" Even if he pulled through, "What kind of life would he have?" I could not help but think of disabled children I knew growing up, how they had been picked on or made fun of, and how their parents were continually having to swoop in to intervene on their behalf. All these years later, it still seemed so unfair, and now I felt ashamed I had not done more to help them. I worried about Daniel's future and wondered if hospital stays would be our new normal. I'm also embarrassed to say I thought about all the imagined things that would be taken away from our family's future. It occurred to me that I was somehow to blame for our son having Down syndrome. "What had I done wrong?" Suddenly, every part of my life was under a microscope of my own creation.

Those first few days are forever blurred together, but there came a time when I sat in the chapel in total silence. It was only then that I heard God's answer. "Why are you not pleased with the gift I have given you?" God continued as if pretending to have been caught off guard by my naive reaction, "Do you not understand what has been given? I have given you a precious angel. You are one lucky guy, and Judi is one lucky gal, as I chose YOU to be his parents." Quite frankly, I was still in no mood to be thankful. However, a certain level of understanding crept into the corner of my mind, and I acknowledged a willingness to continue our dialogue the following day. But first, I needed to figure out if our car was still in the parking deck.

Slowly, Daniel's condition improved, and each day, he was able to breathe more and more on his own. We were soon able to hold him and feed him. Each new day also brought a string of visitors, and *Momma* and *Papa* Bear made sure everyone took the soap to heart, as we wanted to get our little guy out of the NICU and back home where he should have been days before. Looking around the rooms during our time in the unit, it was hard not to wonder about the other babies. They all had blue or pink name tags, so we could see their names, but we knew nothing about them except for a few pleasantries shared with their parents. What condition might they have? Would they make it? Right now, as you read this, there are armies of babies clinging to life throughout hospitals, just like the one where we spent so many days with our son. There are also armies of soldiers, better known as neonatologists, who care for them, and if you saw them in action, you would be left in awe. I know we were. Some babies, without visitors, were lovingly held and fed as if they were their own. He saw what you did. It did not go unnoticed.

Genetic testing was done to confirm the suspected diagnosis of our son. One day, as we strolled towards the sterile hospital cafeteria, which had become another daily hangout, we ran into the geneticist in a hallway, and he told us, "I will meet with you later to discuss the results of our testing." We ate the latest helping of bland macaroni and cheese in total silence, as we surmised, he wouldn't wait to share good news with us. Later that day, in an unknown office, we were told genetic testing had confirmed Daniel had Down syndrome. The geneticist then told us our child would have many serious limitations in his life and that "higher education was completely out of the question." A strange comment, to be sure. It also came across as grossly inappropriate. Who did he think he was? I'm a lawyer, and my wife received her master's degree from Case Western Reserve University. Clearly, communicating with people was not his forte and, although I was tempted to tell him to get back in the lab where he so clearly belonged, I did manage to say, "Well, that's not so bad. If you ask me, higher education is completely overrated." As new parents, here we were, already defending our kid, and he wasn't even out of the NICU yet.

One day, Daniel finally came home. It was wonderful to have him in his own room and in his own crib. My law partner at the time, having been delayed like the rest of us in celebrating the new arrival, threw a party for me at a local establishment frequented by lawyers from the local bar association, complete with blue balloons attached to stools, plenty of beer, and boxes of bubble gum cigars. It was the first "normal thing" I had experienced in weeks, and it was the first time the outside world celebrated our good news. There was no discussion of higher education; instead, we were asked questions about

Daniel's height and weight at birth, as well as whether we were getting any sleep.

As new parents with no prior experience, my wife and I were naturally nervous. Daniel's diagnosis initially terrified us and, although he had been cleared to come home, we spent many nights checking to make sure he was breathing. I've been told this is common even if there are no fireworks in the delivery room, as we experienced. Being a new parent is always scary stuff. Although Dan was born with many of the characteristics typical of babies with Down syndrome, there was one he seemingly did not share. Our son was noticed to have an unusually good muscle tone. He was not floppy but solid. Had he been lifting weights while in the womb? It appeared so, or maybe it was the orange juice, after all, that had him doing constant calisthenics.

His heart was our biggest worry, and unfortunately, it remains so to this day. Daniel was born with a mitral valve defect, a common heart condition for children born with Down syndrome. As such, not only did we make regular trips to the pediatrician, but we also made the rounds with a heart specialist. Another unexpected outcome in our journey was the introduction to numerous outstanding pediatric physicians and specialists. First, his primary pediatrician monitored Daniel's health like a hawk perched on a nearby tree and, secondly, his heart specialist, an affable chap with a bow tie, gave us peace of mind when we needed it most. He was also fond of drawing diagrams of hearts on any paper he could find in an examining room, some of which I still have tucked away in a drawer in my office.

Initially, Daniel did not exhibit any obvious signs of delay. However, in time, while other children learned to stand and walk, Dan did not. Rather, he scooted along the ground on his butt while flapping his legs in a motion evocative of a butterfly in flight. He was quite proficient at it and could get across a room with great speed. Friends and relatives alike marveled at his ingenuity. It also helped that, like many children born with Down syndrome, he was incredibly limber. While others marveled, we just wondered when, if ever, he would stand up and walk. Initially, Daniel was able to say a few words, but over time, his delays became more pronounced as his vocabulary did not continue to expand at the same rate as that of other children his age. Soon, his peers were walking and talking, making his delays even more pronounced to those around him. On the other hand, early on, we also received wonderful news concerning his heart condition, as it had healed on its own. He would not require surgery, and we need not see the heart specialist again for several years. Hallelujah!

It has been said that "communication is key." Daniel had much to say but no clear way to say it. Many people with Down syndrome have difficulty speaking clearly for a host of reasons. First, poor facial muscle tone affects speech rate, intonation, and stress on words. Secondly, many have diminished hearing or otherwise struggle to process tones effectively. Lastly, cognitive issues may impact understanding and remembering. With our son, we regularly engaged him in facial exercises—including using a small brush to rub around and inside his mouth—along with formal speech therapy from an early age. Since children with Down syndrome are strong visual learners, we used picture books, and my mother, my wife, and I enrolled in a local sign language class. For our final class, we had an informal get-together, along with a potluck dinner, with a group of hearing-impaired individuals and, although our signing skills were found to be terribly wanting, we enjoyed communicating in a whole new language and being introduced to a group of beautiful people we would not have conversed with otherwise. As for our son, he developed a unique vocabulary supplemented by signing, and since some words and signs were uniquely his own creation, we dubbed his language *"Danglish."*

One morning before our daughter was born, as if sensing he was about to be a big brother, Dan stood up against the side of the bed. By nightfall, he was walking across the room.

"Woo Pig Sooie"

Before our visit to Fayetteville, Arkansas, nobody in my family had ever called hogs. At least, not that I know about. On November 5, 2011, that all changed. People love animals, and, as such, it is little wonder why so many sports teams are represented by a cornucopia of critters. Indeed, all creatures, great and small, are represented. There are lions, tigers, and bears. Oh my! There are eagles, yellow jackets, panthers, wolves or packs thereof, gators, cardinals, buffalo or thundering herds thereof, huskies, cougars, frogs, longhorns, gophers, terrapins (turtles), ducks, beavers, owls, rams, and penguins. The list goes on. There are Great Danes, greyhounds, bluetick coonhounds, roadrunners, coyotes, gorillas, wombats, sand sharks, kangaroos, spiders, slugs, boll weevils (beetles), and geoducks (saltwater clams). You get the idea. Almost every college has a nickname and usually a mascot. Sometimes they are the same, and other times, they are not. There are some 1,850 college nicknames and a breakdown compiled by Jason Kirk of *Banner Society* reveals that animals make up the vast majority, followed by people, non-fighting and fighting, with sword guys—knights, pirates, Spartans, Trojans, cavaliers, and the like—making up the largest slice of people mascots. Not surprisingly, cats lead the way with 15.9% of all mascots, followed by birds at 15.5%. These two alone make up nearly one-third of all mascots. Dogs are a distant third at 6.8%. Among bird mascots, colleges play fast and loose with hawk names, as many are not really hawks or birds at all, for that matter. On game day, mythical creatures seem to run rampant in more than just the imagination. One school, Hollins University, proudly has no nickname or mascot. As for the University of Arkansas, they proudly call themselves the *Razorbacks*.

A razorback is a term used to describe a wild or semiwild hog common in the southern US with a sharp ridge of hair along its back. When the University of Arkansas was founded in 1871, it had no known connections to feral pigs. In fact, like many universities, their mascot was derived from the bird family, as they were originally known as the *Cardinals*. This all changed in 1909 when Arkansas football coach Hugo Bezdek fatefully called his players "a wild band of Razorback hogs" after a huge win over LSU. The team's tenacity, along with the tough, fearless animal, led the student body to change the official mascot the following year and, starting in the 1960s, a live mascot began attending football games and other university events.

Today, *Tusk VI*, the Razorback mascot, has season tickets to all Arkansas home football games. Born on April 19, 2018, the Russian boar—born under the zodiac sign *Aries* and weighing in at 350 pounds—makes the fall trek from the *Stokes Family Farm* near Dardanelle, Arkansas, to Fayetteville and Little Rock, much to the delight of his adoring fans. Game-time snacks include apples, corn, and watermelon and, when the home team scores a touchdown, *Tusk* enjoys a grape or two. All right, all right, or *twenty*! In 2011, the year of our visit, we saw *Tusk IV*, who was in his inaugural season as the live mascot, and, in time, he would compile a 44-44 record. Yes, they keep records of such things in Arkansas. Generally considered the most docile of the *Tusk* clan, after being handled frequently by people since birth, "our" *Tusk* made headlines by sending flowers to retiring Texas Mascot *Bevo* upon learning of the longhorn's cancer diagnosis. Yep, a true gentleman, but sadly, our *Tusk* passed away in 2020.

The name "Big Red" was once used for the animal mascot, but it is now exclusively applied to the costumed human mascot, *Big Red.* Starting in 1997, the *Tusk* name has been associated with Arkansas football, and all *Tusks* to date have been males, as female swine do not have tusks. Until recently, Keith Stokes of the *Stokes Family Farm* was the long-time breeder and handler for the live mascots. He passed away on August 18, 2023, at the age of 59, just barely missing another upcoming college football season, with a United States Senator serving as one of his pallbearers at his funeral. *Tusk VI* is now lovingly cared for by Keith's wife, his two children, their spouses, and his beloved grandchildren. And, for anyone who does not believe a mascot is important, Keith's obituary recommended that in lieu of flowers, donations could be made to the *Tusk Fund*—a fund established in 2008 by Razorback Athletics through the *Razorback Foundation*, with donations going directly to assisting in the care and feeding of *Tusk* and to provide even greater living and travel accommodations.

So, how exactly does one go about calling hogs? It's simple, really, and once you've done it, there's no going back. Trust me. We learned quickly and often. First, raise your arms above your head during the Hog Call, yell "Woo," and wiggle your fingers for a few seconds. Next, bring both arms straight down with fists clenched while yelling, "Pig." Then, extend your right arm with the "Sooie." Repeat these steps twice and finish by yelling, "*Razorbacks.*" Got it? It should sound something like this: "Wooooooooo. Pig. Sooie! Wooooooooo. Pig. Sooie! Wooooooooo. Pig. Sooie! *Razorbacks*!" Since I'm just a "*Buckeye*" from Ohio and fearing I might get it all wrong, I lifted those instructions directly from the University's website. Regardless, it is one of the most entertaining things we have ever done at a football game. We loved it, and when we got home there were many demonstrations, usually led by my son, for friends and family alike.

Although it was the first time anyone in my family had called hogs, it was not my dad's first visit to the *Razorback* State. With his engineering work, he had been there many times, including multiple visits to the Rose Law Firm, which gained notoriety in the 1990s with stories of intrigue surrounding Vince Foster, Web Hubbell, and former First Lady Hillary Clinton. Foster committed suicide and Hubbell pleaded guilty to wire fraud in connection with the Whitewater investigation, all while Clinton went on to be a Senator, Secretary of State, and presidential nominee. Years later, as we drove from the airport towards Fayetteville and our rendezvous with the hogs, we reminisced about Dad's visits to Little Rock. Still, given his work in product liability, he was certain he had never met any of those memorable characters. Dad had also visited Arkansas years before, when my brother and I were still little kids. Growing up, our garage, much to my mother's chagrin, housed two old, rusty 1960 Jaguar Mark IXs. One of them was from Arkansas and, as we drove down an unfamiliar highway, our father described how he had driven out from Ohio with a friend—and a flatbed truck—to pick it up. Between the two rust buckets, he hoped to create one fully functional car, and, at one point, he had told me and then my brother that it would be restored in time for our senior high school proms. This had become a family joke and as we ribbed him over his slow progress and those seriously delinquent deadlines, even Daniel jumped in, telling him, "Grandpa, that thing won't drive as it does not even have wheels." As we all had a good laugh, Dad told us, "One day, I'm going to restore that car and if you're nice, I might even take you all for a ride in it. Who knows, maybe one of your kids will drive it to their senior prom."

Dad's delays in finishing the car had nothing to do with his lack of mechanical expertise. Far from it. He had worked as a mechanic at a gas station while putting himself through college and always had a fondness for the automotive world. As kids, we would regularly find ourselves with our father at a nearby racetrack, usually in a garage or near the pit row with plenty of greasy car parts and beef jerky. No, as a mechanical engineer with a drawer full of patents—including the first patent for a run-flat tire—he could finish the car if he could find the time and the parts. From an early age, Dad had a gift for making things and fixing things that broke. He also seemed to know how to do almost anything, and his hands were unnaturally strong. Heck, my brother and I watched him build a garage from the ground up by himself and refinish nearly every corner of the house. His collection of tools was impressive, as was his resume, which not only included B.S.M.E. and M.S. degrees from the University of Akron but also included completed coursework and certifications from Caltech, MIT, and Northwestern, among others. As a registered Professional Engineer, he served as a member of countless professional organizations and was the President of *The American Society of Mechanical Engineers*. Though I never recall him ever reading a book for pleasure, it was numbers and equations that danced in his head.

"The Boy in the Plastic Bubble"

In 1976, the year of our nation's bicentennial, John Travolta starred in a made-for-TV film (Netflix, before Netflix, for you younger readers) called *The Boy in the Plastic Bubble*, where he played Tod Lubitch, a teenage boy with a severely compromised immune system. Forced to live inside a sterile plastic pod, he attends a Houston high school via a closed-circuit television system (Zoom before Zoom for you younger readers) eerily like classroom arrangements created during the Covid pandemic. Faced with the prospect of potentially losing his young love forever after learning she is going off to art school in New York, he must decide if he is willing to step outside his house, unprotected and, in so doing, risk illness or death. The final scene, which depicts the young man climbed atop a horse with his girlfriend, offers a classic and equally symbolic "riding off into the sunset" ending. Although we have no idea about Tod's fate, his choosing to live outside the plastic bubble seems an obvious choice. What kind of life was he really living anyway? It was terribly suffocating and unmercifully sterile. As for Travolta, previously best known for his television role as *Vinnie*

Barbarino on *Welcome Back Kotter*, he would re-emerge as a mega star when he rode onto the sets of *Saturday Night Fever* and *Grease*.

For many, this movie left quite an impression, so much so that we still use its language. This is especially true in politics and culture. How often have you heard the phrase "living in a bubble" or "getting outside of your bubble?" Where do you think these came from? When we brought our son home, we were terrified that any illness might be catastrophic to him. However, in the back of our minds, *The Boy in the Plastic Bubble* played on a continual loop. Much like the story of Moses leading the Israelites out of Egypt in the book of *Exodus*, should one live a certain life in captivity or risk an unknown future in the wilderness? For Daniel to have a full life, we decided we must let him step outside our home and comfort zone. He must live outside the plastic bubble, even if it involves risk.

Early on, before his second birthday, we thought we had made a horrible mistake with this approach. The wilderness, it turns out, can be a scary place, especially for new parents of a disabled child. We had taken Daniel with us to Colorado for a January ski trip. Though everything had gone well, when we got home, he developed a fever. A few days later, he was admitted to the Children's Hospital as he had developed an infection in his heart. I was furious at my decision and was pained with guilt as I paced about his room and the nearby hallway. How could I have been so stupid as to put him on a crowded airplane? What was I thinking by letting him be in an airport during the winter with cold and flu viruses on nearly every escalator handrail and hovering above every food court table? I felt like I had put our son through an unnecessary stress test and vowed that when he got better, I would be more protective. But what if he didn't get better? It was too much and right when I thought I might freak out, Dan's pediatrician told us he was on the mend. He also asked us where we had gone skiing and said we had made the right decision to take him with us. He said, "You can't leave him in *a bubble*. He needs to build his immunity and that only comes through time and exposure. So, where are you going next year?"

We took the doctor's words to heart the following year as we flew our little boy across the pond to visit England. After a wonderful stay in London, we traveled to Oxford to relive a few memories. While in law school, I was given the opportunity to study international law and European Community (EC) law at Magdalen College. My brother had spent the same semester at New College studying English literature. After showing our wives and parents our colleges, dorms, and daytime hangouts, we were more than willing to share our evening haunts as well. One pub frequented by both my brother and me was *Turf Tavern*, located down an alley called St. Helens Passage. The place is a classic English pub complete with low ceilings, wood beams, rock walls, and a dozen taps featuring various bitters neatly arranged in a semicircular design. Crammed in the pub, next to a drunk self-proclaimed Welsh boxer, I was glad we had decided to leave Daniel at the bed & breakfast with my mom.

Later that evening, after we had several pints in our systems, we saw a young man in a wheelchair—who was also severely disabled—being lifted across the pub to a back table. A man, clearly his father, led the successful effort to get him situated near family and friends. At that moment, I found tears had formed in my eyes and then streamed across my cheeks. Several pints of bitter can do that for you. My father asked me if everything was all right, and I told him it was tough to see the struggles of the neighboring family. I told him it was irrational, but it made me sad. Dad, who always had a way with words, said to me, "Jim, that's not what I see. What I see is a loving father with a wonderful family and a young man who is right here where we are—at *The Turf*. How cool is that?" It was exactly what I needed to hear, and I remember it like it was yesterday as I made a vow to myself, right then and there, that I would be like that young man's father. If need be, I would carry Daniel through, and literally over, a crowd so that he might experience everything we did.

As for the rest of our evening, things got downright dicey. The "Welsh boxer" became belligerent with all of those around him.

Eventually, he was cut off and then inexplicably tried to start a fight with Dad. He even went so far—in some lame and archaic attempt to question our father's masculinity—as to ask Dad if "he had ever been with a woman before." Dad, without hesitation and while pointing to us, responded, "They don't call me Pops for nothing!" This left the provocateur dumbfounded. Like I said, our *Pops* always had a way with words.

The Gamecock Game

The trip to Arkansas was the first official "guy trip." Largely a creation of my mom and dad—with my father looking for any excuse to get away with his sons and grandson, and my mother acting as a willing accomplice—the idea had been hatched the year before after an impromptu visit to a South Carolina *Gamecock* game. Sitting at lunch in a restaurant on Bay Street in Beaufort, South Carolina, and, on a whim, my son, my dad, and I decided to drive up to Columbia for the South Carolina-Arkansas football game. At the time, Daniel was 12 years old. In retrospect, it was an unintended test run, which, in the end, gave us a list of "dos" and "don'ts." Ryan Mallett threw for over 300 yards, while Knile Davis racked up over 100 yards rushing and scored three touchdowns in a convincing 41-20 *Razorback* victory over the *Gamecocks.* With kickoff at 7:00 p.m., the weather was chillier than expected and the late-night drive home through a thick, unrelenting fog in the low country was a bit like the final score—undesirable.

However, there was also much that we greatly enjoyed on our visit, with those 78,000 fanatics crammed into *Williams-Brice Stadium*. The pre-game festivities provided our first introduction to a quirky tailgating variant wholly unique to South Carolina—*The Cockaboose*. Yes, that's correct, I said, *Cockaboose.* Lined up just outside the stadium, on what's called the *Cockaboose Railroad* in *Cockaboose County*, sit 22 train cars/cabooses, which have been converted into mini-party centers. On any given Saturday, whether the *Gamecocks* are playing right next door or on the road, the cars are packed with fans, food, and booze. Children dangling from the back of a caboose make for quite a sight, as do the spiral staircases and crowded rooftops built atop the train cars. Inside the cars, fans and other lucky tailgaters can mosey up to a full-length custom bar or relax on a leather couch with a flat-screen TV. The railcars have been there since 1990, when a Columbia businessperson and real estate developer, along with a partner, bought the cabooses from the Illinois Central Railroad. If you ever make it to the South Carolina capital, make sure you find a way to get an invite, as unexpected guests are not always welcomed, even in this otherwise hospitable southern city. And if you ever win the lottery, a *Cockaboose* might make a nice addition to any real estate portfolio. With prices exceeding several hundred thousand dollars, make sure to bring your checkbook and plenty of your best-behaved friends.

Columbia sits right smack in the middle of the *Palmetto State.* For much of the year, it is home to warm, wet weather, and in the summer, things are downright sticky. Hardly a place you would expect to encounter a sandstorm. Yet, that's exactly what happens shortly before every kickoff. Imagine thousands of fans jumping up and down while waving white towels and chanting "USC" to an instrumental piece by Finnish DJ and record producer *Darude.* This ultimate club banger was followed by a classical music piece entitled *Also Sprach Zarathustra* or *Sunrise* by Richard Strauss, which is now better known as the theme music for Stanley Kubrick's 1968 cult favorite movie, *2001: A Space Odyssey.* As the music builds, one is introduced to *Cocky*—the costumed mascot, along with *Sir Big Spur*—a live Old English back-breasted red gamecock.

A super quick history is needed to better understand these mascots and the school's name. If history is not your thing, I promise not to run afoul of or ruffle any feathers. So, here goes. Founded in 1801, the school's nickname is linked to a town just a little over 40 miles away.

Sumter, South Carolina, is named after General Thomas Sumter, a fierce combatant in the American Revolution and de facto leader of South Carolina during the war. As a constant thorn to the British forces, he was dubbed *"The Fighting Gamecock"* for his never-say-die attitude and straightforward military tactics. Hundreds of years before, in 1521, during Magellan's circumnavigation of the world, the Portuguese explorer and his crew first saw a betting man's sport that had been in existence for centuries at various corners of the globe—cockfighting. In the years that followed, the British came to use the term "cock of the game" to describe this "sport," eventually shortening the term to "gamecock." There is some indication that Sumter himself may have also had an unhealthy fascination with cockfighting.

Which leads us to *Cocky* and *Sir Big Spur*. Somehow, inexplicitly, the costumed human claims to be the son of the live bird, and one is left to contemplate not only the size of the egg for which *Cocky* was hatched and whether *Big Spur*, a male gamecock, might lay such an egg at all. However, with modern science rolling down the tracks with a *Cockaboose* in tail, anything is possible. What we know for sure is that the regal red-winged, black-breasted Old English Rooster made his debut in 1998 at a baseball game and was originally named *Cocky Doodle Lou*, after then-head football coach Lou Holtz. Under a new name, *Big Spur* finally made a football debut in 2006, and since then, there have been multiple *Big Spurs,* the latest being *Sir Big Spur VII.* All Big Spurs were originally raised and trained by Mary Snelling and her husband, Ron Albertelli, of Aiken, South Carolina. In fact, *Cocky Doodle Lou* was given to Snelling by her father on the recommendation of a friend who was known to have taken part in illegal cockfighting. As such, the first mascot was essentially a rescue.

Feathers were ruffled in 2019 when Beth and Van Clark—South Carolina alums living in Edgefield, South Carolina—took over the role of caretaker of *Big Spur* after Snelling and Albertelli retired and handed over the reins. The Clarks—pressed into duty—faced immediate difficulty after *Big Spur VI*, raised by the previous handlers, passed away at twelve years of age. Thereafter, the Clarks auditioned three roosters they had raised to determine which one might best handle the heat, noise, and mayhem of *SEC* college football. When *Sir Big Spur VII* finally made his debut, not everyone was pleased, including his prior handlers. There was something a little different about the rooster, which would have gone unnoticed by most but not diehard *Gamecock* fans. *Sir Big Spur's* head was not clean-shaven. Instead, he sported a bright red comb. Now, another quick historical detour is needed, as over time, those who trained roosters for fighting adopted a practice called "dubbing," which involved trimming or removing the bird's comb—the floppy, crown-like protrusion on top of the bird's head. It was primarily done to prevent excess bleeding for those unfortunate creatures trapped and made to fight. To many, this new *Sir Big Spur* looked more the part of a dandy than a seasoned fighter.

In August 2022, feathers were further ruffled when the prior handlers made it clear they would rather retire the name than have *Sir Big Spur* resemble "Barney the Barnyard Rooster." Soon other names were bandied about, with the University initially endorsing "The General," while the student body, perhaps willing to be a bit more provocative, rallied behind "Cock Commander." Along these lines, my father and I had chuckled several times when seeing and reading certain "unofficial" merchandise worn by the younger crowd at the game. Some, although devilishly clever, shall not be repeated. In the end, Ray Tanner, a former beloved baseball coach who became the athletic director, acting as mediator, got the warring factions together in a room 48 hours before the 2022 season opener. The result was that *Sir Big Spur* would remain the official name and when the beloved bird arrived before kickoff, he was without a comb, leaving many to wonder if *Sir Big Spur* had been "dubbed" or if the world gazed upon *Sir Big Spur VIII.*

Our perch for the game was in the lower bowl section near the goal line and, like most college football stadium seating, was nothing more than a faded number stenciled on a bench. It really didn't matter since my back end seldom touched the cold metal as we never sat down. In fact, nobody sat down—ever. The seats may have been frosty, but our hearts were warmed by a halftime visit from Ryan—a good family friend—who was attending South Carolina en route to ultimately becoming a doctor specializing in sports medicine and pain management. Although he was young and no doubt spending a Saturday night with his college friends, he still had taken the time to find us, come chat with us, and share his favorite *Gamecock* stories. It gave us our first glimpse of things to come, including gracious and unparalleled local hospitality.

Once home, we discussed how much we enjoyed spending the weekend with just the guys. My wife and my daughter—Claire—seemed to enjoy the time without us as well. Imagine that! In discussing this phenomenon, we were reminded that Daniel was the only boy in the family, as my brother also had daughters. Furthermore, his special needs seemingly surrounded him with even more women. His teachers, therapists, and school aides were, for the most part, women. Even his friends in his special education classes were girls, and our local play group with other children with Down syndrome was also mostly girls. In searching for a little guy time, we naturally veered towards sports and, given our trip to the *Gamecock* game, college football seemed the perfect fit. From the outset, I was more than a willing convert. Not only do I love football, but I love to travel. A vagabond at heart, roaming through college towns was right up my alley, and my brother, who lives in Virginia, was also on board from the start.

After we had coalesced around the idea, our next question was, where should we go? As an Ohio State graduate—along with my brother—and an enthusiastic *Buckeye* football fan—along with my dad, my brother, and Daniel—the *SEC* Conference seemed intriguing. Why do they always seem to get the best of us and all *the Big 10* teams for that matter? Dad was drawn to the *SEC* for a completely different reason—the weather. Next, where should we start in the *SEC*? The answer was easy. While seated in the corner of the endzone at the South Carolina game, many of our neighbors had been Arkansas fans, and they were more than happy to give us an introduction to Fayetteville and *Razorback* football. We were also directly behind the Arkansas cheerleaders, and Daniel clearly caught their eye as several strands of cardinal and apple blossom-colored beads were personally delivered and wrapped around my son's neck by more than one young woman. Given our positive experience, making Arkansas our first game with my brother made sense.

Fayetteville, Arkansas

The night before the game in Fayetteville, we arrived at our hotel a little later than expected. Lodging in a college town on a weekend with a home game is no easy feat. This first trip with the entire gang was also before the proliferation of alternatives provided by the advent of *Airbnb* and *Vrbo*, so unless you wanted to crash at a frat house, hotels were the only workable possibility. Our hotel was outside of the downtown area and more than a few miles from campus. It was also right next to a *Wendy's*. After unpacking, we debated heading downtown, but given the late start, we decided to dine in at the hotel, as they had a small open bar, resembling a diner with an open grill against the back wall. This first official guy trip Friday night dinner, far from fine cuisine, brought a great deal of levity to all.

After straddling up to the bar, the four of us were greeted by our bartender, who just happened to be the same woman who had checked us into the hotel. It was a short walk from one end of the lobby to the other and, as the husky but well-kept worker asked us for our drink order, we saw her motion to a person with a suitcase who had just entered the hotel that she would be there in "just a sec." When we asked her what type of beer she had, she literally rolled out a cooler from some unknown back storage area and rummaged through it. The words she uttered are still repeated by my brother and me to this day. She said, and trust me, this is the exact quote, "We have *Budweiser, Bud Light, Busch, Busch Light, Natural Light, Natural Ice*, and *Boulevard IPA*." First, we openly wondered how many beers could be housed in the medium-sized orange cooler hauled out from behind the counter. Second, we did not expect the IPA to be the final option, as the options she provided were generally going from bad to worse. Why in the world did they have this high-end beer? It just seemed so odd. So unexpected. Not surprisingly, in unison, my brother and I blurted out, "*Boulevard IPA*!"

When we get together, silliness often ensues, and this dinner was about to give us a lifetime of laughter. After we ordered our drinks and when the bartender could finally break away from the front desk, we ordered a round of cheeseburgers. Again, called into duty, she turned on the grill behind the counter and set about making us our grub. Who else would be the chef, right? Now, much of what happened next was not her fault. In retrospect, it was pretty darn amazing that she essentially ran the entire hotel as a one-person operation. The burners, which resembled an antiquated Coleman camping stove from the 1950s, turned to their highest setting and were barely browning the meat. We could see it from our front-row seats. As we sat for over half an hour and watched her run back and forth from the front desk, check people in, take phone calls, take another couple's drink order, and check on the uncooked burgers, we could not help but see the comedy in our situation. As we approached the 45-minute mark and after our second *Boulevard IPA* had set in, we got punchy. Remember *Wendy's* next door? Well, as other people streamed into the hotel lobby with bags of food, it just made our situation that much more preposterous. My dad, always quick to make a joke, proposed we take turns running next door to grab a snack as we waited—prompting our neighbors at the bar to burst out laughing. We eventually got those burgers, and I must say they were quite yummy and almost completely cooked. Of course, by that point, we would have probably eaten a gummy bear off the floor mat of our rental car.

The next day, my dad insisted that we correct our false start. After strolling about in downtown Fayetteville, he proposed a late lunch at *Doe's Eat Place* on Dickson Street. It turned out my father had been to the original restaurant in Greenville, Mississippi, a handful of years before. I'm glad he had. Established in 1941 by Dominick "Doe" Signa and his wife, Mamie, the original restaurant was a grocery store called "Papa's Store" run by Doe's father, which started in 1903. The family lived in a house behind the store. When Mamie got her mitts on a recipe for hot tamales, the couple began running a honkytonk in the front part of the store. Although white themselves, the joint was strictly for Black people and served those wonderful tamales, along with buffalo fish and chili. In the back, "Big Doe," as he was known by locals, soon found himself cooking steaks for a local doctor, who, in time, brought other doctors and lawyers to share in his discovery. Say what you want about lawyers (and I can say this because I am one), but they (we) always know a wonderful place to eat. In fact, it was a group of lawyers who had first taken my dad to *Doe's Eat* in Mississippi. Regardless, in time, *Doe's Eat Place* was born. The original place is still going strong and has been joined by other "franchises" throughout the south, including Fayetteville.

Seated near the front windows, we could watch countless families walk by dressed head to toe in Arkansas garb and yet we were still hours away from the kickoff. The rock wall closest to our seats was covered with framed pictures and other Arkansas memorabilia, while another was dedicated as a *Razorbacks* sports player's signature wall. With a slogan of "*Meat me at Doe's*," our gang split a few steaks and had several orders of the famous tamales. Everything was delicious and easily made up for the shenanigans from the night before.

After lunch, we made a decision that would become a crucial staple of our football trips. If we were really going to do things right, we needed to go all in for the hometown team. We would not attend as casual observers—with our Ohio State mindset and preconceived *Big 10* notions—but instead as local diehards. What better way to do this than a visit to the campus bookstore? We would also share this newfound love for the home team with the women in our lives, as what better way to say "I love you" than to bring home a shirt from Arkansas with a hog on it? We quickly learned we were not alone as the place was a madhouse, and, at first, I was glad we did not have any Arkansas gear as I could more easily track my son in what felt more like a train station in India. A campus bookstore is reminiscent of a visit to Las Vegas or Disney, forcing you to suspend reality—at least when it comes to the cost of a sweatshirt. In the end, we did emerge with the requisite *Razorback* t-shirts, caps, and other assorted merchandise.

As we strolled along the *senior walk*—those sidewalks engraved with the names of now more than 200,000 University of Arkansas graduates dating back to 1876—we embraced the joy of acknowledging other college traditions beyond our own. In that moment, we were *Razorbacks*, ready to call hogs and embrace traditions we had known little about just the day before. It was good, and Saturdays at home in the fall would never be the same.

One oddity we observed on campus, not fully understood at the time, was groups of young men, along with some younger kids—boys and girls—donning black framed eyeglasses. It was only after we returned home that we better understood the local fashion statement. These young *Razorback* fans were paying tribute to Brandon Burlsworth and his trademark glasses. These kids, who all seemed to be wearing number 77, were *Burls Kids*. In time, Hollywood would also pay tribute to this offensive lineman—who went from walk-on to All-American—in the 2016 movie *Greater*. The podgy youngster was redshirted as a freshman in 1994, but after transforming his physique with a relentless workout regimen, he received a scholarship and a starting position at right guard on the offensive line in 1996. The following season, he was named a captain and in 1998—the year my son was born—he was selected for the College Football All-American Team, making him one of the greatest walk-on stories of all time.

Tragically, eleven days after being drafted by the Indianapolis *Colts*, Burlsworth was killed in a car accident on his way back to his hometown in Arkansas. His jersey number—77—was permanently retired in a ceremony at Arkansas's first home game in the 1999 season. His locker, originally untouched for years, is now on permanent display for all to see. Brandon's story is no doubt heart-rending, and the movie requires a box of tissues to be readily at hand. Why do bad things happen to good people? Why was this young man's life cut short right when he was about to enter football's greatest stage? His story certainly shakes our sense of fairness. However, through the pain, we are buoyed by the young man's unyielding faith. By his example, we are also reminded to seize every opportunity that comes our way. Along these lines, friends and family established the *Brandon Burlsworth Foundation* in honor of his work ethic and Christian values to provide underserved children a chance to attend *Razorback* and *Colt* football games as *Burls' Kids*; to provide eye care—in partnership with optometrists and Walmart/Sam's Optical Department—to thousands of students; to provide football camps to third through ninth graders; and to offer awards and scholarships. Not surprisingly, the foundation's logo prominently features Burlsworth's signature black-framed glasses and number 77 will always be a *Razorback* whose legacy lives on to this day.

Later, after walking across campus and as the sun began its final descent across the western Ozark sky, Daniel, my father, *my brother*, and I settled in to watch Arkansas host South Carolina. The game we had chosen was in Fayetteville, but the University of Arkansas football team still plays some games in Little Rock, making it a team with essentially two home fields. Like the year before, the *Razorbacks* got the better of the *Gamecocks* in a comfortable 44-28 victory. Not only did Arkansas gain over 400 yards, but they also managed to force four turnovers. Bobby Petrino—who was in his fourth year as head coach—had a pretty darn good team that would finish 11-2, ultimately would go on to win the Cotton Bowl (29-16 over Kansas State) and finish fifth in the country. In fact, their eleven wins are a feat that has only occurred three times in their 117-year history and was their best finish since 1977. With a combined record of 21-5 over their past two seasons, the future looked bright for Petrino and the Arkansas football program.

Uncle John

The dark skies had turned chilly, and a stiff wind greeted us as we walked out of *Donald W. Reynolds Stadium* following the Arkansas win over South Carolina. We were tempted to find a spot near campus to grab a bite, but Daniel was clearly exhausted. So, we decided to head back to the hotel bar and lobby to watch No. 2 Alabama host No. 1 LSU in Tuscaloosa in what was fatally being dubbed as "the game of the century." After my dad dropped us off, he ran next door to *Wendy's* for more burgers. (The learning curve is a wonderful thing, while our emerging Atkins diet, maybe not so much.) Our friend—God bless her—had pulled the remaining *Boulevard IPAs* aside for my brother and me. "My goodness, does she ever get a chance to go home, and is there some other stash of IPAs in another cooler we don't know about?" we pondered. In the hotel lobby, with my son dressed in his pajamas and ready for bed, we were joined by other Arkansas faithful, along with a smattering of South Carolina fans. This, too, we learned, is part of the college football tradition, as when your team is not yet playing or has already played, you join countless others in watching other games.

Unfortunately, the much-hyped game, with an exceptionally large national TV audience, was a snoozefest, with neither team seemingly wanting to win. These heavyweights, even with relentless coaxing from coaches and referees alike, barely sparred in the ring. In the end, in overtime, when the bell finally rang to call the fight, LSU's kicker bested Alabama's kicker three kicks to two. Like many others at the hotel, my dad and son ditched the game long before the conclusion to avoid sleeping in a chair with a bed so invitingly nearby. As for my brother and me, we grabbed the last *Boulevards* and went back to our room to talk and reminisce. After we could talk no more and had dimmed the lights to allow silence to finally creep into our room, we heard from outside our hotel window, "Welcome to *Wendy's*. May I take your order?" Each outrageous order made and taken, and the confusion of changes and add-ons that inevitably ensued, made us laugh and giggle like schoolboys in the darkness. In that moment, we were kids again, and I was alone again with my little brother, and tomorrow would have to wait.

My brother was born four years after me. I have been told I kept watch at the foot of his bedroom door when he first came home, although I honestly do not recall doing so. I do remember when he was young, he had his share of chapped lips and sore throats. Then, one day, he no longer licked his lips, and he got his tonsils out. John— with his brown hair and brown eyes— was a slender kid and still is as a grown man. We grew up at the end of a red brick dead-end street in a dark olive-green split-level house, played outside until the streetlights came on, and rode our big wheels (later bikes and skateboards) down the middle of that same street and in our neighbor's driveway. In hindsight, our neighbors were incredibly patient with us. We also had a brown and black dog named *Bingo,* who, in a world before leashes and doggie-poop bags, followed us everywhere, including into the woods and onto the playground of our nearby grade school.

Growing up, my brother was always by my side. We were typically joined by a gang of other kids in the neighborhood, along with *Bingo* and a few other local canines, as we explored nearby areas called "*the ravine*," "*the field*," "*the cave*," "*bottle-land*," "*the oasis*," and the most feared area of all, "*Kodiak cliff*." The latter still sends shivers down my spine, although *Bingo* loved it. "*The oasis*"— a cluster of tall trees right smack in the middle of "*the field*"—still gives me the willies but for entirely different reasons, as this was a known hangout spot for older teenagers and a boatload of malfeasance. We dared enter only during daylight and never on weekends, as they carried cigarettes, switchblades, condoms, and BB guns.

One day, when other neighborhood kids told us Mr. Remy's house (in "*the field*") was haunted, my brother and I protested. We knew he was a sweet old man, as every Christmas, we walked over a box of chocolates from *Mary Coyle*. When we told him "Merry Christmas," he always smiled and told us, "Indeed, Merry Christmas, boys. Oh, and tell your parents, I mean your mother, thank you for the Christmas gift." Later, after he had passed away, and when kids threw rocks at the windows of his dilapidated house, my brother and I would not partake. How could we? A few years later, when other kids told us Mrs. Bermbach was a witch, we finally had the reinforcement to confront such heresy, as a group of us had been regularly stopping by her large stone porch for punch and cookies after a long day of running through "*the ravine*" and her backyard. She was certainly no witch, at least not that we could tell.

As we grew older, my brother and I regularly walked the nearby railroad tracks—much to my mother's chagrin—and we often played sports in a nearby lot located at the rear of a block of houses. In the neighborhood, it was simply known as "*center field*" (not to be confused with "*the field*"), and for whatever reason, which is still not entirely clear to me, this large grass lot was usually mowed, making it the perfect spot for games of soccer, football, baseball, tag, and in the evenings "ghosts in the graveyard." It was here where my friends and I first noticed that my kid brother was athletic and could usually hold his own, even with a group of much older guys. He never seemed to mind being the youngest, and I did my best to make sure he was always included. As brothers, we had a few dustups, and in hindsight, I was too rough on him, especially when my parents were out in the evenings, and I was left in charge. He still reminds me of my shortcomings in those moments, and I believe rightfully so.

Looking back at my high school years, I wish I had spent more time with my brother, especially since I went away to college. Except for one overlapping quarter at Ohio State and a summer in Oxford, England, we have not lived in the same town since the early 1980s. I guess, like most teenagers, I was trying to look cool and hanging with my kid brother seemed anything but. Still, there were moments. I remember one weekend, my brother approached me and asked if we could do something together—as he did nearly every weekend around that time. I had been invited to a party and initially told him I could not, but for whatever reason, I changed my mind. Maybe it was looking at his face after I had turned him down yet again. At the last minute, I decided to ditch the party for dinner at a dine-in *Pizza Hut*, where we split a large pepperoni pizza and a pitcher of *Coca-Cola* and then saw the movie *Dark Crystal*. The funny thing is, I cannot remember a single party from high school, but I can recall that night with my brother as if it were yesterday.

John excelled in most athletic endeavors, and while he enjoyed tennis and skiing, he was particularly gifted on the soccer pitch. Not only did he have a great touch on the ball, but he also had a nose for the goal. When he was younger, he managed to get my father and I involved with soccer on his little league team when my brother's coach—a former player at the University of Akron—took his ball and literally went home after he grew frustrated when the 8-, 9- and 10-year-old kids didn't understand his European league formations and strategies. Who could blame him? The team was terrible and could barely grasp his vision of the Dutch Orange Clockwork. They were literally "*The Bad News Bears*" of kid soccer and, not surprisingly, did not win a single game in their first season. However, the kids did not quit, nor did our father. He went out and secured team sponsorship, provided the kids with patches for their uniforms, and assigned the players nicknames. In the second season, the team finished second after a heartbreaking defeat in the championship game. The final season for my brother, the team played other teams outside the league—scheduled by our dad (long before club soccer existed)—went undefeated and walked away as league champions. After the final whistle blew, the team gathered to celebrate at a local pizza joint, where my father was presented with the game ball signed by all the kids on the team. Today, that ball sits on a shelf in a cabinet in my dad's home office, along with his most prized professional mementos and accolades. As for my brother, he went on to become the first four-year lettered athlete in soccer at our high school and, although he finally hung up his boots, he is still running marathons.

Since we grew up in the same house and attended the same schools, we experienced many of the same things: We both played *Dungeons & Dragons*; we both caught the punk music bug; and while we never smashed our disco records, we certainly talked about it. Thankfully, we never ditched our *D&D* dice, any Gary Gygax writings, or our carefully painted, metal miniature figurines, even if we did not continue to publicly profess our love for the game. In high school, we took slightly different paths, as John was far more popular and even served as Vice President of his class. It never occurred to me to run for office, and if I had, the student body would have responded with, "Who is he? Is he in our class?" Heck, my brother even had a steady girlfriend when I was still afraid to even talk to girls. Do I need to say more?

While my brother followed me to Ohio State, he would then head to the East Coast and the New York metropolitan area for his legal studies, where he ultimately met his wife. Today, he and his wife have three wonderful daughters and a thriving law practice in Virginia, yet he always finds a way to spend a long weekend with the guys on our college football adventures. All I can say is I love my little brother, and I'll always keep guard at the foot of his door.

The following year, long after we had returned home and resumed our everyday lives, on April 1st—April Fool's Day—the then 51-year-old head coach of the *Razorback* football team crashed his Harley-Davidson motorcycle. Thankfully, nobody was seriously hurt. Later, when it was discovered that he was not riding alone, it set off a series of events that would cause untold embarrassment to a young woman, her family, the University, the athletic department, and the football program. It also led to his dismissal. Human frailty aside, the events that quickly unfolded are a stark reminder that in football and in life, things can often change in an instant; highs are usually followed by lows, spring follows winter and, long after we say goodbye, traditions and memories remain. Lastly, if you wait long enough, things come back around. A decade later, Bobby Petrino was hired as the offensive coordinator of the Arkansas *Razorbacks*. As Mark Twain may or may not have said, "History doesn't repeat itself, but it sure does rhyme." As for the *Razorbacks*, their offense is running on a high octane again.

A Table at Luigi's

One night in mid-December, in the early 2000s, when the kids were still little and long before our college football trips, my parents had taken Daniel and Claire on a ride on the *Polar Express*. Dressed in their Christmas PJs, along with countless other families and a smattering of friendly elves, the four of them made the surprisingly fast journey from the downtown Akron, Ohio, train station to the North Pole. Geeked up on hot chocolate and candy canes, with faces smashed against the frosty passenger windows, children and a few adults yearned for an up-close look at Santa's workshop. Later, my father chuckled when he told me that although my daughter was interested in the workshop and elves, she seemed completely preoccupied with discovering the North Pole had its own *Winking Lizard* restaurant, especially since we regularly frequented the same place on weekends. He told her there was more than one restaurant, which was sort of true, as there are a few others throughout Northeast Ohio, and Santa obviously enjoys his share of chicken wings. Just look at him!

Before the black locomotive carrying the packed and steamy Cuyahoga Valley Railroad passenger cars cut through the Cuyahoga National Park on a dark, snowy night—and before the big man himself made an appearance in the train car carrying my children—all had gathered for dinner across the street from the train station at a well-known Akron restaurant called *Luigi's*. Opened in 1949, this beloved establishment has been serving classic Italian dishes for over 75 years and is a must-stop for visitors to Akron or for those returning home. When friends or workmates visit town, you inevitably end up there in a booth, snuggled up against a wall with autographed pictures of famous patrons and mounds of fresh mozzarella atop your salads as you await their delicious pizza pie.

That evening, Vern joined the table for dinner. An affable Texas lawyer, he was a long-time business associate and friend of the family who was in town for work at Firestone with my dad. Far from Dallas, Vern undoubtedly enjoyed the familiar surroundings, catching up with my parents, the great food and, presumably, my excited children dressed in their Christmas PJs. In the dim light of the restaurant, at some point during the meal, he noticed my father had a bloodshot eye and asked him about it. Dad told him the eye had given him problems for several days and when he originally thought it had gone away, it came back again. Mom joined in by commenting that he seemed to get bloodshot eyes more often, but they did seem to go away. Taking a sip of *Coca-Cola*, all while my kids chattered about Santa and the North Pole, he told my dad, "Jim, I'd get it checked out; you never know." As for the *Polar Express* and the wisdom of my parents' decision to soon board a train with hundreds of children, the otherwise talkative trial lawyer remained mute.

A few years before, my Aunt Jill—Dad's little sister—had found herself sitting across a table from Frank Jessie at this same Akron hangout following a mini-reunion for a local catholic high school in Akron now known as St. Vincent-St. Mary. As I said, it's where you usually find yourself when visiting the area. St. Vincent-St. Mary—like the city—is best known over the last twenty years for being the home of Lebron James. Frank—like Lebron—had played basketball at St. Vincent—albeit a few years before—while my aunt had been a cheerleader there. Both were good students and even though they shared a ninth-grade algebra class in 1961, they managed to graduate, hardly knowing each other. It had been over thirty years and while not everyone looked quite the same, *Luigi's* had hardly changed at all. At one point, after sharing local memories and a few good laughs with those at the table, Frank asked Jill if he might get in touch with her again in the future. When my aunt told my future uncle, "Sure, I'd like that," little did Frank know that he was sitting across the table from his future wife or that he'd soon be returning to his old high school to share in the madness surrounding "the chosen one." He also could not possibly have known the enormous impact he would one day have on my son's life.

Rowan Oak

Our second official "guy trip" took place in the first week of October 2012. The game we picked was Texas A&M at Ole Miss in Oxford, Mississippi and when we rolled into town in the early morning hours, we knew exactly where we had to go first.

Along white walls—scrawled in graphite pencil and a red-grease pencil—is the plot outline of *A Fable*. Written in large letters by hand and positioned about 2 or 3 feet from the ceiling, is every day of the week, starting with Monday on one wall and ending with Sunday on another. Below each day, and in smaller print, is additional scribbled detail. William Faulkner literally mapped out his working plan for the novel from one wall to the next, which is set during Holy Week and World War I. The week, much like the story itself, is now forever frozen in time as the novel was published in 1954. He spent over a decade working on it, hoping to make it one of his greatest works and, although it was met with mixed reviews, the novel did ultimately fetch him a Pulitzer Prize. Below the plot-lined walls of the famous author's office—set atop a small table—rests a typewriter. It was given to him by his mother and, though it has long since gone silent, at one time, Faulkner banged out nearly every finished word he ever wrote on this mechanical device.

For me, our college football journey began anew in this room. As I stared at the walls and then back at the typewriter, I imagined the author locked in this writer's den in the early morning hours when he was prone to write, searching for his next great word. When the mood struck him, he was also known to take the typewriter to a neighboring porch to enjoy the outdoors and write from a favorite Adirondack chair. In this study, as I walked across its creaky wooden floors, I caught a glimpse of a beautiful story not yet told. It was our story, and it was immediately etched across my mind. Each football trip, much like Faulkner's days of the week, could be mapped out through time. Each with its own tale, but part of a larger narrative. Right there and then, I knew we had embarked on something uniquely special, and if properly nurtured, it would only grow in time. What I did not see, and could not possibly know, is that one day I would write about it.

For October, the average temperature in Oxford, Mississippi, is usually between 75 for a high and 51 for a low. However, when we drove up to the former author's Greek Revival house behind a double row of ancient cedars, it felt more like 35 degrees tops. The short-statured writer—with his pinched mouth, prominent brow, deep hazel-brown eyes, beaked nose, and trademark mustache—would have opted for his office over the neighboring porch to write a few words this fall morning. Luckily, we had brought obligatory Midwest gear, including coats. The sky was bright white, but since the forecast called for rain, we decided against a stroll through the nearby *Bailey Woods Trail*, where Faulkner was known to wander in the evenings and afternoons.

Staring at the beautifully maintained white house, built in the early 1840s by the wealthy Irish planter, Robert Sheegog, we were immediately drawn to the central pedimented portico supported by paired columns with Doric capitals. Faulkner bought the house in 1930, during the early days of the Great Depression, when the house, like the country, was in disrepair. The first thing he did, besides applying a fresh layer of paint, was to rename his new home *Rowan*

Oak. Taken from Frazer's *Golden Bough*, Faulkner localized the Scot's legendary Rowan Tree—a symbol of peace and security, with the live oak—a symbol of strength and solitude. This place, renamed, would be his home for the rest of his life, and this home, this town, and her famous writer would soon capture our hearts.

Truth be told, as a young man, I was never a big fan of any of William Faulkner's works. Like most, I was made to read—with the help of Cliff Notes—*The Sound and the Fury* and *As I Lay Dying* while in high school. I much preferred Hemingway and Steinbeck, as I could better navigate and decipher their stories, while the poetry of Frost was downright soothing in comparison. In college, when I embarked on my own self-directed American literature binge, I picked up *Absalom, Absalom!* and *Mosquitoes* at a cool campus bookstore full of hippies and artists. However, after making myself read the former, I still felt as if I had barely understood a single word. Faulkner's love of whiskey and tobacco was far easier to discern. Cleanth Brooks, the renowned professor and American literary critic, reminds us that Faulkner works well in classrooms as it requires a kind of active reading, as "there was so much to do with each exact text by Faulkner, so much to unfold that has been carefully and ingeniously folded by the author." There is little doubt his works demand a reader's unwavering attention. His writing style is unpredictable, terribly uneven, and, at times, for me, downright annoying. Reading Faulkner demands patience—patience many young readers do not have. However, as Jay Parini reminds us in *One Matchless Time-A Life of William Faulkner*, "The confusions of the text almost always dissolve after several readings…Faulkner cannot be read, he can only be reread."

The night before, approximately 85 miles north, we had stayed and dined in Memphis, Tennessee. The weather was good, but the ribs were better. Before our trip, we had a big decision to make. Knowing that our flight took us to *Blues City*, the home of *Graceland*, we had to decide where to have our Friday night dinner. More importantly, we had to decide if we were going to indulge in wet or dry ribs, and, in the end, we went with the obvious choice—the closest rib joint to where we were.

Tucked in a narrow alley across from the *Peabody Hotel*, down a short flight of stairs in what is a basement, Daniel, my father, my brother, and I found ourselves seated at a cozy table with a Vichy-style tablecloth. It was another Friday night in America, and *Charlie Vergos Rendezvous* was hopping. *Charlie Vergos* has been making ribs since 1948, when my dad was but a wee lad. Legend has it that Charlie started selling ham sandwiches and beer at *Rendezvous*, turning an old elevator shaft into a smoker. He later added his famous ribs. It is little wonder that the place has been in business for over 75 years, as the food is delicious, while the atmosphere is classic Americana. Outside, smoke billows across the downtown Memphis rooftop of the industrial-looking structure, while inside, a whirlwind of food and activity unfolds. Outside, a small sign, partially encased in wrought iron, proclaims "Charcoal Ribs," while inside an open kitchen, along with servers hauling trays full of grub, proclaims order in chaos. The walls are crammed with pictures of famous guests and with a quick perusal, one can locate pictures of past Presidents Ronald Reagan, George H.W. Bush, and George W. Bush. A photo of Bill Clinton, not surprisingly, shows the 42nd President hamming it up in the kitchen surrounded by smiling staff.

Dinner included orders of ribs—cooked on racks for an hour and a half, some 18 inches from the fire, washed in vinegar, and seasoned with a Greek chili recipe and paprika—along with orders of slaw and beans. The meal was washed down with several beers from *Ghost River Brewing Company* while Daniel sipped a Coke under a pen light he had brought from home. Dad, dressed in his navy sports jacket, light blue shirt, and jeans, probably also enjoyed a wild turkey with a "splash of soda." It was his typical Friday night libation, but I just cannot recall if he ordered one that night or not. What I can recall is his black hair, dark brown eyes, contagious smile, clear voice, and optimistic attitude. I can also remember we spent nearly two hours eating, drinking, laughing, catching up, and planning our next day at Ole Miss. It was also one of the best dinners the Gardner men ever shared together and set in motion a tradition that is a major part of what we endearingly call "Friday night dinner on the guy trip."

Oxford, Mississippi

Literature permeates everything in Oxford like an early morning dew. After our morning run to William Faulkner's home, we found ourselves in the charming town square, where we enjoyed a cup of black coffee followed by a bit of shopping. Our first stop was *Square Books*, which is a mammoth bookstore made up of three separate buildings and, given the chillier-than-expected temperatures, we managed to procure a few Ole Miss stocking caps and pullovers to wear to the Ole Miss-Texas A&M game scheduled later in the day. Still, hours before kick-off, the square was packed, but our crew (Dan, Dad, my brother, and I) found a place—upstairs—for a pre-game meal consisting of burgers, fries, and cokes. As we looked out over the landscape, we quickly realized this town, especially in the cracks, angles, and shadows, revealed a story we could never fully comprehend. Much had happened here and long before we ever came around.

Elijah Evan Edwards served as the Chaplain of the 7th Minnesota Volunteer Infantry during the Civil War. Before his military service, he was a professor of ancient languages and even served as a college president. He had long brown hair and an untamed beard to match. However, he may be best remembered for his diary, which provides a detailed account of his wartime experiences, which are a thousand miles away from his home. One such experience occurred on August 22, 1864, years before our visit to the *Magnolia* State, when Oxford, Mississippi, was deliberately set ablaze by the Union Army under the command of General Andrew Jackson Smith. Edwards describes the scene as follows: "*I saw everywhere scenes of riot and wildest confusion. Many houses were in flames, and others were being plundered relentlessly by the mob consisting of mostly of soldiers, without guidance but acting as any unruly mob would do. They carried from the buildings all kinds of plunder most of which could not be any use to them. They carried mirrors, rocking chairs, vases, articles of wearing apparel, bedding, books. As the smoke grew denser the scene grew more weird and more like Hades. This piece of diabolical tomfoolery was capped by an exhibition that would scarcely be deemed possible, in a CIVIL war. A drunken man on horse-back came galloping through the smoke, holding before him a grinning skeleton which he had stolen from a Doctor's office. It is said this vandal was a Surgeon's Assistant. Whoever he was, and I did not want to know more, his act was the most revolting that I have to chronicle.*"Today, what the Chaplain describes would clearly constitute war crimes.

By the time the Union Army marched out of town, much of Oxford had been left to glow in a bed of embers. Designed to, among other things, lower morale, the pillage of Oxford, Mississippi, was not unique, as many cities in the South suffered a similar fate. In fact, Hampton, Virginia; Winton, North Carolina; Baton Rouge, Louisiana; Donaldsonville, Louisiana; Randolph, Tennessee; Fredericksburg, Virginia; Celina, Tennessee; Greenville, Mississippi; Jackson, Mississippi; Austin, Mississippi; Hernando, Mississippi; Bluffton, South Carolina; Darien, Mississippi; Eunice, Arkansas; Vicksburg, Mississippi; Old Columbus, Tennessee; Meridian, Mississippi; Alaxandria, Louisiana; Rome, Georgia; Atlanta, Georgia; Griswoldville, Georgia; McPhersonville, South Carolina; Orangeburg, South Carolina; Columbia, South Carolina; Charleston, South Carolina; Petersburg, Virginia; Tuscaloosa, Alabama; and Richmond, Virginia, were all either torched or ruthlessly bombarded. If you are not familiar with all those places, it is not surprising, as a few were never rebuilt.

Oxford, Mississippi, like much of the South, was left traumatized by the war. The scars run deep. Most of the American Civil War took place on Southern soil and, while the South sought to defend territory, the North aimed to conquer it. Edwards and others may have written about what they did and saw, but Southerners lived through the events and the aftermath. Not only were cities destroyed, but the entire infrastructure was left in ruins, and with the "total war" tactic employed by Union General William Tecumseh Sherman and others, crops were burned, and homes were systematically sabotaged. Many were literally left with only their shirts on their backs.

This result was all but inevitable as not only was the South on the wrong side of history, but it was also completely outmatched. The North had a population of over 20 million people, while the South had a population of 9 million people, with 5.5 million free and 3.5 million enslaved. The North had a commercial and manufacturing economy, while the South was primarily agricultural. In fact, by 1860, the North produced 90% of the nation's manufactured goods, including 32 times more firearms than the South. The North also had a well-developed rail system and abundant natural resources, including coal, iron, and gold. Again, the result, like the cause, in hindsight, was a foregone conclusion, and we are left to imagine a grinning Alexander Hamilton—with locked eyes—staring across a room at the face of a downcast Thomas Jefferson.

The year before Oxford was burned to the ground, in 1863, Abraham Lincoln announced the *Proclamation of Amnesty and Reconstruction*—known as the Ten-Percent Plan—which required 10 percent of the Confederate states' voters to pledge an oath of allegiance to the Union to begin the process of readmission to the Union. However, reconstruction is a long and slow process, especially when it involves rebuilding your home, your community, your stained history, and your present identity. At times, it can also be downright tricky.

Following the war, and long after the Union armies had gone home, the South remained largely frozen in a state of shock. The North no longer occupied her lands, but most certainly occupied her mind. Edward A. Pollard, the editor of a Richmond newspaper, published *The Lost Cause: A New Southern History of the War of the Confederates*, which he championed as a "New Southern History" and which he hoped would serve as a vehicle for presenting the Confederate version of the war to the world. Pollard's hunch was certainly correct, as the victors of war are left unabated to write their history. Still, while he vainly searches for justifications in the Confederate cause, not surprisingly, he is left empty-handed. Ironically, his book title—*The Lost Cause*—has become a cliche phrase used by Northern journalists, and Southern academics for that matter, as a ready-made soundbite used to explain the aftermath of the Civil War. Of course, such a monolithic view fails to appreciate the complexity of having an entire war fought in one's backyard, the actual process needed to create a new community/identity and blatantly ignores the brutality witnessed by a Minnesota Chaplain in the Union army who described the happenings as being *like Hades*. In the end, comprehending the sins of a father is not an easy exercise. It takes time. Furthermore, humility is needed by everyone, regardless of locale, as man's fall from grace occurred long before the United States was even a whisper. Lastly, lest we forget, revisionists stand on both banks of this river as the war was not fought entirely on the issue of slavery, even if in the North, we wish it had been.

Trisomy 21

Years before our run-in with the charismatic hospital geneticist—remember the guy who told us in the hospital that our son would essentially never amount to anything—I sat in a high school (or maybe it was in junior high) science class listening to a teacher explain chromosomes. Yes, it's a trip down memory lane, right? What we learned then, and maybe still remember now, is that they are normally together in 23 pairs—46 in all—half of which come from the mother and half from the father. Our bodies have instructions encoded in our DNA and these instructions are carried out by our chromosomes. Probably the best known, and certainly the most talked about in any high school, concerns the two sex chromosomes, with one carried by the sperm of the father and one carried in the egg of the mother. The egg typically carries an X chromosome, whereas the sperm might contain an X or a Y chromosome. If the combination is XX, you have instructions for a girl, but if the combination is XY, you have instructions for a boy. This instruction is in the 23rd pair of chromosomes. Since I carried a Y chromosome, Daniel's instructions were to build a boy. His eyes and hair color were contained in the 19th pair and his height and build were most likely included in the 17th pair.

These carefully written instructions, akin to a recipe passed on from one generation to another, might also contain a predisposition to certain diseases or ailments during a lifetime. For instance, the first set of chromosomes has been linked to prostate cancer/breast cancer, the 2nd to autism, the 3rd to lung cancer, the 6th to diabetes, and the 14th to Alzheimer's disease.

Modern genetics has identified thousands of chromosomal abnormalities, including trisomy 21, which is characterized by an extra chromosome 21. The third 21st chromosome, commonly referred to as trisomy 21, is what typically causes 95% of all Down syndrome. The two other types are called translocation and mosaicism; although rare, errors in these patterns can create Down syndrome. Individuals with a mosaic cell pattern, where some cells have trisomy and others do not, may exhibit less pronounced characteristics of Down syndrome.

Chromosome 21 is the most well-known trisomy, occurring in approximately 1 in every 700 to 800 births, although the rate increases with maternal age. However, there are other lesser-known extra copies of these chromosomes, including trisomy 13 (Patau syndrome), which leads to birth defects, as do trisomy 9 and 22. Sadly, many affected by trisomy 18 (Edwards syndrome) do not survive beyond infancy and pregnancies with trisomy 16—the most common trisomy usually occurring in 1% of all pregnancies—typically result in miscarriage. Each trisomy results in a person having 47 chromosomes, not 46, thus inevitably altering the delivery of encoded instructions in DNA.

Three years before players from Princeton and Rutgers held the first intercollegiate football contest in America, John Langdon Down delivered his research paper to the *London Hospital* in England. It is not known what, if anything, he might have made of America's newfangled creation or if he approved or disapproved of the changes made to his native Britain's rugby and football (soccer). However, when the British physician presented his findings in 1866, he most certainly hoped to reshape medicine and anthropology, at least in merry old England. As the superintendent of the *Earlswood Asylum for Idiots,* he had long been a visiting physician at *London Hospital.* In "*Observations of an Ethnic Classification of Idiots,*" Down put forth the theory that it was possible to classify different types of conditions by ethnic characteristics. He further took specific aim at the great Mongolian family, believing a very large number of congenital "idiots" are typically Mongols. John Langdon Down also believed the great Mongolian family represented a reversion of Caucasian children to earlier racial types and, although blatantly racist through a modern lens, in retrospect, these statements were not merely provocative but quite liberal for the time. Yes, he suggested Caucasians were more developed, but in doing so, he was also breaking from Victorian science by suggesting all races shared a common ancestry. His misguided aim at the Mongolian family, although feeble by today's standards, represents a breakthrough in attempting to find the commonality of physical features among the disabled. Further, his lifetime of work in assisting people with disabilities easily eclipses any early misguidance.

In 1858, before the American Civil War, John Langdon Down had been appointed Medical Superintendent of the *Earlswood Asylum*. It was here, starting in earnest in 1862, that he cataloged the characteristics of a genetic condition that would one day bear his name. The first and most common symptom of Down syndrome is a disability in intellectual development, known previously as being "mentally retarded." This symptom, although best known, is also the most difficult to generalize as the intellectual capabilities of those people with Down syndrome vary greatly. Those with Down syndrome also share a laundry list of potential medical issues, including congenital heart defects, with roughly one-third being born with Atrioventricular Septal Defect—a large hole between the upper filling chambers (atria) and the lower pumping chambers (ventricles) of the heart—which occurs when the heart does not usually develop in the womb. Instead of having two separate valves between the atria and the ventricles, there is only one valve. As a result, more blood flows from the left side of the heart to the right, increasing pressure and ultimately causing the right side to work harder and, thereby, less efficiently. Other developmental cardiac problems include mitral or aortic valve regurgitation, which occurs when these valves do not close properly, causing the backflow of blood. Many born with Down syndrome require life-saving surgery or surgeries to correct these defects. Those born with Down syndrome might also battle vision problems, hearing loss, susceptibility to infections, hypothyroidism, blood disorders, hypotonia (poor muscle tone), sleep apnea, problems with the upper part of the spine, especially in the cervical spine near the skull, dental issues, digestive problems, epilepsy, Celiac disease, dermatological complications, and obesity. For those who live into advanced adulthood, dementia and Alzheimer's are also a known risk.

John Langdon Down was unaware of many of these now-identified medical complications, but he was nonetheless able to catalog many of the physical characteristics of those with Down syndrome, as it is largely recognizable to the naked eye. In 1866, he identified a group of his asylum residents as having common facial features that differed from those of the general population and the other residents. This, in part, is why he believed they must be from the same family. The doctor identified a flattened face, especially the bridge of the nose and almond-shaped eyes (commonly referred to in early Western medical circles as "Mongoloid eye fold"). He further identified a "long, thick, and much roughened" tongue. Later, in 1924, Thomas Brushfield, a medical student at Cambridge University, identified tiny white spots on the iris—the colored part—of the eye—which came to be known as "Brushfield spots." A short neck, small ears and an overall small stature are also common physical characteristics in many with Down syndrome. In 1908, Reginald Langdon Down—the son of John Langdon Down—correctly identified a single crease across the palm of the hand now known as a palmar crease or simian crease. In a peculiar, if not wholly implausible twist of fate, Reginald's only son, Jonathan, was born with Down Syndrome. Sometimes, the truth is stranger than fiction.

While a cluster of agreed-upon common characteristics continued to form, the root cause of Down syndrome remained unknown at the start of the 20th century. An initial breakthrough in unlocking this mystery started when, during the 1920s, a medical doctor named Lionel Penrose began to grapple with the role of heredity in the mental deficiency of his patients at an Institution in England. In collecting statistical analysis, he was able to identify that the incidence of Down syndrome was much greater if the mother was more than 35 years of age. Simultaneously, he found no correlation between the age of the patient's father. Penrose was unable to take his query further but believed race and mongolism had nothing to do with the known deficiencies. In 1961, Penrose, along with Norman Langdon Down—a grandson of John Langdon Down—and a group of prominent scientists, penned a letter to the editor of the British medical journal called *The Lancet* urging the medical profession to abandon the term "Mongolism." The editor of this publication believed an appropriate alternative might be *Down syndrome,* and the rest, as they say, is history.

In the early 1950s, across the English Channel, in nearby France, a French pediatrician and scientist named Jérôme Lejeune, working in Raymond Turpin's laboratory, and in conjunction with Dr. Marthe Gautier, discovered a connection between an individual's characteristics and one's fingerprints and lines on their hand. In 1956, biologists from Lund University in Sweden announced to the world the discovery that mankind has 46 chromosomes. In the world of genetics, this discovery was a quantum leap forward and two years later, on May 22, 1958, after first noticing a discrepancy in the chromosome count in those with Down syndrome, Lejeune and Gautier reported the discovery that Down syndrome was caused by an extra copy of chromosome 21. This incredible discovery would be later disputed as Turpin and Gautier believed that their contributions had not been adequately acknowledged and in 2014—two decades after Lejeune's passing—Gautier was appointed the rank of Officer of the French Legion of Honor for her role in the discovery. As for Lejeune, during his life, he earned the Kennedy Prize, and his unyielding love and tenderness towards the disabled put him on a path toward sainthood. Although Down syndrome has an English name, it was most certainly bequeathed a French heart.

Just Three Years before I was Born

Ole Miss is no stranger to controversy. Originally derived from the plantation days in Mississippi, the name, through time, would become synonymous with the University of Mississippi. Chartered by the state legislature in 1841, planners chose a rural site in Oxford to build the school, and in 1848, the school welcomed its first class of 80 students. During the burning of Oxford in the Civil War, several buildings at the University were spared destruction as they were being used as a hospital for both armies. The University reopened in 1865 and to avoid rejecting veterans, admission standards were lowered and costs decreased by eliminating tuition. Current students, no doubt, wish this were still the case. Later, in 1882, the university began admitting women and was the first college in the Southeast to hire a female faculty member. However, the student body remained entirely white for over 100 years.

The school's sports teams were initially called the *Red and Blue* and for a brief period in 1929 became known as the *Mississippi Flood.* A contest run by the student newspaper in 1936 resulted in *Rebels* being the new nickname, which beat out *Stonewalls* and *Confederates*. Some lobbied for *Democrats,* but to no avail. The mascot became *Colonel Rebel*—an old white guy with white hair and a matching white goatee, who donned a red suit, big red hat, and a dark string tie. However, by the 1950s, campus life hardly resembled a rebellious lifestyle and the student body—unless dressed for an antebellum-themed party—most certainly looked nothing like *Colonel Rebel.* Charles Eagles, a history professor at the University of Mississippi and author of *The Price of Defiance*, writes, "Instead, Ole Miss stressed social life, encouraged conformity, and emphasized institutional traditions." The school further developed the aura of an exclusive club or a finishing school for Mississippi's finest. Adored by students, alumni, and locals alike, and resembling an aspired cultured living, the school also became known for beauty queens and winning football teams. Both became institutional traditions. Both became a way of life.

Mary Ann Mobley came to the university in 1955 as a prestigious Carrier Scholar. She was not only an excellent student but was also a trained singer, dancer, and model. Mobley even served as an officer in student government and had been selected for Mortar Board, an honorary leadership group. In 1959, the "brown-haired Southern belle" won the Miss America beauty pageant. The following year, Lynda Lee Mead, another "dark-haired beauty," took home the crown. She was from Natchez, Mississippi and was Mobley's sorority sister at Ole Miss. In 1962, Annice Raye Jernigan traveled to Atlantic City to compete in the Miss America pageant and, although the Ole Miss student did not win the crown, she was one of eight other Ole Miss students to be crowned Miss Mississippi during a ten-year stretch.

Ole Miss was equally dominant on the football field. In fact, the 1959 team not only won a National Championship but is also considered by many as the greatest team in the history of the *SEC*. The *Rebels* outscored their opponents 350-21, and the defense posted eight shutouts in eleven games. Perhaps even more remarkable, the defense never allowed a single touchdown drive during the entire season. The next year, in 1960, taking a play from the playbook of the Chi Omega sorority house, the football team won a second undisputed National Championship. Winning games, like crowns, had become commonplace with the arrival of legendary coach Johnny Vaught in 1947 and *Sports Illustrated* took notice with an article in 1960 entitled *"Babes, Brutes, and Ole Miss."* One excerpt read, "The young men at Ole Miss are astonishingly broad-shouldered and happily carefree. They are friendly and courteous, but there is a slight swagger about them…The young women at Ole Miss are softly pretty, …and it is no wonder at all that in rapid succession, two of them have been chosen Miss America. The wonder is that girls from other regions even have a chance."

With the convergence of great football teams, Miss Americas, and the dawning of the television age, Ole Miss was clearly in the national spotlight. On September 24, 1962, a special college football issue of *Sports Illustrated* featured the University on the cover. In retrospect, the picture taken the season before at the Cotton Bowl in Dallas, Texas, is surreal. Five flag girls—with matching grey tops, grey miniskirts, and white boots—all have one hand on their hip while the other arm hoists a Confederate flag high above each of their heads. Within a week of this cover hitting newsstands across the country, the entire nation would be focused on Ole Miss, but it would have nothing to do with football or beauty pageants. Instead, it would involve an infinitely more significant endeavor.

Eight years before, in 1954, the Supreme Court ruled in *Brown v. Board of Education of Topeka* that segregation of public schools was unconstitutional. James Meredith graduated from high school in 1951 and enlisted in the United States Air Force, where he served until 1959. Thereafter, he attended classes at Jackson State University—a historically Black University. In 1961, following the inauguration of John F. Kennedy, Meredith applied to the University of Mississippi but did not identify himself as an African American until midway through the application process. In response, state officials delayed and otherwise blocked his application, and Meredith ultimately sued the University. On September 10, 1962, the Supreme Court ruled that Meredith must be admitted for the fall semester. The next few weeks that followed would not only be downright raucous but also historic.

When we approached the life-size bronze statue hours before kick-off, it was hard to imagine what it must have been like for James Meredith on October 1, 1962, when he entered *The Lyceum*—an academic building at the center of campus and previously spared destruction during the Civil War—to register for classes as the first African American in the university's history. The statue depicts Meredith walking towards a nearby 17-foot limestone portal, with the words "courage," "knowledge," "opportunity," and "perseverance" inscribed around the top; there are no statues of the federal agents who accompanied him that morning. There is also no replica of the riot-battered border patrol car in which he was driven from his dormitory at Baxter Hall. You cannot hear the slurs hurled against him, but unfortunately, you can easily imagine. They still echo. Gone is the debris from the riots that shook the town, the state, and the nation the day before his triumphant walk into history. Gone are the tear gas and Molotov cocktails, as are the stolen bulldozer and the commandeered fire engine. There is also no statue of Dr. L.G. Hopkins, a lone country doctor who cared for the wounded throughout the night. However, there is clearly still a Faulkner aroma, especially since his nephew—Captain Murray Faulkner—served with the 67 guardsmen of Troop E and helped to form a perimeter around local marshals and *The Lyceum* until daylight finally won.

Wearing a buttoned suit and tie and with a faint mustache, the statue gives no clue as to the genuinely precarious situation Meredith had found himself in. The day before, on September 30, 1962, as the riots raged, President Kennedy considered using a helicopter to extract Meredith but feared he would be assassinated. Ultimately, as a last resort, the President invoked the Insurrection Act of 1807 and ordered the U.S. Army to suppress the riots. There is a plaque marking the site of the riots, where two people—French journalist Paul Guihard and 23-year-old jukebox repairman Roy Gunter—lost their lives. It is now designated as a National Historic Site. The Ole Miss football team went undefeated that same year, winning their third National Championship in four years.

At the front of the statue, near his feet, an inscription reads, "*James H. Meredith, a Mississippi native of Kosciusko, stepped onto the pages of history on October 1, 1962, when he opened the doors to higher education at the University of Mississippi and in the South. As a major figure in the American civil rights movement, he helped lead the way to justice and equality for all citizens.*" As we walked towards *The Grove,* it seemed hard to believe this had all occurred just three years before I was born, and I thought about those words, "lead the way to justice and equality for *all* citizens." I squeezed Daniel's hand extra tightly.

While Meredith walked into a firestorm in Mississippi that same year—1962—another individual entered a campus thousands of miles away in California and, although he could not physically walk, his actions were another giant step toward justice and equality for all citizens. His story also shares another special link to our family and the battle for integration. Edward Roberts was born in 1939, and, like most young boys, he enjoyed playing football and baseball with his friends. By the early 1950s, he had also become the star athlete at his school. However, one day in 1953, when he was 14 years old, Ed came home saying he wasn't feeling well. The next morning, he woke up with a fever and a sore backbone and after a house call from a family doctor, he was taken to a nearby hospital. The young man, who walked into the hospital, was admitted that same night but never walked again. Two days later, he couldn't breathe without assistance.

A 1952 survey found that Americans feared only nuclear annihilation more than polio. The virus, seemingly random and without a known cure at the time, struck fear in nearly everyone, especially parents. They felt helpless and for good reason. It was still two years before the Salk Vaccine would be rolled out, allowing moms and dads to finally sleep peacefully again. Polio is a highly infectious disease that attacks the nervous system. The symptoms are typically pain, weakness, fatigue, and muscle loss, and the disease can lead to paralysis or death. During the first half of the 20th century, the disease paralyzed hundreds of thousands of children, and Ed Roberts was one of them. The year before Roberts was admitted to the hospital, 21,000 Americans contracted a paralyzing form of polio and 3,000 died from it. Ed, no doubt, contracted a mutated version of this same polio virus, and his family was soon quarantined as the only defense against the disease was avoidance or "social distancing." Sound familiar?

There are countless images of young children, many with nervous smiles, being treated for polio in what was called the *iron lung*. The big machine, which resembled a small tubular submarine, assisted in breathing when muscle control was lost. It was a lifesaver for thousands, including a young Ed Roberts, but unfortunately, he would never be able to breathe without assistance again. Paralyzed in most of his body, he could only move two fingers on his left hand and two toes on his left foot. He remained in hospitals for years before returning home to live in a makeshift bedroom set up in the dining room of a new house because his old house was not big enough for the machine in which he slept every night and often rested during the day. When not in the iron lung, Roberts survived by "frog breathing," a technique for forcing air into the lungs using facial and neck muscles. This technique also allowed him to speak and otherwise communicate effectively.

While at home, Roberts attended classes by telephone. Then, when he was not quite twenty, his mother loaded him into their station wagon, drove a few blocks, unloaded his wheelchair, lifted him up, strapped him in, and wheeled him through the doors of his high school. She insisted that her son go to school in person. Although he was terribly frightened by the prospect, he managed to gain acceptance from his fellow students, and along the way, his confidence ballooned.

Having battled polio, paralysis, lung failure, and the fear of being seen in public, his fight was just beginning. Although Roberts had completed all his academic work, the school initially refused to let him graduate with a high school diploma as he had neither fulfilled his gym requirement nor learned to drive. Thankfully, the school board ultimately reversed course. Next, the California Department of Rehabilitation refused Roberts' financial assistance for college, as they determined he was not employable. A decision, in retrospect, which is richly ironic if not a wonderfully karma-laced event, as he later became the director of the California Department of Rehabilitation. I know, rich, right? Lastly, Edward Roberts successfully entered UC Berkeley in 1962 after initially being told the school was not able to "accommodate cripples." At first, the administration argued it was simply not feasible, as the campus was built on hills, and the dorm rooms were not nearly large enough to accommodate Roberts and his iron lung. However, by coincidence, the Director of Student Housing was also a physician who had worked previously with individuals suffering from polio. After meeting Ed, the doctor said, "You say you want to enroll here as a student? They're quite a few of you (with polio), you know. You're the first I've seen here, but I venture to say you won't be the last. Let's see what we can work out." The infirmary would be his dormitory, and the doctor was correct as although Edward Roberts was the first profoundly disabled student to attend UC Berkeley, he was not the last; within a year, he was joined by others and the third floor of the infirmary would later become known as the "Rolling Quads"—ground zero for Disabled Students Programs (DSP) with Roberts at the helm.

Edward Roberts passed away several years before my son was born. He was 56 years old. Besides being a trailblazer, he is also considered a founding father of the Independent Living Movement and hundreds of Centers for Independent Living around the world are based on his original model. Located at a fully accessible transit hub, the Ed Roberts Campus is a national and international model dedicated to disability rights and universal access. If we ever get to a Cal football game, we intend to visit the center and see *The Disability Mural*—a community artwork by people who have experienced or been touched by disability. As for Ed's mom, she celebrated her 103rd birthday in April of 2023. And James Meredith? He celebrated his 91st birthday in 2024. He originally opposed his statue at Ole Miss and believed it should be removed along with a nearby Confederate monument. However, he has since changed his mind. Our family appreciates his change of heart as we may never have fully comprehended his independent story, nor the story of Edward Roberts, and the inflection point that was 1962, without the statue as our starting point. It turns out Ole Miss football players were not the only champions that year.

The Grove

Envy is defined as a feeling of discontent or resentful longing aroused by someone else's possessions, qualities, or luck. For years, we knew very little about Ole Miss traditions and tailgating at *The Grove*. If we had known then what we know now, we would have surely felt a twinge of envy every Saturday for those lucky souls in Oxford, Mississippi. The truth is, we had heard whispers of a legendary tailgating spot in northern Mississippi, but much like the grainy black and white photographs of the *Loch Ness* monster or *Bigfoot*, we proudly played the role of skeptics. Perhaps clouded by our northern prejudice, we questioned how such a place could exist without it being a part of the *Big 10* or Notre Dame. Surely, if such a grand place could even be found in the South, it would be in Tuscaloosa at the University of Alabama and not in Oxford, Mississippi. No, this reeked of mythology and unlike those explorers who dreamed of finding *El Dorado*, we would not legitimize the fantasy of stumbling upon a city made of gold. However, pride and ignorance can be dangerous, and lessons are readily available for all who are willing to acknowledge the errors of their ways. Personally, I still do not believe in the *Loch Ness* monster, *El Dorado*, or even sometimes *Bigfoot*. However, when it comes to tailgating, we discovered the holy grail and like willing disciples, we are out to spread the good news. Envy can be as destructive as pride and prejudice, and we want no part of it.

We had no clue about the true extent of tradition and pageantry that awaited us, especially in the center area of the Ole Miss campus near a cluster of oak, elm, and magnolia trees. Early Friday morning, before every home football game, on what is affectionately called *Trash Can Friday*, the University places red and blue trash cans throughout campus in anticipation of the impending party. A plethora of those iconic cans are put in the 10-acre, tree-lined area known as *The Grove* and serve as a signal that "spot holding" is now open. From 6:30 a.m. until 8:00 p.m., students, student groups, fraternities, sororities, businesses, academic departments, sports teams, alumni, and even rival fans fill the park to plant their flag on what is considered prime real estate. They set up chairs, bring blankets and picnic baskets, play cornhole and hacky sack (yes, it is a college campus), and do what they can to pass the hours. Some come in groups and take turns occupying their newly claimed turf, while others fly solo and hope that reinforcements will soon arrive. Nobody dares leave a spot unattended, as countless others—resembling crazed parents looking for a dining table at Disney World for their families—will swoop in immediately as if they have been lurking behind one of the beautiful trees the entire time. By early afternoon, for the most part, the park resembles a large board game with a game piece sitting in every imaginable space.

The one rule, which is strictly enforced by campus police, is no tailgating equipment is allowed in *The Grove* or on campus before 8:00 p.m. At 7:59, the campus police carefully remove all road barriers, and at 8:00 p.m., they set off a siren. What happens next is known as the *Running of the Tents*. Trucks and SUVs, lined up as far as the eye can see and reminiscent of a good old-fashioned convoy, stream onto campus. Packed with supplies, these vehicles pull up to curbs and are unloaded quicker than a NASCAR pitstop. From there, the actual running begins, with people using dollies, carts, and their backs to get the tents to the promised land as soon as possible. Every second counts, as by 8:30 or so, nearly every spot, back-to-back and neighbor-to-neighbor, has a tent set up or clearly taking form. In the business world, it would be considered a construction miracle and would no doubt perplex residents of any major city. At Ole Miss, it's just how they do things. It is not known how boundary disputes are managed or if there is a "border sheriff" who patrols the park. Maybe it is best if that remains a mystery, as we are spared potentially unsavory details. One more thing to mention, if it all seems to be a little too much, a multitude of local outfits will help stake out spots, set up tents, and provide a variety of rental options. We guess that such an option is expensive, but let's face it, good stuff seldom comes cheap.

By the time we arrived on campus, *The Grove* was a sea of red and blue as far as the eye could see. A smattering of maroon tents, say one in a hundred, showed the admirable commitment of a few of the visiting contingent, but make no mistake about it—we were deep in *Rebel* territory. Originally called "the Glade," *The Grove* earned its name in 1935. However, despite the first home game at Ole Miss taking place on November 11, 1893, *The Grove's* tailgating story did not begin in earnest until the 1950s. In those early days, tailgaters began parking their cars and RVs in and around the park just a few times a year. This was partly because very few games, including home games, were played in Oxford. Most big games were instead played in the state capital in Jackson, Mississippi, approximately 170 miles away, while others were played in Memphis and as far away as Birmingham, Alabama.

The building of *Vaught-Hemingway Stadium* started in 1915 as a federally sponsored project and was originally named after Judge William Hemingway, a professor of law and chairman of the university's committee on athletics. In the early 1980s, legendary Ole Miss coach Johnny Vaught had his name added to the stadium and, in 1998, the field was named after longtime supporter Dr. Jerry Hollingsworth. Today, the official title is *Vaught-Hemingway Stadium at Hollingsworth Field.* As the field was improved and expanded, the number of games played in Oxford also expanded, along with the massive game-day experience at *The Grove.*

After a series of massive rainstorms in 1991 that turned the park into a muddy mess, the tradition of parking cars and RVs was figuratively taken to the junkyard and stopped the following year. The tradition of parking in *The Grove* was already on a slippery road. In 1982, before the season opener against Memphis, protesters, as part of a "Save the Grove" movement, snuck into the park and sat on blankets near the cherished trees, blocking prime spots for tailgaters. Three weeks before, the university had cut down three dead trees. University botanists believed the trees had perished due to "asphyxiation by root collapse," and the weight of parked vehicles had hastened their demise. Lighter vehicles, like their heavier brethren, were ultimately prohibited. Everyone and everything, including the trees, is thankful for these changes as they make a wander through this grove of oak, elm, and magnolia magical, even when there is no game.

A favorite saying at Ole Miss is, "We may not win every game, but we ain't never lost a party." Truer words may have never been spoken. A journey into *The Grove* is not only a spiritual walk, but it is also an invitation to Mississippi's number one social event. However, this is not an exclusive party for members only. No, this party is open to all and at this party, hospitality reigns for friend and foe alike. Whatever you have heard about Southern hospitality, double it. Within minutes of entering *The Grove*, we were welcomed—like long lost friends—into tents, given beads and pins, offered seats, and offered food and drink. In fact, at one point, my brother and I found ourselves unable to keep up with the unopened beers we had been given from the first few tents, so we "re-gifted" a few at subsequent tents. Never come to a party empty-handed, right? Not to be outdone, a family whose son played for Texas A&M invited us into their tent for a *Shiner Bock* and a taste of brisket. At that point, we realized there would be no need for dinner, and we had better start pacing ourselves!

The place was packed. On more than one occasion, I lost sight of Daniel, but he was inevitably found under a tent with strangers and treated like one of their own. Once, I found him seated with a group of Ole Miss fans, holding a Coke in his hand. At another tent, he was being introduced by a young woman to her sorority sisters. Not surprisingly, he was in no hurry to leave. Several years later, my brother and I got on an elevator with an elderly woman dressed head to toe in Ole Miss garb. When we told her we had seen a game at Ole Miss and visited *The Grove*, she reached out and grabbed my brother's hand, saying in the most beautiful and dignified southern accent, "Please tell me you enjoyed your stay." Please tell me you were treated well." After we assured her that we had enjoyed the game and that we had been treated like family, she said, "Oh, good. If you had told me otherwise, it would just break my heart." Her words, as much as anything, sum up our entire weekend in Oxford, Mississippi, and we are forever grateful to be part of the Ole Miss family.

Until now, I have referred to the happenings in *The Grove* as "tailgating." Perhaps a better description would be a high-end cocktail party. True, a canopy may be nothing more than a glorified open tent, but what is under the posts can make all the difference in the world. What we witnessed rivaled the furnishings of the finest homes I've been in, with chandeliers, curtains, rugs, white linen tablecloths and napkins, actual glassware and the finest dinnerware and silver usually reserved at my house for our formal Christmas dinner. Atop highly decorative dining room tables, there were mounds of food, including the usual game-day fare of hot dogs, brats, hamburgers, chicken wings, chips, salsa and dips, fried chicken, and the obligatory assortment of barbecue. However, more unexpected were the mounds of shrimp, ornate vegetable trays, and charcuterie boards. There were cookies and watermelon, right alongside edible fruit arrangements and decorative *Rebel* cupcakes that would have made Martha Stewart proud. The tents, adorned entirely in Ole Miss paraphernalia, sported flags, helmets, ceramics, plants, ferns, and fresh-cut flowers. Even if plastic cutlery or paper napkins were on hand, it was meticulously arranged and tied with ribbon or bows in Longaberger baskets.

Now, I need to say this loud and clear: When it comes to how *Buckeye Nation* comes dressed to the *Horseshoe*, we need to up our game, and, in case you're wondering, that includes yours truly. Granted, those attending games at Southern schools, for the most part, need not wear parkas or hooded sweatshirts. However, we all could do a little better, even when bundled up on a cold or rainy November afternoon in Columbus, Ohio. Maybe we could do a better job with color-coordinating our layering? Just a thought. In comparison, a trip through *The Grove* presented a mixture of a Sunday revival, a *Taylor Swift* concert, and a photo shoot for *Ralph Lauren*. Women were dressed in skirts and dresses, and the shorter the dress, the higher the boots. Going without make-up was like skipping church. You just don't do it. Going without jewelry was also considered a sin, and while some opted for completely bedazzled looks, others chose a simpler, more classic vibe, such as wearing a family heirloom pearl necklace. As for the guys, I offer a few observations: khakis outnumbered jeans; button-downs and polos outnumbered T-shirts; Sperry topsiders outnumbered tennis and running shoes; and blazers outnumbered sweatshirts. Who knew belts and ties could be worn outside of the courtroom? If it seems like a bunch of unneeded effort, or at least unnecessary itching and sweating, you might be right, but comfort is not everything in life. It is also how "you never lose a party."

Attending an Ole Miss football game also requires learning an entirely new vocabulary. If we had known this before our journey south, we might have looked up local sayings or checked online to see if *Rosetta Stone* offered a language learning program for Ole Miss. In this regard, we did not immediately feel like family but rather more like strangers in a strange land. For example, earlier in the day, when arriving on campus, we encountered countless fans wearing pins and shouting a most peculiar phrase—"*Hotty Toddy.*" At first, when we saw multiple young women wearing *Hotty Toddy* pins, we surmised that the quarterback or another player on the team must be named Todd and must be one darn good-looking dude. However, when guys began greeting us with "*Are you ready,*" we noticed others would help break our stupefied silence with yells of "*Hotty Toddy.*" We soon wondered if the entire campus was simply enamored with mixed cocktails, known as "hot toddies," made with whiskey, water, honey, and lemon, and usually served hot. Maybe it was another gameday tradition in liquid form. So, what exactly does "*Hotty Toddy*" mean and where did the term come from? We intended to find out.

It turns out that it is not entirely clear to anyone. But here is what we do know. In 1925 or 1926 (depending on the source), the *Mississippian*—a student newspaper now known as *The Daily Mississippian*—printed a cheer that went like this: "*Heighty, Tighty! Gosh A Mighty! Who in the hell are we? Rim! Fam! Flim! Flam! Ole Miss, by Damn!*" Could "*Heighty Tighty*" have morphed into "*Hotty Toddy*" over time? Many believe this is exactly what happened, while others have alternative theories. One such theory is that *Hotty Toddy* is simply a play on the phrase "*hoity-toity,*" used to further embrace the high-style tailgating and fashion unapologetically on display in *The Grove*. Remember the heirloom pearl necklaces I mentioned? Hoity-toity, indeed! Others maintain that a military connection exists as the cheer bears a resemblance to military chants popularized in World War II. Legend also tells of a trip to Richmond to honor Field Marshal Foch—the supreme allied commander of World War I—when the drum major in the Ole Miss Corps, during the parade, dropped and then recovered his baton while giving his salute. This effort was greeted by someone in the crowd who shouted out, "hoity-toity." Lastly, many believe our gang was not far off the mark when we surmised a connection to hot toddies, as whiskey and other cocktails are known to pour freely during a Saturday in *The Grove.* Regardless of how it started, it represents the spirit of Ole Miss. They yell it. They feel it. And, above all, they live it. "*Are you Ready*? ... "*HOTTY TODDY*!"

As we wandered about campus and in *The Grove,* we were drawn to the sounds of The University of Mississippi Band, affectionately known as "*The Pride of the South*." We were also lucky enough to get right next to the band as they belted out the Ole Miss fight song "*Forward Rebels*," and in the process established another important piece to the guy trips. Any pre-game activities must include spending quality time with the school's marching band, and even if we have no idea what everyone is singing, we act like we do. When in doubt, we do a little lip-syncing, *Milli Vanilli* style.

Cutting straight through the middle of *The Grove* and right into the heart of Rebel Nation is a brick walkway called *The Walk of Champions*. About two hours before the game, the Ole Miss football team, much to our delight, walked down this path on their way to the stadium. They do it before every home game, even in the spurts of drizzling rain that had decided to pay us all a visit. Things were tight, with the players often walking single file and although other teams do "walks" before games, the intimacy of this encounter was truly unique. You literally could reach out and touch the players. Even pre-Covid-19, we wondered if it might be a good idea to have a giant hand sanitizer for the players at the end of the walk as they high-five thousands and shake hands with half the citizens of the great state of Mississippi.

The Walk of Champions was established in 1983 by newly hired head coach Billy Brewer, who sought a way for his players to participate in the excitement of gameday in *The Grove*. In the process, he created another wonderful tradition at Ole Miss. Starting in 1998, the team began walking under a *Walk of Champions* arch that was donated by the 1962 undefeated National Championship team. After the team walked through, we scampered to a larger road to watch the Ole Miss band march by on their way toward the stadium and, when fans gathered in the street to follow this festive parade, we were more than happy to join them.

"Johnny Football"

Pinned in at the 1-yard line, down by ten points, and with less than eight minutes remaining in the game, Texas A&M was on the ropes. Ole Miss, who had forced six turnovers, including four fumbles and two interceptions, appeared to be on the verge of snapping a 15th straight conference loss. Sporting our newly purchased blue Ole Miss stocking caps as it had gotten downright cold again, we, along with the *Rebel* faithful, yelled with what was left of our voices to support the Ole Miss defense. Surely, a stop here would go a long way in sealing the game. The *Aggie* quarterback, a 6-foot-1, 200-pound freshman from Kerrville, Texas, had shown moments of brilliance. For instance, on the opening drive of the game, he burst through a hole and scampered 59 yards for a touchdown, and he managed some other highlight-reel scrambles throughout the game. Still, it was not the 557 yards and four touchdowns he had amassed the week before against Arkansas. As he trotted onto the field, it felt like *we* had him.

Today, as I write this, I don't recall what happened on first or second down, but I do recall what happened on the third play. Johnny Manziel rifled a 32-yard pass to Mike Evans. First down, *Aggies*. Two plays later, Manziel, dancing by a cadre of Ole Miss defenders, rushed for a 29-yard score. And, just like that, after a lightning-quick march down the length of the field, the lead had been severely cut. Hugh Freeze, the Ole Miss coach, perhaps feeling the impending doom if Ole Miss did not keep the ball and run out the clock or even manage to score again, hastened the collapse when he went for a fourth-and-1 in his own territory. Stuffed at the line of scrimmage, it was a disastrous call. Four plays later, *Johnny Football* found Ryan Swope for what would be the game-winning touchdown. The 30-27 win gave the *Aggies* a 4-1 record, while the *Rebels* slipped to 3-3 overall and 0-2 in the conference.

We were witness to a shooting star, burning white-hot, across an October Mississippi sky. Surveying the landscape that night, it was blatantly obvious that he was the best athlete on the field—by a mile. At one point, during one of his acrobatic escapes, followed by a darting hop downfield reminiscent of a rabbit in a briar patch, my brother turned to me and said, "He's an animal." Whatever he was, he was not like anything we'd ever seen. Wherever he was, you could not take your eyes off him. As for Ole Miss, they just wished he'd never come to town.

In mid-November, Johnny Manziel took his traveling magic show to Tuscaloosa to battle an undefeated Alabama football team. The *Crimson Tide* was the best football program in the country, with arguably the best coach ever and possessed one of the best defenses in recent history. Operating out of a shotgun, the first-year quarterback completed 10 of 11 passes and rushed for 74 yards—in the first quarter! A national television audience was treated to tight camera shots of defenders out of breath and a secondary frantically trying to communicate with one another while enduring a blistering pace of play. After *Johnny Football* handed Alabama their first loss of the season, the *Crimson Tide* wished he had never come to town—especially the defense. Much of the country was shocked by what they saw. Not us. When I called my brother following the game, all he said was, "No way a big, slow elephant was gonna catch a wild animal." Nick Saban may have been in shock but even if he was, the "process-oriented" and unapologetically maniacal perfectionist wasted no time in acting. In a meeting following the game, he emphasized to his defensive coordinator, Kirby Smart, that they needed to improve their defensive speed. In the spring of 2013, after watching game film of Johnny Manziel and the Texas A&M offense ad nauseam, Nick Saban realized changes were coming to football and the *SEC*. Yes, they must get faster on defense, but he also surmised they needed to be faster and, dare he admit, more unscripted on offense as well.

The colorful trail of light, first spotted in that night sky over Oxford, Mississippi, brought further wonder and excitement to the *Best Buy Theater* in New York City when, on December 8, 2012, Johnny Manziel became the first freshman to win the Heisman Trophy. However, shooting stars are not really stars but rather pieces of space rock and dust that produce glowing streaks of light as they enter the atmosphere at high speed. Flung back to Earth, meteors—whether they come from asteroids or comets—burn up as they enter the atmosphere. Smaller ones, known as meteoroids, melt away at high altitudes, while the larger and heavier ones cannot be completely vaporized by atmospheric friction. When they strike a planet's surface, they form craters and are classified as meteorites.

In the 1985 action thriller film *Runaway Train*, Sara—played by Rebecca De Mornay—says to Oscar "Manny" Manheim, a ruthless bank robber and hero—played by John Voight— "You're an animal." He stares back at her and shouts, "No, worse …human." Johnny was no animal. Rather, he was human like the rest of us.

In hindsight, his meteoric rise was pre-set on a course to fall. Like an obvious movie plot twist, we really should have seen it coming. First, there was the fight before the beginning of his historic season and then the Halloween picture of a seemingly inebriated Manziel in a *Scooby Doo* costume. The following summer, his removal from a frat party at the University of Texas seemed unusual for an *Aggie*, if not daring, and was followed by an NCAA suspension for receiving payments for his signed autographs. Although analogous to Ohio State players getting tattoos as "payments" for trading little yellow pants pins for beating Michigan, the rules, at the time, did not allow student-athletes to benefit from their name, likeness, and image. Please, don't get me started.

In 2014, when drafted by the Cleveland *Browns*, his flashing the "money fingers" appeared naive, especially since he would soon be lining up against some of the most elite athletes in the world, whose job it was to quite literally bring him down. You could already imagine the mocking celebration after every sack. Being spotted in Las Vegas during training camp, giving the finger to the Washington bench in a preseason game, and his involvement in a fight in downtown Cleveland at 2:30 a.m. during the football season were troubling for a rookie at best. Entering a rehab facility in January of 2015 provided hope, if not some relief. Instead, things got worse. Allegations of assault, domestic violence, and a hit-and-run followed, as did a suspension for violating the league's substance abuse policy. At one point, while he was supposed to be with the team, even though he was out with a concussion, he was absent from the week 17 game against the Pittsburgh *Steelers*. Instead, he donned a disguise and partied in Las Vegas like it was 1999. On March 11, 2016, during this madness, the Cleveland *Browns* released him.

More recently, Manziel has discussed his lonely ride through the stratosphere, his immeasurable dislike of the NCAA (he is not alone), his issues with substance abuse, and even a suicide attempt. The young man, who has seemingly lived hundreds of years in the public eye, is still only 31 years old as of the time of this writing. It would seem he has time to find a new purpose so that he might bolt again across a starlit night. In *Runaway Train,* Manny, the ruthless bank robber, turns hero in the final scene, sacrificing himself to save countless others. He was, after all, *human*. As for those of us who saw Johnny play, we know what we saw when he lit up the ink-black sky, and we will never forget it. Nick Saban knew what he saw, and being a great coach, he learned from it. As for me, I am still rooting for *Johnny Football* in my now well-worn and slightly tattered Ole Miss stocking cap.

One Snowy Night

Several months after our wonderful visit to Oxford and Ole Miss, during another Ohio winter, I dusted off a few mentally weighty Faulkner tomes and with a cup of tea in hand and a fireplace nearby, I took Parani's advice and cracked a few. He was right. It changed everything. My mistake in college was to assume Faulkner was a realistic writer, but now, as I reread his works as chiefly fantastical, glaring subtexts emerged. More importantly, these subtexts, perhaps more than any I had encountered, captured the essence and purpose of our college football trips. Relations between fathers and sons saturate his fiction, while, like Mark Twain, his exploration of boyhood is conspicuous. What's more, his stories, wandering between myth and reality, inevitably lead us back home. My mind was set afire.

Every boy strives to be a man, but every man resides in the shadow of his father. Some dads are totally absent, while others are present but not truly engaged. Others, thankfully, are not only present but also fully engaged. Regardless, manhood, in some way or another, is largely shaped by this relationship. However, men are not only fathers and sons but also husbands, brothers, grandsons, grandfathers, uncles, nephews, fathers-in-law, brothers-in-law, sons-in-law, cousins, teachers, coaches, pastors, mentors, and friends. Masculinity is also shaped through these relationships and connections. It was only after we had returned from Mississippi, and I reminisced about *Rowan Oak* that these thoughts started swirling around in my head. I suddenly realized our yearly college football sojourns were akin to camping trips of old. The game, the meals, and the festivities, much like time around a campfire, provided ample opportunities for sharing our past through stories, all while making new memories together. In some small ways, it helped all of us figure out who we are as men. In some small ways, it also helped us return home again.

Looking out my window, I could see the snow was really coming down and, although I was half tempted to go outside and shovel my drive, I could just not manage to remove my nose from *Absalom, Absalom!* and William Faulkner's description of a room on a "long still hot weary dead" September afternoon. Besides adjectives—stacked like pancakes, the room is teeming with ghosts. It was my third read of the novel, if you include my college effort, and I kept stopping to reflect upon our visit to Mississippi, which is why I had originally gotten up to peek outside into the wintry woods behind my house. The ghosts of the Civil War appeared everywhere, including Ohio, but especially in the South and in Mississippi and William Faulkner, as a White Southern writer, was confronting the issue of race head-on. Suddenly, I found myself back again at *Rowan Oak* in the writer's study and with the now-silent typewriter front and center in my mind. His bravery, in retrospect, astounded me, and his text had partially unlatched the door to his hometown for me to better spy.

Returning to *One Matchless Time-A Life of William Faulkner*, Parini writes, "A sense of place was everything to William Faulkner and more than any other American novelist in the twentieth century, he understood how to mine the details of place, including its human history, for literary effects." He continues, "Place, for Faulkner, becomes a spiritual location from which he examines a truth deeper than anything like mere locality. Faulkner saw himself as taking part in a great process, moving through history and, in an intriguing way, creating a counter-history of his own." On a snowy evening in Ohio, with a book in my lap, it occurred to me that Oxford was not only a physical location but also a spiritual place with its own human history. The same is true of Starkville, Gainesville, Columbia, Fayetteville, Baton Rouge, Athens, Auburn, and Tuscaloosa, and the entirety of *SEC* football is taking part in a great process, moving through history and creating a counter-history of its own. No wonder they take it so seriously.

Baton Rouge, Louisiana

Finally, on our third college trip together, we got our first southern game without the need for a jacket when we paid a visit to the bayou. In fact, with a 3:30 p.m. kickoff and hardly a cloud in the sky, it was downright hot. We got there early, and since we had just eaten lunch at a joint near campus called *Voodoo BBQ*, we passed on sampling the mounds of jambalaya being prepared in the bowels of the stadium. In retrospect, this was probably wise, given the heat and humidity.

Before the game, we, along with thousands of other adoring fans, paid a visit to *Mike the Tiger*, the famed live Bengal Tiger and the iconic image of Louisiana State University. For those who might be worried, *Mike* was not left to sit in some cramped cage. No, *Mike* resides between *Tiger Stadium* and *the Pete Maravich Assembly Center* in a $3.7 million, 15,000-square-foot environment, which includes a live oak tree, a waterfall, and a stream flowing from a rocky area with a multitude of lush plants and trees.

To date, there have been seven Mikes. During our visit in 2013, we were blessed to see *Mike VI*. "Our Mike" was born in 2005 and was donated to the university by *Great Cats of Indiana*, a nonprofit sanctuary and rescue for big cats. When he got to campus, he was two years old and weighed 320 pounds. He was officially declared *Mike VI* at a ceremony in September of 2007 and served as the university's live mascot for the next nine years. In May of 2016, *Mike* was diagnosed with spindle cell sarcoma, a type of cancer. He underwent radiotherapy at Mary Bird Perkins-Our Lady of the Lake Cancer Center in Baton Rouge. Later, in October of that same year, it was discovered that the tumor had grown and the cancer had spread. He entered hospice care in his night house on October 10, 2016, and was humanely euthanized the next day.

In 1934, a group of people associated with the university—including Athletic Department trainer Chellis "Mike" Chambers—purchased a two-hundred-pound, one-year-old tiger named *Sheik*. The $750 purchase price was raised by collecting 25 cents from each student. On October 21, 1936, throngs of onlookers, many of whom were students playing hooky from class, welcomed the new tiger mascot to campus. In honor of Chambers, *Sheik* was renamed *Mike* and, though he would serve as mascot for the next twenty years, *Mike* never completely took to his name as he would only roar when his trainers called him *Sheik*.

The second *Mike* is shrouded in mystery, as he reportedly died of pneumonia at eight months of age and was buried, perhaps secretly, under a willow tree along the Mississippi River by the newly appointed Athletic Director Jim Corbett, the campus police chief C.R. "Dick" Anderson, and LSU Athletic Department business manager Jack Gilmore. Scrambling to find a replacement, a statement was issued on behalf of the University, stating the new *Mike* was having issues adjusting to his new surroundings and would be kept inside to become better acclimated to his new home. Legend has it, and photographs would appear to confirm it, another cub of appropriate age was eventually located at a zoo in Seattle. Unfortunately, the replacement only served as the official mascot for one year, as he died in a local zoo from complications associated with multiple fractures to his left rear leg. The past three mascots have been donated, and the university has not purchased a tiger since *Mike III* in 1958. Today, *Mike VII*—who has both Siberian and Bengal characteristics—was donated to the university by a sanctuary called *Wild at Heart Wildlife Center*. He enjoys a tiger habitat animal care plan licensed by the USDA, and the facility, tiger, and animal care programs are inspected annually in compliance with the Federal Animal Welfare Act. Perhaps one day, in a more perfect world, there will be no need for sanctuaries or rescues. Until then, we love you, *Mike*!

With endzone seats for the game between LSU and Florida, we were directly behind one of Tiger Stadium's "H-style" goalposts. Constructed with two parallel upright bars with a cross bar perpendicular to each, this style differs from the "T-style" or "slingshot" goal post, which has only one post as a base and is the style of choice for most college football stadiums and all NFL venues. LSU installed these "H-style" goalposts in the stadium in 1993 for a game against Tulane to celebrate 100 years of LSU football. The unique-looking goalposts, unlike their NFL counterparts, are not bright yellow but instead are white, presenting another visual that differentiates the college game from the Pros.

Another oddity noticed while waiting for the game was that there were no nets behind the goalposts. As the field goal kickers warmed up for the game, we were treated to a barrage of incoming footballs landing all around us. Reminiscent of a baseball game and the need to stay alert for foul balls, we had to always keep one eye on the kicker. Equally odd to these visiting Yankees was that the game was played in its entirety—netless.

Coming into the game against the *Gators*, LSU was the defending *SEC* champion and boasted a 5-1 record, with their only loss coming at the hands of the Georgia *Bulldogs* in a 44-41 shootout in Athens.

Zach Mettenberger and the *Tiger* offense were putting up some big numbers, averaging nearly 46 points per game. It helped that he had a platoon of running backs he could rely on and could chuck the ball to two outstanding future NFL receivers, Jarvis Landry and Odell Beckham, Jr.

The night before the *SEC* showdown, the gang, at the recommendation of several acquaintances in Baton Rouge, had our Friday night dinner at *Jubans*. Known for its timeless Southern dishes and classic style interior, the beloved establishment did not disappoint. The meal and service, along with the must-have *Abita* beer, were marvelous. The restaurant was established in 1983—the year I graduated high school—and, after a brief closure during the dreaded Covid pandemic, it reopened in 2022 with a new design and rave reviews. My father and I enjoyed the décor of the place so much that we went back later the same night, as my dad had forgotten his credit card and only discovered this once we got back to the hotel. While we left my son and brother behind, with the goal of returning for a nightcap at the bar next door, this plan was shattered when we returned to the hotel and discovered both sound asleep. A satisfying evening indeed.

The next day, pre-game, brought the usual dose of levity that has become a hallmark of our trips. We were warned about the traffic near the stadium, so we took a shuttle from a parking lot well outside of campus. However, this was no ordinary shuttle! The hand-painted white shuttle was more like a minibus, with a millennium of miles under the hood and a husband and wife acting as owner-operators. The elderly Black couple had a system—he drove, and she collected the fees. As we got closer to the stadium, we kept picking up more passengers until it reached a point where there was no more room; at least, that's what we thought. Finally, to accommodate one final passenger, the driver ordered his wife off the bus. Over her initial protests, he left her on an unknown corner with assurances that he would come back for her later. As we pulled away, she was clearly not happy, and my father openly wondered what type of reception the driver would receive when he finally returned to find her. We half imagined him stopping at that corner hours later, opening the door to pick her up, and her getting on board, followed by the doors reopening with him being kicked to the curb. My brother and I also found ourselves chuckling when a young female fan in the seats in front of us, locked arm in arm with her boyfriend by desire and, quite frankly, necessity, told him, "We are so lucky we go to LSU as purple is my favorite color. Imagine if we went to another school? We would have to wear something else."

On October 12, 2013, before nearly 93,000 fans, LSU defeated Florida 17-6 in Death Valley. A defensive struggle, to be sure. LSU, which was trailing at the end of the first quarter 3-0, scored two touchdowns in the second quarter and never looked back. The running attack, along with a stout defense, carried the day but left little in the way of fireworks for the *Tigers'* dynamic receiving duo. However, plenty of defense for the home team also meant plenty of noise from the fans, and we played a small part in what was originally called "Deaf Valley." Crowe Peel, a former LSU boxer and a 1949 national champion, named his gas station "Deaf Valley" because of the noise that boomed from Tiger Stadium. It officially became the nickname for the stadium in 1959 following a Tiger victory against Clemson in the Sugar Bowl. Clemson also calls their stadium "Death Valley," but that story will have to wait a few more pages. Regardless of when or how it started, opposing teams, finding it nearly impossible to hear, clearly struggle when visiting LSU. Les Miles, the man who coached the *Tigers* to victory when we were there, summed it up by saying, "That was Death Valley. That was the place where opponents' dreams go to die."

Following the game, with the party famished, we legged it back to our car but soon found ourselves in the mother of all traffic jams. It was in the early days of Google and GPS, but we were early converts, as through a cell phone, we tracked down a nearby restaurant and a shortcut through side streets to get there. On the route, atop a bluff above the Mississippi and under a fanciful moonlit sky, we passed one beautiful Southern home after another, with glimpses of brick and cedar, wrapped-around porches and the flickering of gas lamps. To this day, I long for this street, unknown.

Baton Rouge, the capital of Louisiana and the seat of Louisiana's most populous parish, is French for *Red Stick*—a reference to a cypress pole used to settle a border conflict between the Houma Indian Tribe and the Bayogoula Indian Tribe. It was first coined by a French-Canadian explorer named Pierre Le Moyne, who spied the pole while making his way upriver in 1699, long before the Mississippi resembled a glorified drainpipe, when the river, like the lands around it, ran wild. As for the town, it was founded in 1810 and became part of the colonies in 1817. Today, a commemorative sculpture on Scott's Bluff near the Southern University campus marks the spot where the original Red Stick is said to have been located.

Louisiana is known as the *Bayou State*, derived from extensive marshy, slow-sluggish streams and waterways that meander and snake throughout the state, reminiscent of spin art on canvas or a Rorschach test. These shallow waters, fashioned like a mixed drink—part fresh, part salt—and populated with vast cypress trees often scarved in Spanish moss, are lovingly or unlovingly better known as swamps. They provide warm ecosystems encompassing millions of acres and are home to a dazzling display of wildlife, including wiregrass, bottomland hardwood, mosses, water celery, shrimp, alligators, blue herons, pelicans, white-tailed deer, catfish, and many other types of fish. The people of the bayou also comprise a dazzling display, with Choctaw Indians, Houma Indians, Atakapa-Ishak Indians, African Americans, and Europeans— commonly called Cajuns—who speak a form of French unique to the region.

"The Waterboy"

On November 6, 1998, when Daniel was seven months old, our family was introduced to a fi ctional character straight out of these Louisiana swamps. His name is *Bobby Boucher*, and he would soon become a household favorite. *The Waterboy* stars Adam Sandler as *Bobby Boucher*—a 31-year-old man—who still lives at home with his mother while attending college. Most importantly, he is also the waterboy for the football team. My son, who still lives at home in his mid-20s, was once a waterboy for his high school football team and, like Bobby, he also loves his momma. The film cost roughly $23 million to make, raked in hundreds of millions of dollars, further launched Sandler's career into the stratosphere, and is still played nearly every weekend on cable to this day. It has also, dare I say, become known as a classic. Th is must drive the critics crazy. They hated it. Now, if thin-skinned, one might take offense to a straightforward, if not "simple" young man who stutters and admittedly has anger issues. He is also regularly called a "moron." The two usually go hand in hand: getting angry and being called a moron. We have seen it over and over in raising our son and with other young people with mental and physical disabilities. The critics never even went there, but instead made it clear they just didn't think Adam Sandler was very funny. Fair enough, but the reviews are what we find to be curious, if not telling. For instance, consider the following critical reviews of the film: "*It's stupid,*" "*Doesn't have much of a brain,*" "*Can't make Adam Sandler fans think,*" "*One of the dumbest pieces of garbage,*" and "*Stupid, stupid, stupid.*" Curious and telling, indeed, but at least they refrained from using the "*R*" word.

My son has probably watched this movie at least fifty times and the rest of the family is not far behind. In fact, my wife and daughter made a point of watching it the night we were in Baton Rouge, and while we searched for a place to eat dinner, they were curled up on the couch with a bowl of popcorn, undoubtedly laughing about "High-quality *H20.*" Little did they know we were having our own *Waterboy* moment as the place we found was seemingly straight out of the movie. Wandering through the night, with only headlights and our cell phones to navigate us, we found ourselves parked in what felt like the middle of a swamp. Upon exiting the car, a chorus of frogs and crickets greeted us, along with a finally cooling air. In the distance, through the silhouettes of cypress and oak, we could make out a cedar-shingled structure with neon beer signs. We could also hear laughter wafting in the air, side by side, with the smoke from grills and fryers.

Once inside, we got our names on a list, and while my father and son grabbed a seat outside on a covered porch, my brother and I inched our way toward the bar. Quite frankly, the idea of getting a drink order seemed utterly preposterous. However, even though we were ten rows back, a bartender, with a look eerily like *Vicki Vallencourt* in appearance—Bobby's love interest, played by Fairuza Balk—made eye contact with us and lipped, "What can I get you?" Suddenly, we loved this place as much as the movie. As for dinner, when we finally did get seated, we had to have the special of the night—fried gator—in honor of LSU's win over Florida. It tastes just like chicken. Well, sort of. Later, when researching for this book, I was unable to identify the name of the restaurant or determine its location. Maybe it is out of business, or maybe we really did wander onto the set of *The Waterboy*

Both of my children attended a red brick elementary school—reminiscent of a Norman Rockwell painting—right up the road from our house. Daniel's teachers were marvelous. Every one of them. They cared for him. In fact, his second-grade teacher—Mrs. Roman—over a decade later and during the Covid pandemic, stopped by our house and dropped off a gift on our front porch on Dan's birthday. She even sang *Happy Birthday* from outside the house. She said she "had been thinking about him," and Mrs. Gray, his gym teacher at this first school and again in high school, attended his most recent birthday party. She also gives him personal tennis lessons. I mean, come on!

Early on, Daniel was placed on what is called an "IEP," which stands for Individualized Education Program. This concept was formally introduced in 1975 with the passage of the Education of All Handicapped Children Act (EHA), which legally recognized the rights of students with disabilities to attend public schools. Our son had both a special education teacher and a regular teacher, along with an aide. For the most part, his special education teachers were exceptionally creative in finding ways to help our son learn. His high-school special education teacher, Mrs. Zimmerman, had a profound impact on Daniel's learning and on his life. She was also with Dan for the longest period, as although Daniel graduated from high school in 2017, he remained at Woodridge for several more years until he "aged out of school." Mrs. Zimmerman is a warrior who relentlessly advocated for her entire special education class. She is also a darn good teacher.

Starting in the fourth grade, Daniel's aide was Mrs. Lacey and except for a brief period in middle school, she would remain by his side throughout his entire time as a Woodridge Bulldog. In another classic example of "*Danglish,*" our son has always called her "*C. Chris.*" She was and continues to be a godsend to our entire family. With a special heart for those with disabilities, she was the perfect partner for Daniel, and, in time, our families have grown quite close. We remain so to this day. One unexpected consequence of this friendship was a crash course in West Africa, and, more specifically, Mali, as we learned that their entire family was heavily involved in a non-profit organization called *African Sky*. Started in 2004 by her son—Scott— *African Sky* primarily focused on community-based projects in rural Mali, including community cereal banks (to assist with food security), water pump repairs, mosquito netting, adult literacy programs, and the building of schools. It was our honor to be included in the annual fundraiser each year, where Daniel acted as self-appointed co-host to the festivities.

When not in class, Daniel had regular visits with an in-school speech therapist and occupational therapist. Progress, albeit slow, was nearly constant. He had few friends outside of class. Further, when together with a group of children, he usually found himself chasing after the others. One day, after growing tired of watching him chase the other kids—only to have them run and scream when he got close—I suggested they take turns playing the role of the monster. A little girl, with complete sincerity, responded, "But why? He's the monster." Those are the moments that pierced our hearts. With his blue eyes and thick sandy-blonde hair, Daniel looked more like a surfer or a country club tennis guy than a monster. Not surprisingly, like many kids with Down syndrome, Dan was short. He still is. This trait he might have also gotten from his parents, but given his father is "follicly challenged," the mane of thick curls is most certainly from his mother.

It was also easy to blame Daniel, and unfortunately, my wife and I witnessed our son become a scapegoat nearly every time something got broken or somebody got hurt. When in doubt, point the finger at the kid who could not defend himself, right? Daniel, on the other hand, is completely incapable of lying. I mean it. Even when he tells a fib, he cannot keep a straight face. I guess it's another characteristic of Down syndrome. One day, he came into the house and started to limp up the stairs towards his bedroom. When we asked him what was wrong and what had happened, he turned and led us directly to the woods, where we found a sled wrapped around a tree.

An unexpected consequence of Daniel having Down syndrome was a major change in our lifestyle. We prioritized what was most important to us, even if it meant having less money. Together, as a team, my wife and I decided that she would not immediately return to the outside workforce, as caring for Daniel's needs was our top priority. It was also downright time-consuming. After he moved on to the next school, we found ourselves miles away, with Daniel regularly taking the bus. Nearly every day, we were summoned by the bus driver about an incident, and Dan often returned home in tears. Staying home would allow Judi to drive Dan to school and pick him up. It would also make it easier to pick him up during school hours when needed and, of course, take him to his private speech therapy following school.

Thankfully, Daniel was a relatively healthy little boy. In fact, the rest of us made more visits to the doctor than he did, but for whatever reason, the insurance company did not see it that way. Rate increases became the norm, and, at one point, we were paying nearly $4,000 a month in premiums with a $7,500 deductible, which was almost twenty years ago. His speech therapy and many other services were deemed "private pay," so we were paying for nearly everything out of pocket anyway. The whole thing made *us sick,* and a stack of bills was left piled on the kitchen table. Having seen enough, I set out to find another insurance plan, but this proved to be easier said than done. Daniel had a "pre-existing" condition, so he was generally not insurable. One night, while at the dinner table, I opened a letter from another insurance company that congratulated my wife, my daughter, and me on being accepted into their program. Another thinner letter regretfully informed us that Daniel's coverage was declined. At that point, I had what could be best described as a "bad dad moment." I tore the letters up at the table, cursing and yelling all the while. When I looked up after my rant, I noticed both kids were crying. It just made me feel even worse about our predicament, and I wish I had controlled my emotions better. In retrospect, I am grateful that we had the means to afford health insurance, while many others did not.

The Ghost in Your Mind

A joke shared regularly among men and particularly enjoyed by my wife's grandfather goes something like this: "There are two types of guys. Those who have prostate cancer, and those who will get prostate cancer." Unfortunately, the best jokes have a kernel of truth, as 1 in 8 men in the United States will receive a prostate cancer diagnosis in their lifetime, making it the most common form of cancer among men (just above skin cancer), and the third most common cancer overall behind breast cancer and lung cancer (as of this writing skin cancer was 4th overall). In fact, it is estimated that 164,000 men will be diagnosed with prostate cancer this year alone. The prostate is a small walnut-shaped gland—behind the bladder and in front of the rectum—that produces seminal fluid used to transport sperm and, for whatever reason, it is also known to lure and sow cancer.

Roughly 1 in 350 men under 50 are diagnosed with prostate cancer, while 1 in 52 men between the ages of 50 and 59 are diagnosed with the disease. However, in males 65 or older, the incidence jumps to nearly 60% of all males. This is also when most men receive the first diagnosis. Yes, unfortunately, the joke holds true as cancer is tied to the aging process and old men are apt to get prostate cancer. With this rather bleak forecast, I suppose another quip might be appropriate: "getting old sucks, but it sure beats the alternative."

In its early stages, a person with prostate cancer may have no signs or symptoms, but as the disease progresses, symptoms can include trouble urinating, decreased force in the stream of urine, blood in the urine, blood in the semen, weight loss, generalized pelvic pain, and erectile dysfunction. This cancer is usually slow growing but can be aggressive and spread quickly, as the disease generally plays by no rules. Rather, it makes them up as it goes along.

Following the holidays and the dinner at *Luigi's* with Vern, Dad decided to get his eye checked out. What followed was a physical and a battery of tests, including a PSA test that measures the amount of prostate-specific antigen (PSA) in your blood. PSA, which is mostly found in semen, is a protein produced by both cancerous and noncancerous tissue in the prostate. Small amounts are also found in blood. The test is a valuable diagnostic tool, as is a rectal exam, and since Dad's PSA was found to be elevated, he ultimately underwent a prostate biopsy. He then got the news nobody ever wants to hear—"You have cancer." Suddenly, a bloodshot eye seemed a million miles away. Before the following year ended, Dad underwent prostatectomy surgery—a common prostate cancer treatment—to remove his prostate gland. This was followed by 6 to 8 weeks of radiation. Later, Dad told me the surgeon told him, "He thought he had gotten most of it, but there might have been a little that got away," and when he heard those words, despite the subsequent radiation treatments, he knew he must battle cancer again one day. He just didn't know when.

While this was my immediate family's first introduction to "the emperor of all maladies," that was not the case for my wife, as she had been introduced to this ghoul before. Her introduction came in 1978, when she was just 14 years old, growing up in the suburbs of Chicago. Like most teenage kids, her summer had been filled with hot-hazy days playing outside, chewing *Bubble Yum*, listening to the *Bee Gees* on a turntable or on the radio while sitting in the backseat of an un-airconditioned car, with windows rolled down, and alongside her cousins. That same summer, the boy in the bubble—John Travolta—had reemerged as hunky *Danny* and, alongside Olivia Newton-John, cast as adorable *Sandy*, starred in the cultural phenomenon known as *Grease*. Although Judi and I had not yet met, we already shared much in common, as we both knew every word to every song on the soundtrack and, like every other American teenager, had already seen the movie more than once. However, we most certainly diverged on whether *Danny* or *Sandy* was our summer big-screen crush and when we would hear the words you never wish to hear about a loved one.

Near the end of summer, her mom, Arlene—much like my dad and his bloodshot eye— had noticed a mole on her neck near her collarbone. One day, it just showed up. She had never seen it there before, or at least not that she could recall. At the urging of friends and family, she eventually decided to have it checked out by a doctor.

My wife was just starting her freshman year of high school. Going back to school and starting a new year can be exciting and scary at the same time. And, in the fall of 1978, as she navigated the school hallways, cafeteria, and her tiny metal locker, my wife was not worried about dating or who might be on the homecoming court. Gossip held no zeal, and the big game coming up on a Friday night didn't seem to matter as much as it should have. Nor was she worried about an upcoming algebra test as much as she should have been. Her mother's lung cancer diagnosis had turned everything, including high school, completely upside down.

Our parents and our families share a story that is in no way new or unique. Far from it. Cancer is a prehistoric disease dating back to the dawn of humanity. Its longevity is alarming if not admirable, as while plagues, black death, leprosy, and smallpox have been largely cast aside, this silent thief remains. Louis Leakey, the renowned anthropologist who is credited with digging up some of the earliest known human skeletons, discovered a jawbone originally thought to date back two million years, which purportedly carried signs of a peculiar form of lymphoma found endemically in southeastern Africa. The discovery has been widely disputed in that many believe the specimen is merely 700,000 years old. However, the lump found in the fossilized jaw has been diagnosed by the Royal College of Surgeons in London as a sarcoma of the bone. This hypothesis remains unaltered.

For the most part, ancient writings make no specific mention of what we now call cancer. Perhaps it was not known, or maybe it was kept private. Then again, perhaps it was just extremely rare. Ultimately, historians and scientists are left to wonder. However, some writings give us clues and reinforce the notion that cancer has always been with us. In 1862, a self-described Egyptologist named Edwin Smith bought a fifteen-foot-long papyrus from an antique dealer in Luxor, Egypt. Smith's reputation as a forger and huckster originally cast doubt on the authenticity of the ancient materials, as did his means of obtaining it, as some believe he stole it. Regardless, it was translated in 1930 and found to contain the medical teachings of the Egyptian physician Imhotep, who lived in 2625 BC. The great Imhotep was a vizier in the court of the Egyptian pharaoh King Djoser of the 3rd dynasty during the Old Kingdom, and was renowned for his interests in architecture, astrology, and astronomy. He was also known to dabble in neurosurgery. The papyrus, which is essentially a surgical textbook, outlines forty-eight cases, including bone fractures, shattered skulls, and skin abscesses. However, one case is of paramount importance for our purposes. Case number forty-five describes, "bulging tumors of the breast mean the existence of swellings on the breast, large, spreading, and hard; touching them is like touching a ball of wrappings, or they may be compared to unripe fruit, which is hard and cool to the touch." A more vivid description of cancer would be hard to imagine.

Mankind's description of cancer may date back to the time of mummies, pyramids, and pharaohs, but the world's introduction to this formidable foe may have begun 150 million years ago, at the end stages of the Jurassic period, when dinosaurs roamed the Earth. Located about 110 miles southeast of my house is the *Carnegie Museum of Natural History* in Pittsburgh, Pennsylvania. It is a wonderful facility and is home to a specimen labeled CM 72656. The specimen—roughly the size of a shoe box—is a fossilized *Brontosaurus* dinosaur bone. This well-known and easily recognizable four-legged herbivore—with a long neck and a counterbalancing long tail—has been prominently featured in films such as *Jurassic Park* and, when living, would have weighed 30 tons and been 70 feet long. Although nobody will ever know for sure, this *Brontosaurus* dinosaur also appears to have had bone cancer, as part of the fossil reveals an oval-shaped, crystallized tumor. It also seems to have grown large enough to encroach on the outer bone.

Perhaps not as flashy as a dinosaur, a prehistoric reptile known as Pappochelys rosinae roamed the Earth nearly 240 million years ago. Though it had no shell, it is believed to be an ancestor of the modern turtle. When researchers in Germany examined a fossil of this prehistoric creature in 2013, they discovered something strange about its left femur—was it a peculiar growth representing a break that did not heal properly, or a form of cancer that still plagues humanity today? Regardless, throughout time, this dark menace has taken aim at nearly every living creature, including mammals, reptiles, birds, fish, and mollusks. Fossils reveal cancer in mammoths, buffalo, baboons, and saber-tooth tigers, and evidence of cancer has been discovered in fossilized Sea Creatures. Plants can even get cancer, although it is rarely fatal. While some animals seldom get cancer, others, including pets, fare much worse. Humans, meanwhile, get the most cancer of all.

In *The Emperor of All Maladies-A Biography of Cancer*, author Siddhartha Mukherjee writes, "Even an ancient monster needs a name. To name an illness is to describe a condition of suffering- a literary act before it becomes a medical one." The word *karkinos*, from the Greek word for "crab," first appeared in the time of Hippocrates, around 400 BC. Examining a tumor with the naked eye reminded the father of modern medicine of a crab burrowed into the sand. For doctors and scientists that followed, the term captured the quick—almost sideways—scuddle-like movement of an unseen disease in the body. For patients, the name explained the sudden, sharp pain produced by the disease, which felt like being caught in the grip of a crab's pincers.

This monster is a disease caused by an uncontrolled division of an abnormal cell in a part of the body. The result is a cell that cannot stop growing, which ultimately becomes mutated. This phenomenon can occur anywhere in the body. Cancer, therefore, is not a single disease but a collection of many different diseases related to certain qualities. Cancers of solid organs or tissues include the lung, prostate, bone, breast, colon, and skin, among others. There are also cancers of the blood—called liquid cancers—such as leukemia, myeloma, and lymphoma. Currently, there are approximately 200 different types of known cancers. Cancer is also a clonal disease, meaning all cancer cells share a common genetic ancestor. In other words, one abnormal cell continued to grow uncontrollably, somehow managing to survive and producing an unlimited number of offspring.

There are over 30 trillion cells in the human body, and almost every one of them is potentially cancerous. At first blush, given this number, cancer seems virtually inevitable, especially when one considers the birth of new cells and the aging and ultimate death of cells during one's lifetime in a never-ending cycle. However, upon closer examination and with the help of a microscope, one is introduced to an eloquent concerto where cells carry on in harmony. Each cell has a specific part to play, with genetic sheet music providing every note. The result is a symphony called life. Sometimes, a cell begins multiplying faster than the others around it, or to use our music analogy, plays faster than is appropriate, or breaks into an improvised solo. When this occurs, mistakes are caught and corrected as cells are highly regulated by powerful genetic circuits, or to again use our music analogy, cells are made to play in concert with others under the watchful eye of a dictatorial conductor. The result is that uncontrolled growth is regularly and seamlessly reined in. If the mistakes cannot be corrected and uncontrolled growth stunted, the cell, sensing further turmoil, will self-destruct, killing itself for the common good. Furthermore, cell mutation, from one generation to the next, can lead to natural destruction over time as cells become unable to survive and are cast aside by the body. Lastly, if the suicide signal has been overridden and offspring have somehow managed to survive, the immune system, much like a squadron of Apache helicopters, is called into action to take out the abnormal cells. On second blush, cancer's eventual obliteration seems equally inevitable. However, having made this quip, I'm now reminded of sitting in a darkened theatre with my wife in London years ago and listening to the haunting lyrics of Andrew Lloyd Weber's strange, yet almost pleasing, musical, *Whistle Down the Wind— "If only it was so, these are the loneliest words I know."*

Describing the mechanics of cancer and the built-in safeguards designed to avoid it does little to explain why it happens. This is especially true for those who are suffering from the impact of this disease. So, why does it happen? The short answer is we still don't really know. An equally important question is why it happens to one person and not another. Again, the short answer is we still don't really know. However, here, in layman's terms and in the form of a cursory summary, is what we do know. The first and easiest place to start is with carcinogens. These are substances or agents known to have the potential to cause or encourage the development of cancer when exposed to them over time. Carcinogens can be chemicals, radiation, or even other illnesses, but the most well-known and certainly most widely discussed carcinogen in the last fifty years is tobacco.

The Tonight Show, Starring Johnny Carson, was another American cultural phenomenon, alongside *Grease*. On January 1, 1971, at 11:59, it was not only the home of *Johnny Carson* but also the time slot for the last cigarette commercial ever broadcast on American television. In case you are wondering, the ad was for *Virginia Slims*. At the time, I was five years old, my wife was not quite seven, and my brother was two weeks away from his second birthday. Studies had revealed the dangers of smoking, and the federal government had finally decided to act by prohibiting television commercials for tobacco products. At the time, not much was made of it, but in retrospect, it was the beginning of the end for America's 20th-century obsession with tobacco. Dad quit smoking several years later after I had thrown his carton of cigarettes in the sewer at the end of our street during a downpour when he was still at work. Earlier that day, a school program I attended had warned us grade-schoolers of the dangers of smoking, and I just knew I had to do something about it. Quite frankly, at the time, he was furious with me, but years later, we both shared a good laugh about it. Judi's mother, who had also been a smoker, also kicked the habit at the urging of her daughter.

That same decade, homes, adorned wall to wall in shag carpeting and with wood paneling, were typically slathered in gold, green, and brown paint. Macramé was back in style, linoleum was the flooring of choice in most kitchens, and new cars, new appliances, televisions, and stereos were welcomed into suburbia like a celebrity sighting. My mother-in-law was especially proud of her new side-by-side olive-colored refrigerator and to protect the linoleum floor, a small mat had been placed underneath it. She came from an Italian family, and another cultural phenomenon was a generally healthy obsession with keeping a clean house, especially the kitchen. Judi recalls her mother regularly moving the refrigerator out to clean under and behind it and getting down on her hands and knees to clean the floor and the small rectangular mat, which was primarily made of asbestos.

Asbestos was originally heralded as a miracle. The fibers were not only soft and malleable but also fireproof and great insulators. Given those qualities, not surprisingly, it was soon found in insulation, clothing, and countless household products, including a grey-colored mat in a home in the suburbs of Chicago. Asbestos consumption peaked in the United States two years after the last televised cigarette commercial. Unfortunately, as we now know, asbestos, like tobacco, is a carcinogen, and exposure can cause cancer. Workplace exposures to asbestos, decades later and given lengthy latency periods, are still being unpacked and otherwise litigated as of this writing. Today, joining these two behemoths (tobacco and asbestos) are hundreds of other chemicals currently identified by The International Agency for Research on Cancer (IARC) as suspected human carcinogens.

Long before the suburbs of Chicago spiraled dizzyingly out and away from the original city and Lake Michigan, nearly a century earlier, a young medical student named Emil Grubbe used an X-ray in a tube factory on Halsted Street to treat an elderly woman with breast cancer. For three weeks, starting on March 29, 1896, he blasted his patient with radiation using an improvised X-ray tube and, while the tumor did shrink, the patient died shortly thereafter, in large part because the cancer had already spread to her brain and spine. What Grubbe nonetheless realized, as evidenced by the shrunken tumor, is that X-rays (radiation) could be used to kill cancer cells locally. With this knowledge in hand, he began treating other patients with local tumors and, in doing so, along with others, gave birth to a new branch of cancer treatment—radiation oncology. However, what the ingenious medical student failed to initially understand is that the sword he wielded was sharp on both sides, as radiation can also produce cancer.

Marie Curie, born in Poland in 1867, is one of the most renowned scientists in the fields of X-rays and radioactivity. In fact, she might be considered one of the greatest scientists overall, as not only did she win a Nobel Prize in Physics in 1903 for her discovery of radioactivity, but she followed it up with a Nobel Prize in Chemistry in 1911. Curie is still the only woman to have won the distinguished prize in two fields and is the only person to win in multiple scientific fields. She is also one of the first known to die from these discoveries. Starting in February of 1898 and working alongside her husband—Pierre—in Paris, France, Curie isolated and named a new radioactive element called Polonium (in honor of her native Poland). Several months later, the couple isolated Radium, which was the most radioactive substance that had ever been discovered. It also just so happened to glow in the dark. The scientist later wrote how she and her husband enjoyed entering their lab at night as "the glowing tubes looked like faint, fairy lights."

The birth of the atomic age captured the public's eye, especially since it glowed in the dark, and soon, Radium was a marketer's dream, used in a variety of consumer products, including wristwatches. Manufactured by the millions, the watch dials and numbers were painted by hand, with *3*, *6* & *8* requiring particularly intricate work. Believing the paint was harmless, women known as *Radium Girls* would moisten the tip of their brushes, thereby inadvertently ingesting Radium-laced paint. Still others—long before Go-go dancers, disco, or *Spencer Gifts* in its heyday—were known to purposely decorate their teeth and fingernails with the paint just for fun.

Starting in the 1920s, it all went terribly wrong as some *Radium Girls* started losing their teeth while others were treated for deteriorating jawbones. Confusing Radium for Calcium, their bodies had allowed this radioactive substance to become part of their bones, where it ruthlessly killed cells, mutated others and, eventually, gave many of the women cancer. At the time, this was all a bit confusing as Marie Curie was promoting Radium as a therapy for shrinking tumors, and Emil Grubbe had been performing X-ray treatments on his patients for over twenty years. Radiation was supposed to destroy cancer, not create it. However, by the 1930s, it was well established that chronic radiation exposure caused cancer and, to make matters worse, radiation was seemingly everywhere. Where you live may result in greater exposure to potentially damaging radiation, especially at higher altitudes and sunlight itself may cause skin cancer, as it contains ultraviolet radiation (UV).

While Pierre Curie died after being run over by a horse and carriage in Paris in 1906, Madame Curie died of leukemia in 1934. Her exposure to Radium is speculated to be a potential cause, as is the X-ray equipment she and her daughter, Irène Joliot-Curie, operated as medical volunteers during World War I. Her daughter, who also won a Nobel Prize for her work on radioactivity, succumbed to the same disease. Madame Curie was originally buried in a wooden coffin, which was placed inside a lead-lined coffin, itself contained within another wooden coffin. In 1995, Marie and Pierre's bodies were transferred in lead-lined coffins to the Panthéon in Paris. Her notebooks are kept in a lead box, and if you wish to review them, you must first sign a waiver. As for Emil Grubbe, by the 1940s, his fingers had been amputated one by one, and his face was later left heavily disfigured from repeated operations to remove tumors. He treated thousands of patients and is believed to have undergone as many as ninety surgeries himself. Although he died in 1960 from multiple squamous carcinomas with metastasis, he was eighty-five. Lastly, the *Radium Girls* are buried throughout our lands, but with much less fanfare and hardly a lead coffin to be counted. Many died from cancer. Many did not.

Whether tobacco, asbestos, or radiation played a role in our parents getting cancer, we are forever left to wonder. The disease is insidious in that way, as it makes you ask questions for which there are no easy answers. It makes you replay the same movie in your mind, even though you know the ending, but wish you didn't. While you find imagined significance in certain frames or scenes, it is only in retrospect, when it no longer matters, as the script cannot be changed anyway. Cancer is a ghost trapped in your mind, and it follows you everywhere you go.

One day, when she got home from her classes, on a Thursday, Judi's mother had sat her down to share the terrible news. A few months later, as my wife did her best to doggy paddle through high school, her mom visited the world-renowned *MD Anderson Cancer Center* in Houston, Texas, to chart a treatment plan that would ultimately include surgery, chemotherapy, and radiation. Arlene had always been thin, if not lanky, and in a world before the proliferation of fast-food restaurants, her daughter later recalled her mother's love of making sandwiches. She once told me, "My mom would have loved all the places we have now. I could see her going to *Jersey Mikes* for lunch and then *Panera* for dinner." In any event, at first, her mother's sandwich building went unabated, but then she quit making them. Her mom soon lost weight she really couldn't spare, and after several rounds of chemotherapy, she lost all her hair. While other teenage kids attended high school parties, my wife often spent weekends helping her mother with basic household chores. Fortunately, by that point, the mat below the refrigerator had been discarded.

Judi knew things looked bleak, but what she could not fully comprehend as a fourteen-year-old girl was that her mother had been specifically diagnosed with malignant mesothelioma. This cancer is an aggressive and deadly form of cancer that most often affects the tissue that surrounds the lungs (pleura) and the survival rate is typically a mere 4 to 18 months after diagnosis. When her mother heard her diagnosis and that her condition was terminal, the doctors asked if she wanted to know "how long she had to live." Being told you have cancer is terrible, but being told it is terminal and being asked if you wish to know how long you have must be unbearable. In 1978, there was no internet to surf and cancer was seldom discussed in public. Arelene told the doctors she would rather not know.

Although we share a birthday, I never met my mother-in-law. One day in early April 1980, about two months following my wife's sixteenth birthday, Arlene was taken to the hospital. She was frail and tired. She had undergone a battery of treatments, further battering her body and mind, but nothing had slowed the quick march toward the inevitable. It was a world before hospice was widely known or fully utilized. It was also a world before oxycodone and other modern painkillers we now take for granted, leaving her to endure unspeakable pain throughout her ordeal. Not only did the hospital offer round-the-clock care, but it also offered morphine. At one point during her fight, she had even been prescribed marijuana, probably more for nerves than for pain.

One week after her mom's admittance, Judi received a phone call and was told to get to the hospital as soon as possible so that she "might get an opportunity to say goodbye to her mom." She later recalled walking into her mother's hospital room, telling her mother she loved her and saying goodbye. Her mom could not speak, but most certainly heard her daughter's words. On April 12, 1980, her mother quietly passed away. She was only 41. Forty-four years later, as my wife reminisced about those awful times, she said to me, "I lost my best friend that day. She was my biggest fan." Her mom never got the opportunity to see her daughter graduate from high school, attend college, or earn a master's degree. She never saw her get married and she never met her grandchildren. Of course, she also knew nothing about our guy trips. Truth be told, cancer pilfers all we hold sacred.

The 12th Man

Before nationwide radio or television broadcasts, an enterprising Texas A&M cadet named David J. "Mike" Finn obtained a telephone lease and rights for a direct, uninterrupted line to the A&M campus. He then arranged for the use of the college's stock-judging pavilion, where he set up several amplifiers. Below, on the arena floor, he created a makeshift football field to track play-by-play action and enlisted another cadet, William "Doc" Tolsen, to help him. Two other cadets, Othman C. Thompson and Arthur C. Keith, were 180 miles away at Fair Park in Dallas, Texas and relayed the events unfolding on the gridiron between Texas A&M and SMU. A former student, William B. "Bean" Harkrider, provided the actual play-by-play commentary for the crowd in the arena. Finn's sales pitch was simple- "Why go to Dallas for the game when you can hear it called play-by-play at the Pavilion." At 35 cents, it seemed a bargain, and on October 8, 1920, many students, along with the university president and the Dean of Engineering, did just that. Sensing his success and having better gauged his expenses, he doubled the price for the next broadcast.

The first live football broadcast would happen the following year, after several other entrepreneurial cadets, using surplus US Army Signal Corps equipment left on campus after World War I exercises, set up an experimental station. Later, the station was moved to downtown Bryan, Texas. They used the call letters 5YA and then later 5YB, which was a forerunner to WTAW. When A&M battled against Texas in a Thanksgiving game, a telegraph line was rigged up between *Kyle Field* and the electrical engineering building across campus, while another line ran all the way to Austin. A little over a month later, additional lines were opened between Dallas and Danville, to Louisville and Lexington in Kentucky, and to Boston and Cambridge in Massachusetts. This pioneer radio, in early 1920s Texas, would capture wire-to-wire and play-by-play one of the most famous games in *Aggie* history—the *Dixie Classic*—and in doing so, helped create perhaps its most legendary tale.

The first *Dixie Classic*, which was a precursor to the *Cotton Bowl*, was scheduled for January 2, 1922, and would pit Texas A&M against the seemingly invincible Centre College from Danville, Kentucky. Although Centre College is now a successful Division III team in the Southern Athletic Association (SAA), at the time, they were unbeaten and the top-ranked team in the entire nation. Coming off a stunning victory against Harvard, the *Praying Colonels* had also won a National Championship in 1919 and blown out Texas Christian (TCU) 63-7 in the 1920 *Fort Worth Classic*. When the Centre football team rolled into Dallas, not only did they bring more than a handful of players born and raised in Texas, but they also brought the former Texas A&M coach—Charley Moran.

Texas A&M was no slouch either, having entered the game with a 5-1-2 record that season and 35-3-3 over the prior five years. The *Aggies*, who had been playing football since the early 1890s, were coached by Dana Xenophon Bible—better known simply as "D.X." Except for a stint in the US Army in France during World War I in 1918, Bible had been at the helm since 1917. Quite frankly, it is hard to imagine a head football coach stepping away to serve, but that is what he did, along with most of his team. The same thing happened throughout the nation, and, in fact, Centre only managed to play four games in 1918 with the slew of college athletes uniformed as doughboys and hurled overseas. What seems equally amazing is that Coach Bible got no preferential treatment and, once overseas, was assigned to the 22nd Aero Pursuit Squadron. In his new role as an unarmed scout pilot, thousands of miles from Texas, he helped with targeting the field artillery by flying at low altitudes over the Western Front.

Although Coach Bible had a strong squad going into the game against Centre, he also had a problem. The final two games against Rice and Texas had taken a toll on the *Aggies,* as injuries were piling up. With eighteen *Aggies* on his current roster, including Buck Buckner, who was relegated to crutches, D.X. could hardly afford a single mishap. With his players outweighed by 10-20 pounds by the *Praying Colonels*, this seemed improbable. Reading the game-day tea leaves, the *Dallas Morning News* carried the headline "Centre Is Favorite to Win Battle," and most of the twelve thousand at Fair Park that day, from Kentucky and even Texas, would have readily or grudgingly concurred.

Shortly after 2:30 p.m., before a cheering and mostly standing crowd, the ball was kicked off to Texas A&M. The *Dixie Classic* was underway. A few plays later, tragedy struck when Heine Weir, the captain and star running back for the *Aggies,* suffered a broken leg and was carried off the field. After a flurry of punts and counter-punts, at the end of the first half, thanks to a safety, Texas A&M clung to a 2-0 lead. However, the first half had come at a heavy cost. Not only was Weir out, but he was joined by Sammy Sanders, who was knocked out cold and suffered a twisted knee; fullback Bull Johnson, halfback Louis E. Miller, and quarterback A.B. "Bugs" Morris. Not surprisingly, D.X. was legitimately worried. Not only did his short-handed and thoroughly exhausted team have a full second half to play, but if the second half was anything like the first, and more injuries ensued, the *Aggies* might have to forfeit the game.

E. King Gill was from Dallas, Texas and attended the game that day. He was also a former member of the Texas A&M *Aggie* football team. In fact, the sophomore cadet had started the season with them, but as a running back in an already crowded backfield, he left the team mid-season to focus on basketball. Prior to the game, Jinx Tucker—a sportswriter from nearby Waco—asked Gill if he could help him in the press box as a "spotter," aiding in player identification and statistics. Gill agreed and had a bird's eye view for the first half of the game.

As Bible fretted about his thinning bench, he suddenly remembered Gill being at the game and in the press box. Gill, later offering his recollections of the events in a 1956 interview, recalled looking down and seeing D.X. waving towards the press box. There are other reports that many of the *Aggie* faithful and Aggie yell leaders helped make certain Gill knew he was being summoned. Gill further recalled, "I knew what he wanted. I ran down through the bleachers and jumped onto the field." Coach Bible was noticeably relieved and said to Gill, "It doesn't look like I'm going to have enough players to finish the game. You may have to go in there." Gill immediately ran under the bleachers to put on the uniform of the injured running back, Heine Weir, before returning to the sideline, where he stood ready to play. There, as the only player left on the team's bench, he stayed standing. In that moment, with the selfless act of a fellow cadet, a star was born, as was the tradition of the *12th Man*. Gill never did enter the game. The *Aggies* did finish with enough players and with an enormous upset victory, 22-14. Over one hundred years later, the Texas A&M student section stands united for the entire game as a symbol of unity, loyalty, and the Aggies' willingness to serve when called upon to do so. And it is the reason that Texas A&M has earned a name that embraces Gill's simple gesture of service: *Home of the 12th Man.*

Although I will always cherish the Ohio State Marching Band and "*dotting the i,*" it is but a faint dot compared to the *12th Man*. This Texas A&M tradition is also larger than Florida State's *Chief Osceola's* riding out onto the field and planting his spear near midfield or *Ralphie's*—Colorado's 500-pound buffalo (bison)—leading the team with his thunderous run (with the help of 5 handlers) from one end of the field to the other. *The 12th Man* is bigger than *Traveler*—USC's white horse ridden by a Trojan warrior—or when Wisconsin fans, young and old, decide to *Jump Around* between the third and fourth quarter. The playing of John Denver's *Take Me Home, Country Roads* may sound like a rousing chorus at West Virginia games, but it is just a whisper compared to the *12th Man*, and Howard's Rock at Clemson is but a tiny pebble in comparison. And, although the *12th* Man makes the Oregon Duck entrance on a motorcycle look more like a duckling on a tricycle, for now, to hedge my bets, I'll leave Notre Dame's *Touchdown Jesus* out of the discussion.

You might be thinking, "How can you say such things?" A faint dot? A whisper? A tiny pebble? A duckling on a tricycle? Yep, I stand by these written words as *the 12th Man* is one of the biggest traditions in all of college football, or all sports for that matter. It is, as some might say, "*numero uno,*" or at the least, "*numero dos.*" It has always been and will always be. For you see, we—the fans who stream into stadiums and arenas to support our teams—are all the *12th Man*. Texas A&M, thankfully, just gave us a name and, in doing so, acknowledged us as *the* most important tradition in all of sport. Now, imagine *dotting the i* in an empty stadium or singing *Take Me Home, Country Roads* alone in the woods without fellow fans or friends joining you in that rousing chorus. Not the same, right? Imagine someone planting a flaming spear in your backyard or someone dressed like a duck recklessly driving a loud motorcycle down your street. Call the cops, right? What about secretly touching a rock in the darkness of the night or jumping up and down by yourself without music or an autumn Wisconsin sky? These, no doubt, would be relatively forgettable, if not highly questionable, experiences. However, when you bring together others to share these moments, it resets the entire equation. It refracts the light in a completely different pattern. We, the fans—past and present—have created and continue to create these many wonderful and unique traditions. They are our sinew, and we are what gives them meaning.

It has been said that college football programs represent the front porch of the university. This is also true for the towns where the University resides and, although it may not be the most important room in the house, it is certainly the most visible. If the porch is well-maintained, a passerby assumes the entire house must be equally impressive. The front porch is a perfect spot for any college with national ambitions to attract attention and increase enrollment. Put another way, money spent fixing up the porch, including hiring professional contractors to get the job done right, may prove to be a most prudent expenditure. More students translate into more money for the entire school, and ultimately, the entire community. What if you hired a beloved builder or, in the case of football, a celebrity coach? Furthermore, what better way to sell your school—to potential football players or those seeking degrees in chemistry or accounting alike—than to showcase the history and traditions of the front porch and the entire house? Lastly, what if you knew a whole film crew from *HGTV* would come to visit your house every other Saturday in the fall, at the start of classes, to feature stories about the front porch, its history, and how it gathers folks from around the country with a common purpose and a beautiful view? Traditions, it seems, serve an enormous financial purpose as well.

Unique customs not only unite fans and potentially harness mass financial resources for a college but also serve to remind the opposing team and their small band of followers that they are not welcome in this house, at least for the next sixty minutes. When the Michigan football team runs onto the field in the *Big House* with their *winged football helmets*, jumping up and touching the *GO BLUE* banner, all while over 100,000 fans belt out *Hail to the Victors*, it screams to the visiting contingent—this is our home, not yours. When Penn State gathers over 100,000 fans in *Beaver Stadium*, all wearing white on a dark Pennsylvania night, it is a stark reminder to the opposing team that they are "not in Kansas anymore, Toto," and when Virginia Tech enters the stadium to *Sandman*, visitors might just start clicking their heels and repeating, "there's no place like home, there's no place like home." The funny thing is, those fans who are at home are saying the exact same thing.

As the *12th Man*, nobody really believes they might have to suit up and play. After all, even young Gill never got in the game. However, as a home fan, you have figuratively suited up and pledged that you will do all in your power, or at least all in your voice, to help the home team come away with a victory. In other words, you will be a human conduit to what is known as "home-field advantage," even if it results in a ringing in your ears long after you have left the stadium.

Statistically, teams playing at home win significantly more games than when traveling to opposing venues. In fact, a study by *Bleacher Report* revealed that between 2001 and 2011, roughly 63% of all Division I-A football games were won by the home side. Furthermore, the same report found that the number jumps to a whopping 67.27% when broken down to only BCS teams and Notre Dame. These numbers, besides Major League Soccer (69.1%), are the highest in all American sports. In 2020, *FanSided* reported that in the past ten years (2010-2020), the following teams recorded the best home records: Georgia 56-9; Notre Dame 51-13; Oklahoma 58-11; LSU 61-8; Wisconsin 61-8; Michigan 57-13; Clemson 64-5; Penn State 62-15; Alabama 65-5; and Ohio State 67-5. Although these numbers have no doubt changed, given Georgia and Michigan's recent race to the top, you still get the idea. However, given these stats, it also appears that lesser-known Division I-A programs clearly have more success at home as well.

Typically, if you're the betting type, the national average for home-field advantage hovers around three points. Suppose two teams are closely ranked and have the same record. Money, which always talks, says take the home team! Granted, the better teams will win more away games simply because they have better players, and truth be told, the bigger schools tend to lure smaller schools into their homes with the promise of a big payday. This pads the home wins for many bigger programs and serves as "test games" or "warm-up matches" early in the season. As for the smaller schools, the money might just be used to paint their front porch or cover hospital bills for their brave players. The crowd noise is often considered the primary reason for home-field advantage, as it can literally "pump up" the home team while disrupting the opponent's communication, making it harder for them to coordinate plays. Bigger programs, typically featuring better (and larger) players, often have larger stadiums that naturally generate more noise. But how did they get there? You know the answer. They achieved this by building a beautiful front porch, admired by many, and then sharing their story with all who would listen about how they did it. Every nail came with a story, and along the way, the front porch became a mythical place to behold. Along the way, the fans became a mythical force—*the 12th Man.*

A Library and a Former First Lady

Typically, the "guy trips" are from Friday to Sunday. We get in, enter a state of total immersion and get out—all within forty-eight hours or less. However, College Station offered our group a unique learning opportunity, as the George H.W. Bush Presidential Library and Museum is situated right on the Texas A&M University campus. With this discovery, we knew this trip needed a detour from the ordinary. What we needed was an extra day and after sharing this proposal with our wives, that is exactly what we got. They really are the best! After flying out on Thursday evening, we rendezvoused for dinner at *Pappadeaux Seafood Kitchen* in the Houston (IAH) airport. Now a restaurant dynasty with over ninety locations spanning eight states, the *Pappadeaux* story more properly began in 1897 when H.D. Pappas left Greece for America with nothing more than a dream. Cozied up in a booth against the back wall, we enjoyed an assortment of adult beverages, along with orders of crab and spinach dip, crawfish étouffée, and blackened catfish. This was followed by a round of spoons to share, featuring cheesecake and key lime pie. Luckily, after much food and drink, we decided to stay at an airport hotel for the night as we could barely move.

The following morning, after downing a pot of black coffee, we drove ninety miles from Houston to College Station, Texas. Along the way, we passed big ranches, big homes, big fences, big gates, and countless big Lone Star flags. It's true; everything really is bigger in Texas. After checking into our hotel, we hopped next door to an adorable Italian restaurant for a quick bite before heading off to campus to relive the mid-1980s and the father Bush presidency.

George Herbert Walker Bush was the 41st President of the United States. He served the highest office, for one term from 1989 through 1993 and, along with John Adams, is the only man to have his son also become President. Dedicated November 6, 1997, the George H.W. Bush Presidential Library opened to the public shortly thereafter. Coming in at an initial cost of $43 million and located on 90 acres on the west campus of Texas A&M University at 1000 George Bush Drive West, the contemporary and monolithic design, featuring large limestone, presents a timeless elegance. Outside, as we approached, we were greeted by a large bronze sculpture featuring five horses leaping to freedom over the ruins of the Berlin Wall. Anyone, a member of Generation X or older, remembers that on November 9, 1989, the Berlin Wall fell, ending the Cold War and decades of lives lost behind ill-conceived political philosophies, unrealistic notions of human nature, and unmitigated brutality. The sculpture, created by Veryl Goodnight, represents the pursuit of personal freedom and the triumph of the human spirit. It also represents one of the single greatest political achievements from the Reagan-Bush years.

Much like a toy store for a child, the museum and library provide a treasure trove of artifacts for any history buff, offering a concise chapter in the story we call *America*. Exhibits presenting perspectives on the life and work of President Bush include a World War II Avenger Torpedo Bomber, a 1947 Studebaker, a slab of the Berlin Wall, the Presidential Limo, and replicas of President Bush's Camp

David, Situation Room, and Oval Office. After snapping a few photos of my son behind the desk of the former president, we roamed the halls of the museum, hopelessly trying to take in the thousands of exhibits on display. Regardless of your politics, Presidential Museums are well worth the price of admission, as they are giant time capsules. Still, unlike other museums with untargeted boundaries, the person chronicled is neatly organized within a set time frame—their life. Overall, the experience is truly enjoyable, unique, and highly recommended.

Long before the Iraq War, Saddam Hussein's invasion of Kuwait, Dana Carvey's wildly popular impersonation and the former president's insistence of "Read my lips" on no new taxes, George H.W. Bush played first base for the Yale baseball team, where he led the squad to two College World Series. Having been the captain of his prep school soccer team, he also played a year of football at Yale. Although Bush served as Vice President, a U.S. Congressman, Director of the Central Intelligence Agency (CIA), and Ambassador to the United Nations, he also enjoyed participating in various athletic endeavors. In fact, he has been described as one of the "most sporting Presidents in American History." Consider his enjoyment of golf, matched only by his love of fishing and quail hunting. The man was also a competitor through and through. Once, after Bush had gone fishing in Maine with Russia's Vladimir Putin, he remarked, "I don't think he could be called an accomplished fisherman." The president also enjoyed tennis, biking, and jogging, and when he needed a rush of adrenaline, he would jump out of airplanes.

George H.W. Bush was, by all accounts, "a man's man." Both my grandmother and my mother, who both saw him in person at different points, also insisted that he was "incredibly handsome." Although looks can be disputed, and beauty viewed through the eyes of the beholder, bravery has less room for variance of opinion. The man, a Yale graduate and the son of a U.S. Senator, flew 58 combat missions as a torpedo bomber pilot in the Pacific Theater during World War II. He was brave, alright.

On September 2, 1944, his plane was hit by anti-aircraft fire during a bombing run on the Japanese island of Chichi Jima. With smoke pouring into the cockpit and flames rippling across the crease of the wing, he dropped his 500-pound bombs on the target and bailed out over the ocean, but not before striking his head on the tail of the plane and ripping his parachute. Tragically, two other crew members—the radio operator and gunner—did not survive. Splashing into the water, Bush watched in horror as his plane struck the ocean. Floating by himself for hours, stung by jellyfish, nauseous from being struck in the head and tossed about with a belly full of seawater, the 20-year-old pilot managed to evade capture. Eventually, a submarine crew fished the future president out of the water. He would be the lone survivor. For the others, they were not so fortunate. Known as the "Chichijima incident," eight other pilots were captured, beaten, tortured, and eventually executed. Shockingly, some of the men were beheaded, with at least one cannibalized.

The World War II exhibits are enthralling, made even more so by taped interviews with President Bush, which we watched repeatedly in a state of mesmerized fascination. His deferring his admission to Yale to join the U.S. Naval Reserves and his becoming the youngest commissioned pilot at just 18 years old to earn his wings were impressive, as was his flying additional combat missions after the harrowing escape. For his service, he was awarded a Distinguished Flying Cross, three Air Medals, and a Presidential Unit Citation. Impressive indeed. However, it was his humanity that left us inspired. When retelling the story as an older man, he still choked up and cried when talking about his lost crew members.

Also lost at sea were the letters from his fiancée, Barbara Pierce, which he had kept in his plane for luck during combat missions. The battered and bruised pilot, while on the bridge of the submarine, made a pledge to himself to get home safely and to marry Barbara Pierce before she fell for some other guy. He need not worry as the future first lady once declared, "I've loved George Bush almost since the day I laid eyes on him." Upon his return home, what followed, quite frankly, was a love story for the ages.

The senior Bush was known to cry. As I've said, it's what I liked about the guy. It made him human. After meeting a boy in Poland who had leukemia, the then-vice President stood before the little guy with tears running down his cheek, hoping it went unnoticed by the boy, but if he did see the tears, he'd feel that he loved him. Although it had been thirty-five years since the loss of his three-year-old daughter, Pauline Robinson "Robin", from the same dreaded disease, he and his wife remained heartbroken their entire lives. On April 17, 2018, former First Lady Barbara Bush—the only woman besides Abigail Adams to have both her husband and son serve as President—passed away. She was 92. Within the year, her husband, the 41st President of the United States, passed away on November 30, 2018. He was 94. They were married for 73 years and are buried on the museum grounds, side by side, with modest matching headstones. Also, by their side is Robin.

Presidential Libraries have become both a colossal undertaking and a fanatical obsession for those who hold the office. A president need not have a presidential library. Still, today, it would be unfathomable to imagine a president opting out of this newest form of what might be considered self-love. These "Presidential Temples" are created through a mix of private donations and taxpayer dollars. The construction is typically funded by private foundations, with the operation and maintenance subsequently transferred to the National Archives and Records Administration (NARA). That's you and me, folks. However, given the enormity of the structures and documents contained therein, Congress passed the Presidential Libraries Act of 1986, which required the libraries to provide endowments to NARA to defray costs. Consider, for instance, that the George W. Bush Library Foundation reportedly raised nearly $500 million; and the final costs topped $250 million for the 207,000-square-foot structure located on the campus of Southern Methodist University (SMU) in Dallas, Texas. Although not completed, the Barack Obama Presidential Center is projected to clock in at 225,000 square feet and cost somewhere north of $700 million. The center will likely need an endowment of $1.5 billion. Whoa! Now, that would take just about anyone's breath away, even one not on a windy, wintery street corner in downtown Chicago.

So, how did we get here? Believe it or not, the story begins on a platform at the Baltimore and Potomac Railroad Station in Washington, D.C., on the morning of July 2, 1881. The story also begins with the murder of a president and the perseverance of his wife. President James A. Garfield had been the nation's 20th president for only four months—four tumultuous months. Not only had he battled with power brokers over a barrage of patronage appointments, but the former Union general and Ohio congressman was equally exhausted after his wife, Lucretia Garfield, contracted a near-fatal case of malaria. As he waited to board a train along with his two teenage sons, it was for a much-needed vacation. In a world before bodyguards or security detail, he was joined only by the Secretary of State, James G. Blaine, who had ridden over in a carriage with the president to see him off. Unbeknownst, they were also joined on the platform by a seriously disturbed 39-year-old man named Charles Guiteau, who carried a .44 caliber pistol and who snuck behind Garfield and fired two shots at him. The first lead bullet grazed the president's arm, while the second ripped into his lower back, causing him to stumble forward with hands outstretched to break his fall. There, slumped on the floor, with a bright red stain on the back of his suit, the president remained relatively motionless while screams erupted throughout the station. As for Guiteau, his efforts to flee were thwarted when a man blocked the door, allowing a ticket agent and a policeman to apprehend him. He was then whisked away to avoid an angry mob that began to take shape.

The president's eyes remained open, but in a confused state as if trying to take in what had happened to him. Both his sons, now sobbing, knelt beside him, along with Jacob Smith, a janitor, who futilely tried to get the president back on his feet. The ladies' waiting room attendant, Sarah White, who had rushed over, placed the president's head in her lap. He was conscious as he asked for water but was unable to hold it down as he began to vomit, turning his head so as not to stain her dress. Although in considerable pain, the president was able to tell his sons not to worry and asked that his wife be informed about the unexpected developments. Within minutes, Dr. Smith Townsend, the District of Columbia's health officer, arrived on the scene to assess the situation. Unfortunately, as the president lay on a dirty train station floor, the doctor inserted his finger into the wound in his back. Garfield was then moved to an upstairs room at the train station on a horsehair mattress. Another doctor, who had been summoned for his assistance, was Dr. D. Willard Bliss and, upon arrival, took control of the president's medical care. Bliss removed a long probe from his bag and inserted it into the wound, searching for where the bullet might be lodged. However, after the probe became momentarily stuck near the president's rib cage, he removed it and replaced it with his pinky finger, only to return to his bag for yet another probe. Through it all, the patient managed to remain silent and unflinching.

The forty-nine-year-old republican president managed to survive that day and then the next and ultimately spent the next two months in a makeshift sick room at the White House. Later, he would be taken by train to a cottage on the Jersey shore in the hope that the cool sea breeze might aid in his recovery. Throughout this ordeal, an important question remained unanswered. Where was the bullet? An X-ray machine could not help in solving this riddle, as it would not be invented for another fourteen years and this was before the widespread use of exploratory surgery. On the morning of July 26, the famous inventor, Alexander Graham Bell, arrived at the White House with his assistant, William Taintor. He also brought his *induction balance*—a contraption used to locate metal in the human body. While the doctors believed the experiments confirmed the bullet was in the vicinity initially decided upon, Bell privately believed the experiment had shown nothing.

Throughout the summer, the nation received daily updates on Garfield's condition, and somewhere along the way, the unexpected happened. The United States, still badly wounded from the Civil War, began to heal itself from within. Every citizen, regardless of region or party affiliation, came together to pull for the recovery of *their* leader. However, it was not meant to be. Sadly, on September 19, 1881, President James A. Garfield died, leaving a mourning wife, family, and entire nation. The autopsy found the bullet to the right of Garfield's spinal cord wrapped in a protective layer of scar tissue that had formed around it. In the end, he had not been killed by a bullet but by an infection born from those trying to save him.

The former first lady, pressed into an unexpected role, became guardian of her husband's memory. Lucretia not only set out to correct any inaccuracies written about her spouse but also to organize and preserve his papers. She rightfully believed that an assassin had stolen her husband's life and had robbed her children of their father. She would not let him steal his legacy. When she returned to their home in Mentor, Ohio, she made the second-floor wing into a library and, in doing so, gave birth to the nation's first presidential library.

College Station, Texas

After our visit to the presidential museum, we stopped by a campus bookstore to load up on *Aggie* merchandise for the game the next day. "Gotta looks" the part, you know. We then returned to the hotel to freshen up before our big Friday night dinner, and since we were in Texas, my mom and Daniel had made reservations at *The Republic Steakhouse*, as was rightfully expected. Located on University Drive in College Station, the brick building with a large, cursive "R" etched above the entrance screamed "our kind of place," featuring three black awnings proclaiming "*Steak*," "*Wine*," and "*Whiskey*." Etched across another large black awning is "*The Republic, est. 1836*," a reference to the Republic of Texas that existed as a sovereign country starting March 2, 1836, until it became the 28th state when it joined the United States in 1845.

Inside is a grand setting with dark wood paneling adorned by large Western-style paintings, glass chandeliers, black leather chairs, white linens, and ornate carpeting. A massive display of whiskeys and wines is kept behind glass cabinets, while a steer sculpture breaks your line of vision from table to bar. Although we came to enjoy the Aviance, we really came to chow down and that is exactly what we did. For starters, we had orders of bourbon cherry bacon and Texas fried shrimp, followed by salads. However, the shining star over Texas for us that night was steak. Absolutely delicious! One point of caution is that the chef takes the preparation of steak quite seriously, so any request for more salt or pepper at the table should only be made after due consideration. As for the drinks, several years after our visit, the restaurant introduced Mash Madness, a single-elimination American whiskey tournament featuring 64 hand-picked whiskeys. The staff, with their extensive knowledge of whiskey, rank and seed all 64 whiskeys for the tournament before handing over the selection to the patrons for a blind taste test. Timing can be everything in life, and, in this case, we were a few years too early!

Speaking of spirits, one point of sadness to report is the closing of *New Republic Brewery* in College Station, Texas. Back at our hotel, as we gathered with Ole Miss and Texas A&M fans, we swapped stories and had plenty of local beer, and since my name is Jim, I was especially drawn to a beer named *Dammit Jim*. The red amber, with a toasted malt taste and a bitter finish, was initially called *Bellows* since the owner's father-in-law was a blacksmith. After marketing and selling the beer for approximately two and a half years, the brewery received a cease-and-desist letter from a prominent distillery, indicating that they had held the naming rights since 1830. When a friend of the owner jokingly said, "Dammit Jim, I'm a beer, not a whiskey," the new and improved name was born. This story, like so many others, is another enjoyable part of the football trips, and we hope to learn one day about the brewery's re-opening. It would make for a great story!

North of the university, in an area known as *Northgate*, sits a cluster of stores, bars, and restaurants frequented, patronized, and staffed by

Texas A&M students. One such spot, located almost directly across the street from campus, which claims to serve more beer per square foot than any other in the nation, is *Dixie Chicken*—also known as *The Chicken*. However, we were there for the grub and not the suds. Originally opened in 1974 by two local businessmen, the converted pool hall is a campus institution, and when we walked through the swinging wooden doors, we joined generations of *Aggies* who have previously done the same. Throughout the years, it has also been a hangout for countless aspiring country singers, including Robert Earl Keen and Lyle Lovett.

The outside, made entirely of wooden planks and log beams, resembles a theme park ride one might find in *Frontierland* at *Walt Disney World*, made even more so by a white square sign featuring a cartoon chicken in a cowboy outfit and a large red cowboy hat. Inside, rows of picnic tables sit directly across from a long, never-ending bar. Wood plank floors, covered in dust, bottle caps, and a rattlesnake skin or two, provide the grounding, while vintage signs, antlers, and deer mounts cover just about every corner of wall space. Multiple porches, some covered, seamlessly connect the inside to the outside. Also, just outside, between *The Chicken* and the *Dry Bean Saloon*, sits *Bottle Cap Alley*. A sight to behold, this narrow passage, wall to wall, is knee-deep in hundreds of thousands of bottle caps. The origins are shrouded in mystery, but most believe the decades-old ritual likely started when *Dixie Chicken*, along with other bars, began dumping bottle caps in the alley every night. Besides nostalgia seekers, caps are known to be "borrowed" by the Texas A&M Corps of Cadets, who wear the caps as spurs on their boots when Texas A&M plays SMU.

Another ritual, which would have been more appealing in our own college days, is the unofficial tradition of ring dunking. Starting in the 1970s, after an *Aggie* dropped his ring in a pitcher of beer and was challenged to retrieve the ring by emptying the pitcher, the practice is now reserved primarily for seniors and is limited to a 32-ounce mug of beer on *Ring Day*. The tradition is well-known, with even former President George W. Bush joking about it during a commencement speech to the 2008 graduating class. Although we avoided ring dunking, we did manage to get our fill of burgers and chicken sandwiches. *Dixie Chicken* is a must-stop for any college football enthusiast, bottle cap collector, or ring dropper. It's also a great place if you're just hungry.

Following our late lunch, we moseyed over to campus and walked through the many immaculate pathways lined with miniature *Live Oaks*. The grounds are pristine and, at one point, we saw a young woman walk across a grassy section to pick up a small piece of paper and dispose of it in a nearby trash can. Otherwise, the grass, much like your neighbor's lawn as a kid, was forbidden turf. Texas A&M is the first public institution of higher learning in the state of Texas, established by the Morrill Act, which was approved by Congress in 1862. The Morrill Act, which stated, in part, "(the) leading object shall be, without excluding other scientific and classical studies, and including military tactics, to teach such branches of learning as are related to agriculture and mechanical arts," created many "land-grant" colleges and universities. Signed into law by President Abraham Lincoln that same year, this act was also responsible for creating my brother's and my alma mater, Ohio State University, as well as other schools in the Big Ten, such as Michigan State University. In fact, a good many Universities are "land-grant" colleges and owe their existence to the Morrill Act.

The Aggies

Created on mostly flat grassland with a few rippling hills—on some 2,500 acres in Brazos County—instruction began at the Agricultural and Mechanical College of Texas in 1876 with 40 students and six faculty members. All the students were white males, and all were required to participate in the Corps of Cadets military training. The school was renamed Texas A&M University in 1963, and until 1965, it maintained a mandatory military component for all students. This long-standing relationship with the military remains strong, and today, the school continues to be a senior military college, offering participation in the Reserve Officers' Training Corps (ROTC) programs.

After making a quick stop in the Student Union (an enormous multi-level facility) for a round of bottled waters, we lined up along the side of a street with thousands of *Aggie* fans for *The Corps of Cadets March-In* to *Kyle Field.* The march-in, which has approximately 2,200 members, honors tradition and the university's roots as a military institution. Right alongside the *Fightin' Texas Aggie Band* was the *Parsons Mounted Cavalry*—consisting of over 70 horses and mules, the *Ross Volunteer Company*—the oldest honor guard and drill team of its kind in Texas, and the *Fish Drill Team*—an all-freshman precision rifle drill team with a plethora of National Championships.

Also, in the *March-in* was "*The First Lady of Aggieland.*" She has reigned as the First Lady since 1931 and is the highest-ranking member of the Corps of Cadets. Her name is *Reveille*, but everyone just calls her *Miss Rev,* and this full-blooded rough collie also serves as the school's official mascot. During our visit, we saw *Reveille VIII,* who served as the mascot for Texas A&M University from 2008 through 2015. Born in Topeka, Kansas, she passed away on June 25, 2015, following a brief illness. Her handler—Ryan Kreider—following this sad news, remarked, "*Reveille* is more than just a dog or even a mascot. She's a lady, a former student, a loyal companion, and a perfect representation of why Texas A&M is so great."

Decades before our visit, a group of cadets, while en route back to campus from nearby Navasota, Texas, struck a small black dog (except for its white paws) with their vehicle. Although pets were not allowed on campus, the dog was brought back to school and carefully hidden in a dorm room. The following morning, when a bugler played "*Reveille*" to wake the cadets, the dog's barking quickly shattered any concealment of the pooch. Ultimately, the dog was nursed back to health, was allowed to stay, and was given the name *Reveille.* The pup was named the mascot the following football season and led the marching band onto the field. She would do so for the next 13 years. Upon her passing in 1944, she was given a formal military funeral—including a 21-gun salute—and was buried outside the north end of *Kyle Field.*

Reveille III was the first full-blooded Rough Collie, and every *Reveille* since then has been that breed. Starting in 1960, the dog's free rein on campus came to an end, and she has been cared for by a mascot corporal, a sophomore in the Corps. of Cadets Company E-2, since then. Her handler is chosen by the unit in the spring, and she lives with the cadet for the remainder of that year. The two are nearly inseparable, as she attends classes with the cadet and goes home with her handler for the holidays. The cadet also accompanies her to all her formal *Aggie* engagements. Interestingly, *Miss Rev* is the highest-ranking member in the Corps of Cadets, outranking her handler. This has been known to create colorful moments; for instance, if a dog happens to fall asleep on a cadet's bed, the cadet must move elsewhere, as they are outranked by the dog. Furthermore, if the dog barks in class with her handler, the professor may choose to dismiss the class.

Our *Reveille* is buried alongside the other deceased mascots near *Kyle Field*. There, along with the other *Reveilles,* she is kept abreast of the home game scores as there is a special doggy scoreboard nearby. *Reveille IX,* who replaced our *Rev*, is a *Buckeye* by birth, having been born in Chagrin Falls, Ohio, in 2013. However, she is an *Aggie* at heart and, in retirement, makes her home at the *Stevenson Companion Animal Life-Care Center* operated by the *College of Veterinary Medicine and Biomedical Sciences*. This wonderful facility provides for the physical, emotional, and medical needs of companion animals whose owners can no longer care for them. The animals receive top-notch care as it is a teaching hospital for students in the college. Today, as of this writing, *Rev X* is the official mascot, having assumed her duties in May of 2021. The canine and her predecessor were both present at the dedication ceremony of the *Reveille* statue outside of *Kyle Field* at Texas A&M on March 3, 2023. Things have changed over the years as the latest mascot not only boasts her own website but also has her own Instagram page. But if you message her, keep things clean, as *Ms. Rev* is always a lady.

Nationally acclaimed, the *Fightin' Texas Aggie Band* is the largest military marching band in the nation. Formed in 1894, this 400+ member Corps of Cadets unit operates under strict military guidelines and was once known as the *Noble Men of Kyle*. Today, the legendary band, renowned for its precision and style, is comprised of noble men and noble *women* who work tirelessly at their craft. We were treated to a fabulous show, and *The Aggie War Hymn* still ranks as one of our all-time favorite band performances. It is, quite frankly, darn catchy, and we can all still hum it on cue to this day. Equally stimulating was the speed of the marching, and when the band marched back and forth while maintaining a tight rectangle, it was Houdini-like. If you ever get the chance, you must see this band, as although the football team has had some tough seasons, the band, much like the tailgating at Ole Miss, comes through every Saturday. Trust us, as we know a thing or two about great marching bands. They should not be missed.

Yelling is not the same as cheering, and *Yell Leaders* are not the same as cheerleaders. Five guys engaged in a most peculiar activity were dressed in white, along the sidelines of the playing field and in front of the student section. At times, they moved as if on a dance floor in a highly choreographed manner, while at other moments, it seemed reminiscent of one of my aerobics classes from the 1980s. All the while, these young men, beyond incredibly fit, yelled out letters and phrases to an adoring audience. At a prep rally called *Midnight Yell Practice*, the night before, these same guys practiced the yells and cheers alongside approximately 25,000 fans. Yell practice began in 1913, but the first official Midnight Yell did not occur until 1931, organized on the eve of a game against the University of Texas. Ah, the *Longhorns*, it figures, right? The gathering, held on the steps of the YMCA building all those years ago, has been moved to the stadium and takes place before every home game at Texas A&M, including the game we attended. However, as they yelled that night, we snored. We had thought about going, but Daniel and my father were exhausted from a full day, including our drive from Houston and the trip to the Presidential Museum. However, next time, I'm going as I want to be fully prepared to yell at the game, and I've since learned that practice typically ends at midnight instead of starting then.

As for the Yell team specifics, we must first take a quick trip back in time to the period when college football first found its footing in America. The very first cheerleaders were fans in the stands, who often relied on published school cheers. One such cheer was the *Princeton Locomotive* cheer, popularized in the 1870s, which went like this: *Hurrah! Hurrah! Hurrah! Tigers! S-s-s-T! Boom! A-h-h-h!"* Surprisingly, fan cheering never really morphed into the chanting and singing that is so prevalent in English football (soccer). With alcohol and plenty of younger folk fancying themselves as incredibly clever, in retrospect, it seems inevitable. But, alas, it was not meant to be.

The birthplace of cheerleading is generally attributed to the University of Minnesota and to a student named Johnny Campbell. At a game in 1898, Campbell is reported to have rallied fellow *Golden Gophers* with an iconic cheer that went like this: "*Rah, Rah, Rah! Ski-U-Mah! Hoo-Rah! Hoo-Rah! Varsity! Varsity! Minn-e-so-tah!*" Well, I know, but you had to start somewhere. It was truly historic. You can call it the "big bang" of cheerleading, and Campbell is a bona fide pioneer. Interestingly, it was not until 1914 that a woman cheerleader yelled for the first time. Two years before, Northwestern chose to seat men and women students separately and the University of Kansas quickly followed. The reasoning behind this separation was a belief that the men would be less distracted and would focus their attention, and thus their cheering, on the players on the field. Imagine that. This left the Kansas women's section without a cheerleader, so the female *Jayhawk* fans selected Elizabeth Morrow as their designated yeller for a game against Missouri. This trailblazing moment was followed by Rosa Hart, who was an iconic member of the cheer squad for Tulane starting in 1919. Much like the Texas A&M Yell Team, images reveal Ms. Hart, along with the Tulane male cheer squad, wearing all-white outfits.

Now, briefly returning to Minnesota for a moment, it was not until 1923 that women were allowed to participate in cheerleading for the school. During the Roaring Twenties, women throughout America joined all-female cheer teams, which introduced dance elements and gymnastics into their routines. It was also during this time that the classic college cheerleading uniforms—consisting of sweaters, skirts, and saddle shoes—became the sideline image that largely continues to this day. Interestingly, a cheerleader at the University of Oregon, to garner crowd participation, used the first flashcards around the same time. Pom-poms, as a decorative accessory, gained popularity in the 1930s. Usually made of paper, these originals seldom survived the length of the game. It was not until the 1950s that these accessories were strengthened, ultimately made with handles, and otherwise improved.

Portable megaphones have been widely used for crowd management and mass communication for centuries. As such, it is not surprising that handheld, cone-shaped devices were used early on by cheering and yelling squads at college football games. Once again, the University of Minnesota is generally credited for incorporating megaphones into its routines at the turn of the 20th century. However, the first person credited for using a megaphone at a college football game is Thomas Peebles, a member of the legendary Princeton Pep Club.

The Texas A&M *Yell Leaders*, at least from our vantage point, went without such assistance, relying instead on their voice and movements to communicate to the thousands on hand. This tradition started in the early 1900s, when the *Aggies* were losing badly, and the audience had grown bored. Many of those feeling unenthused were guests from the nearby Texas Woman's University and the upperclassmen, fearing a pending disaster on the romantic front, ordered the freshmen on hand to provide a little entertainment to make up for the lousy game. They found white coveralls and began leading the crowd in yells. The freshmen were an instant hit, but not wanting to lose the future limelight, it was decided that these activities in the future should be limited to upperclassmen. Today, the *Yell Team* consists of three seniors and two juniors, who are elected each year by the student body.

Much like Ole Miss, those in "*Aggie Land*" speak a strange and exotic language. For example, *Aggies* are fond of flashing a thumbs-up while saying, "*Gig 'em!*" This phrase was popularized at a yell practice by P. L. "Pinky" Downs—a member of the Texas A&M Board of Regents and the Class of 1906—when he asked the crowd before a Texas Christian University, "*What are we going to do to those Horned Frogs?*" He answered his own question with, "*Gig 'em, Aggies!*" If you are not familiar with this term, it refers to a long pole with multiple sharp prongs at the end, used to capture fish or small game. It is also perfect for frog hunting and when Downs, for added emphasis, made a fist with his thumb extended straight up, the crowd knew exactly what he meant.

Another peculiar habit is to "hiss" as a sign of disapproval rather than straight-out booing. This is also accompanied by putting both hands flat together and shaking them. I suppose it is slightly more polite but equally unnerving if one is on the receiving end of such dissent. We also heard the phrase *"good bull,"* which in plain English is used to describe anything that embraces the *Aggie* spirit or the traditions at Texas A&M. "*Now that's some good bull.*" Yep, it's a sign of approval, even if that phrase might get you slapped somewhere else. The *Aggie* upperclassman often blurted out, "Whoop!" as an expression of excitement and, though we did it freely, I'm not sure if we were allowed, as apparently it is reserved for upperclassmen. Lastly, and quite frankly, one of my favorites, "Howdy," is the official greeting of Texas A&M. The origins of this campus greeting remain a mystery. Still, as visitors, we were showered with this greeting, which made us feel right at home. I still find myself using it back in Ohio, and occasionally, I'll get a *"Howdy"* back with a Texas drawl and a knowing wink

---

On October 11, 2014, before a Texas-sized crowd of 110,633, Ole Miss whipped the *Aggies* 35-20. After jumping to a 14-0 lead in the first quarter, the *Rebels*, who were undefeated and ranked 3rd in the nation, took a 21-0 lead into halftime and cruised to an easy and early victory. Our favorite part of the game, besides the band, was before the fourth quarter, when singing the third verse of the *War Hymn*, a larger-than-life Texan—with a cowboy hat and a belt buckle the size of a license plate—sitting next to Daniel, hunched down and put his arm around him and began swaying to the right and left. As we looked out across the stadium, we realized all 110,000 fans were arm in arm, swaying back and forth, so we quickly joined them. Rumor has it that when the Aggie faithful sway back and forth, the third deck and press box at *Kyle Field* move two to three inches to the left and the right, leaving the visiting media unnerved by the sensation. Every now and then, to this day, Daniel will gather the guys and lead us in this ritual, no matter where we are or what we are doing.

In the darkness of a Texas night, Ole Miss had played nearly perfectly. However, as good as they were, it was a defensive lineman on the other sideline who caught our attention. At 6'5 and 270 lbs., it was little wonder we could not keep our eyes off him. Yes, he was unnaturally large, but he was also surprisingly fast. Like Johnny Manziel, you got a sense that you were watching someone special, and although his team did not have a monster night, he would have a monster year. As a freshman, Myles Garrett would lead the team in sacks, tackles for a loss, quarterback hurries, and would register at least two tackles in every single game. These exploits earned him Defensive MVP at the annual team banquet. His sophomore and junior years were equally monstrous displays of defensive prowess, and after leaving school early, he was the first overall pick in the 2017 NFL draft. The Cleveland *Browns*, who had finished 1-15 in the 2016 season, had the first pick in the draft, and even though they proceeded to go 0-16 in 2017, when I was asked by anyone about my thoughts on the *Browns* pick, without hesitation, I consistently and unabashedly offered, "The *Browns* comeback is underway." Now, since saying that, the organization has made a handful of rash and inexplicable moves that have become all too common, and, as such, I might need to restate what I originally said to something like, "The *Browns* comeback could be underway if they quit shooting themselves in the foot and give Myles Garrett and Nick Chubb a little help!"

From an Early Age

From an early age, Dan was athletic. He's got a solid build, with well-defined muscles reminiscent of a gym rat. As such, it was not surprising he played organized soccer with his younger sister and then later played pee-wee football in a limited capacity. Our son also developed an early affinity for baseball and his experiences with Little League included both the highest of highs and the lowest of lows. His first team was great, and his coach—Coach H—was a role model to Dan and the other boys on the team. First, the team was good. Darn good. However, the coach treated Daniel just like any other player, regardless of the situation. For example, if there were two outs and bases loaded, Dan would bat if it were his regular turn in the order. The truth is, it scared the heck out of me. His fellow players never complained about putting him in the game. Instead, they cheered for him, and, on more than one occasion, he came through with a hit.

The team was tight, which made them even better and, not surprisingly, they made the playoffs. In a hotly contested game, in which Dan batted and played in the outfield, our guys took a one-run lead into the bottom of the final inning. With two outs, the other team had loaded the bases when their best batter came to bat. He crushed the ball to the opposite outfield—thankfully away from Daniel and his terrified parents—where a fellow teammate sheepishly put his glove up into the air and somehow snagged the ball. For a moment, he gazed into his mitt to make sure the ball was still there. Game over! What an ending! But there was another catch. The other team, as instructed by their coaches, started walking back onto the field as if there was another inning to play. It was surreal. The coaches then met with an umpire and a heated exchange ensued. At that point, Coach H gathered the team together and said, "Boys, you played great, as did the other team. What a game! However, sometimes adults disagree about things and although we believe the game is over, the other coaches do not. We will continue discussing this with the umpires, but I want you to get ready to bat. No matter what happens, I'm super proud of every one of you." It was the perfect response to a very awkward and upsetting situation. Several moments later, the head league umpire, after huddling with the game umpires, yelled out, "Game over!" The team went nuts! As for my wife and I, we knew we had witnessed not only a great game but a great moment in coaching.

In his second year, Dan had a new coach with a different group of boys as the teams were reshuffled from season to season and, although Daniel attended every single baseball practice, he never got into a single game. Rather, he was made to sit at the end of the bench in the dugout and usually by himself. His teammates were not particularly nice to Dan or to each other. The parents were even worse. My wife and I were not used to cheering for dropped balls and hit batters. It was a world we had not seen before and it seemed light years apart from Coach H and the prior season. One day, the coach approached me to inform me that the players and some parents had expressed concerns about Daniel acting up while in the dugout. Under my breath, I mumbled, "You think?" Let me get this straight: a young boy trapped in a dugout for an entire game without any attention whatsoever is acting up. Really? Although seething, I calmly responded by telling the coach that it was because he had never gotten into a game. The coach told me he would not put him in, regardless of the score or situation, and we, therefore, needed to find a solution. For weeks, Dan had asked if he could quit the team, but I felt it would set a bad example. That night, right there and then, I quit for him.

A few years later, Daniel entered *Miracle League* baseball. They don't keep score, and everyone gets to bat. It is a slower game, usually only played for 2 or 3 innings, and every hit is treated like a home run. Best of all, nobody ever cheers for a dropped ball or a hit batter. Instead, they cheer for a player who finally hits the ball after swinging and missing a dozen times. One player, with braces on his legs, would literally fall after each pitch but would pick himself back up and get right back in the batter's box. Yeah, like I said, each hit is treated like a home run. The rules are loose, but you inevitably leave with a smile. Daniel still plays to this day, and his mother regularly volunteers as the play-by-play announcer in the broadcast booth. They make for another great team. Dan has also pursued a plethora of other sporting activities, including skiing, tennis, golf, basketball, bowling, ziplining, swimming, table tennis, and jumping rope. He hikes with his sister and brother-in-law, sometimes through national parks and for miles at a time. Dan has a beautiful golf swing and, although he bats left-handed, he golfs right-handed. His golf coach—Ron—came up with that idea, and it was a brilliant decision to keep those swings separate, as he is known to be a "big hitter" on the baseball diamond as well. More recently, Daniel and his mother have vowed to take up pickleball soon, and I don't doubt them. Not for one minute.

"They Go; We Go"

A month before we visited College Station, Texas, our family had gathered in our family room to watch the *Buckeyes* play Virginia Tech. The game was in Columbus and, although the *Hokies* took a 21-7 lead into halftime, we assumed Ohio State would storm back and win the game. However, it was not meant to be, as the *Buckeyes* fell 35-21. My brother, who lives in Virginia, received quite a bit of ribbing from neighbors and colleagues alike, whereas back home, we just assumed the team had been overhyped, as *Buckeye Nation* has been known to do that on more than one occasion. Still, by all appearances, on paper at least, the team looked like a contender. It was Urban Meyer's third season, and he was joined by Tom Herman as the offensive coordinator/quarterbacks coach and Luke Fickell as the defensive coordinator. Quarterback J.T. Barrett, who had been redshirted the year before, was named the starter after senior Braxton Miller went down with a season-ending injury. In the backfield was Ezekiel Elliott, and the receivers, as usual, were pure class, including Michael Thomas, Devin Smith, and others. Despite giving up 35 points, the defense was billed as being stout and included Joey Bosa and a cast of tough characters.

After the early blemish, the *Buckeyes* rattled off nine consecutive victories, including a 31-24 win in 2 overtimes over Penn State.

The Game, played on November 29, 2014, was in Columbus, but I watched it with my friend Dave at Disney World in Orlando, Florida. We made the trip down to watch our kids perform in the Woodridge Marching Band and with the Woodridge Choir. Both performances were wonderful and the next day, as the kids and wives enjoyed Mickey and the theme park, we snuck out to the ESPN Wide World of Sports to watch the *Buckeyes* battle against that team up north. The game had started out on a most peculiar note, as it was reported Kosta Karageorge—both a wrestler and a walk-on nose tackle for the *Buckeyes*—had been reported missing. As for the game, Ohio State held a 28-21 lead going into the 4th quarter and then the unthinkable happened. J.T. Barrett, a clear Heisman candidate, had his right leg crumpled underneath him when he was tackled on a run. It turned out his ankle was broken, and he underwent surgery the following day. Cardale Jones, essentially the third-string quarterback, entered the game and helped steer the team to an eventual 42-28 victory. Unfortunately, the same day Barrett had surgery, Karageorge committed suicide. The season, even with the victory over Michigan, had ended as poorly as it had started and a palpable malaise had befallen *Buckeye* fans.

The following week, the team, which had been ranked 6th in the country going into the Michigan game, put together a master class in the *Big 10* Championship game against Wisconsin with a blowout win of 59-0. It was the first year of a four-team playoff in the BCS and after Ohio State miraculously squeaked in as the number 4 seed, our reward was playing Alabama. It was a tall order, as not only were they the top-ranked team in the country, but the game was at the Sugar Bowl, which is essentially a home away from home for the *Crimson Tide.* On the first day of 2015, as we huddled up with my father to watch the game in my parents' family room, he said, "I spoke with my friends in Alabama, and they are already buying tickets to the National Championship game. I told them not so fast, and they just laughed. I say if Ohio State wins, we should go to Dallas." He then said, "Our new mantra is, if they go, we go." What happened next was simply surreal, as Cardale Jones, in just his second start and with a bunch of help from Ezekiel Elliott's 230 yards rushing, shocked the world by beating Alabama 42-35, thereby earning a trip to the National Championship.

Since they went, we went. The game, set for January 12th, was a day before my dad's birthday and two days before my brother's. Dad, Daniel, and I had flown out Sunday night, but John had work early Monday morning, and on such short notice, he was unable to change it. With his early afternoon flight, we had our fingers crossed that his flight would not be delayed. Thankfully, it was not. While Daniel and my dad drove out in a limousine to pick up my brother from the airport, I attended a pre-game party with my old college roommate, who also happens to be named Jim. It was a cold, windy day, but the mix of *Buckeye* and *Duck* fans hardly seemed to mind as the Zac Brown Band played outside the stadium. As I waited for my family to arrive, I found myself shivering, although I'm still not sure if it was the weather or my nerves.

On a van ride from the parking lot to the stadium, my brother, my father, and Daniel met an elderly woman who was also an Ohio State fan. Although it was a relatively short ride, they quickly learned that she and her late husband often attended Ohio State football games, and they always carried their "lucky *Buckeyes*" with them. She traveled alone, and she told them she wanted to see the *Buckeyes* play "one last time." When getting out of the van, she insisted our family have her "lucky *Buckeyes*," as we could carry them and keep the tradition going, begun years before with her husband.

Before the game, as we waited for the kickoff, Dad said, "You never know when you'll get a chance to go again, as getting to a National Championship is not easy. You need a lot of things to go your way, and you usually need to avoid key injuries." We were nervous and Oregon was a formidable foe. However, in our hearts, we knew it was ours to lose and despite four turnovers during the game, Ohio State won the first-ever College Football Playoff National Championship 42-20. As gold confetti rained down from the ceiling of *AT&T* Stadium, it seemed like a dream, and Daniel, my dad, my brother, and I posed for a picture, each of us with a smile ear-to-ear and a lucky *buckeye* in our pocket. Dad looked at us and said, "They go; we go."

"If Only It Was So"

Dad's cancer remained at bay for twelve years following his surgery. While each "normal" PSA test was celebrated as good news, the family quietly and collectively held its breath. Then, one day, the cancer strolled back into our world and into Dad's bones. Wandering the corridors of a body—through blood, tissue, or lymphatic vessels—cancer cells can replant themselves and that is exactly what they did. When Dad originally heard he had cancer, he thought it was the worst thing he could possibly hear. Now, he was made acutely aware of just how wrong he was. The only thing worse than hearing he had cancer was being told it was back. Furthermore, the most terrifying word in the cancer dialogue is *metastasis* and, unfortunately, both our parents, at one point or another, found themselves engaged in such dialogue.

Nearly all types of cancers can spread—or metastasize—from the original site to the bones, but prostate and breast cancer, for whatever reason, are particularly adept at this phenomenon. Metastatic cancer can spread to any bone, but most commonly moves to the spine, pelvis, or thigh. Not surprisingly, given the location of the prostate, Dad's cancer was lodged in his lower back. It had not traveled far. Others facing this dreadful disease, on the other hand, might wake up one day to find cancer cells that have invaded the other side of their body. At first glance, metastasis might be likened to weeds popping up in a garden. However, in *The Cancer Chronicles*, George Johnson eerily compares cancer to the pods from *Invasion of the Body Snatchers* landing from some distant star to take over the Earth. Metastasizing cancer, honed for life in a specific tissue, is equally discriminating in the way it propagates. In other words, it can be both a weed in a prized flower garden and a pod deliberately sent from outer space to destroy the earth. Regardless of descriptive verse, metastases are responsible for an estimated 90 percent of all cancer deaths.

Several weeks before my dad's fourth birthday, on an early winter day in December 1947, a young doctor working in the basement of Children's Hospital in Boston received a parcel from New York that included several vials of a yellow crystalline chemical called *aminopterin*. Separated by over 600 miles and four decades of life, this moment would one day play a key role in the little boy's unrealized journey. Sidney Farber, born in 1903, was the chief of pathology at this Massachusetts hospital, specializing in childhood diseases. The coveted package contained chemicals the pediatric pathologist would use in his experiments to fight childhood leukemia. With the help of a microscope, Farber discovered that folic acid played a crucial role in the proliferation of cancer cells in leukemia. After realizing this, he investigated the use of a folate antagonist, aminopterin, to block the function of folic acid in his young patients with leukemia, in hopes of achieving remission. In the process, he would later become the father of modern chemotherapy and thanks to his contributions, along with countless other scientists, chemists, and physicians, this discovery would help millions suffering from different types of cancer. As it turns out, years later, it would also help a grandfather travel to college football games with his sons and grandson.

Long before my dad was born or Sidney Farber experimented with chemicals, innumerable others waged war against cancer and, although initially thwarted in understanding its cause or finding a cure for the dreaded disease, humanity has nonetheless fought valiantly from the start. The first known treatments for cancer date back to surgeries done in the second century AD, when Leonidas of Alexandria described physically removing cancerous breast tissue from an unknown patient.

The surest way to stop cancer was to get rid of it by cutting it out, but historically, this was easier said than done. As a history buff, I recall watching the 2008 HBO miniseries *John Adams*, starring Paul Giamatti as the often-forgotten founding father. I loved nearly every minute of it. However, one specific scene has always haunted me. In 1810, John Adams' daughter, Abigail Adams Smith, known as "Nabby" and played by Sarah Polly in the series, noticed a lump in her breast and was diagnosed with breast cancer. At the time, she was 46 years old and living at her family's farm in upstate New York. After moving back to her parents' home in Quincy, Massachusetts, Nabby underwent a mastectomy without any anesthesia on October 8, 1811, in an upstairs room in the Adams home. The instruments used for surgery, especially at the time, were crude. Take a stroll through any battlefield museum, and you are left with your mouth agape as you gaze upon an assortment of saws, knives, hammers, and chisels. At one point, originally created in the 1600s, there was even a guillotine for breast removal. As for the haunting scene, a daughter's unimagined bravery and the anguish felt by everyone in the house are a gruesome reminder of the reality of early surgeries. Unfortunately, Abigail Adams Smith passed away from cancer less than two years later, making the pain she endured even more unbearable to contemplate.

By the time my dad had his prostate removed, two major breakthroughs had occurred in the surgical world, which were, quite frankly, game changers. First, my father was given anesthesia so that he felt no pain during his surgery. William Morton, a Boston dentist, is generally considered the first to make a public demonstration of the use of anesthesia (Ether), when he made a small incision on a patient's neck in 1846 before a group of doctors and onlookers. The man, who had taken a few whiffs of the vapor and fallen into a deep sleep, told the audience afterward that he "did not experience pain at any time." This was truly revolutionary as surgeons could now perform more complex and time-consuming operations, including the removal of cancerous tissues, without fear of a struggling or justifiably panicked patient.

Secondly, my father, thankfully, developed no infection following his prostatectomy and this was not by accident. Rather, it was an expected outcome built upon diligence and deliberate protocol. Well into the 19th century, surgical instruments were not sterilized and as a result, infection ran rampant and often took as many lives as the original injuries. Starting with Louis Pasteur, this began to change as the French chemist and microbiologist discovered how germs could cause disease. The gnarled teeth of a saw might also contain countless unseen bacteria. In 1865, Joseph Lister, a Scottish surgeon, correctly surmised that if postsurgical infections were being caused by bacteria, then an antibacterial regimen might be used before surgery to curb infection. Later, when Sir Alexander Fleming discovered the first antibiotic— penicillin—in 1928, the protective arsenal was further enhanced, as now, even if patients developed postsurgical infections, lifesaving medications were available.

Following surgery, Dad received radiation treatment. This is a common "one-two punch" approach for treating cancer. First, get rid of what you can see is cancerous and then zap anything you might have missed. The removal of the prostate is considered "radical surgery." Still, suppose he had been experiencing more serious issues at the time. In that case, surgery might have also included taking out more tissue, removal of lymph nodes in the pelvis, or even castration by removal of the testicles. Given those options, I can see why Dad chose radiation.

Radiation, as a potential treatment for cancer, can be traced back to 1895 and to a German mechanical engineer and physicist named Wilhelm Rontgen, who produced and detected electromagnetic radiation waves. His wife, Anna, quite literally lent her husband a hand, as the very first X-ray of a human showed her finger bones and her wedding ring; it turns out that it could not distinguish between bone and metal. Upon seeing the inside of her hand, she exclaimed, “I have seen my death.” An arresting image for certain, Rontgen’s wife most certainly glimpsed the future, as this invisible energy source was so powerful it could pass through objects, including tissue, thereby allowing scientists and physicians to gain a view inside a living human body. Today, X-rays are routinely used by doctors and dentists as a diagnostic tool for a wide range of medical issues. Another—initially unexplained—phenomenon is that X-rays cannot only carry energy through human tissue but also deposit the energy inside the body, where it would kill the most rapidly proliferating cells. In other words, it selectively targets and destroys cancer cells. Scientists and researchers, including Marie Curie and Emil Grubbe, quickly took notice of this potential breakthrough in cancer treatments. As for Rontgen, he deservedly received the first Nobel Prize in Physics in 1901.

Athens, Georgia

Not all Southerners are born in the South. Hugh Acheson was born and raised in Ottawa, Canada and attended Concordia University in Montreal, Quebec. His first kitchen gig was as a dishwasher in Ottawa when he was 15 years old. Later, he moved to Athens, Georgia, so his wife could attend graduate school at the University of Georgia. Although he brought with him his north-of-the-border roots, his menu at *Five & Ten* is a fresh and open interpretation of Southern food, "melding Georgia cookery with French and Italian influences," he's gained along his culinary journey. His restaurant opened in Athens in 2000, and seven years later, it was named Restaurant of the Year by the *Atlanta Journal-Constitution*. Along the way, Acheson has won a cabinet full of awards, including *Food and Wine's Best New Chef.*

On an October evening, after driving in from gridlocked Atlanta, we arrived on the front porch of Acheson's restaurant with the hope of reveling in great food. Located on South Milledge Avenue, the restaurant is situated in a charming, historic red brick home. Literally next door to the University of Georgia's sorority row, the multiple sage green columns make a perfect fit. If not for the white-linen tablecloth covering outdoor tables, the front porch in this neighborhood would not be out of the ordinary.

Inside, there are multiple rooms, each creating a unique but distinctive Southern dining experience. Wood floors, chandeliers, and painted walls in light shades of blue, green, and grey, along with multiple fireplaces, make for a splendid atmosphere. After wandering through several spaces, we were seated in a cozy room, seemingly towards the back, with a half dozen other tables. Dinner included cast-iron cornbread with honey butter and fennel pollen, followed by a cheese and charcuterie board, and lastly, pork chops. For dessert, spoons were passed around to indulge in cookie-cutter ice cream and black forest cake. Did I mention we go big when it comes to our meals?

The following morning, we set out to do a little shopping and explore Athens, Georgia. Quite frankly, the only thing I knew about this town—near the confluence of the North and Middle Oconee River—was the unnatural number of new wave rock bands born there in the 1980s and later in the 1990s. When my brother and I were in college, listening to our "new music," Athens seemed always to be well represented on our playlist, with songs from *R.E.M., The Black Crowes, The B-52s, and Pylon*. Maybe, if we had time, we could do a little digging in these rolling red clay hills of North Georgia to see what we could find on this front. If nothing else, we could at least drink the water. This town, situated just south of the Blue Ridge Mountains, has been renowned for its vibrant music scene for decades, spanning generations and multiple genres. In 2020, the community celebrated this iconic music heritage by creating an Athens Music Walk of Fame, creating yet another reason to return one day.

The old downtown area is laid out on a square grid and features quaint shops, art galleries, restaurants, bars, and fan stores dedicated to the local university and its football team. Athens, Georgia, is a remarkable place to shop and, though we only removed our credit cards from our wallets to purchase *Bulldog* gear, we made a note to ourselves that this would be a wonderful place to bring our wives. With bags full of newly purchased gameday clothing, we searched for a place to eat. Close to our car, at the corner of N. Lumpkin Street and W. Clayton Street, in a brick building with big pane glass windows and a large black sign framed in gold and stretching the entire length of the frontage, we came upon *The Globe*. Hanging on the corner of the building is, of course, an iron globe. Going strong since 1989, the place screamed college hangout with a poet's edge. The place also has a British pub vibe, not just because of its obligatory Shakespeare nod but because the upstairs level was hosting a *Premier League* watch party. Besides *Bulldog* fans, the place was crawling with *Arsenal* holdovers. "Come on, you *Gunners* beat Missouri." Cute, right?

Created by a group of friends and family, the interior of *The Globe* features a horseshoe-shaped bar near the back wall, inspired by an owner's visit to Barcelona. The front of the pub is furnished with wooden tables and chairs, providing additional dining space. The ceiling features a line of black fans, matching the black staircase leading to the second floor, and on our visit, those other "football" fans. The walls have an early American schoolhouse aesthetic with a flag, a clock, a George Washington bust and even a blackboard. Over the bar, on permanent loan, is a giant mural— "The History of Wine Making." When we were there, more pints were being served than glasses of wine, and our gang, although tempted by the fish & chips and *Fuller's London Pride*, stuck with a round of burgers and fries washed down with water and sweet iced tea.

After lunch, we took a short walk from downtown to the northern edge of the University of Georgia campus, stopping at the iconic *Arch* to pose for pictures. Forged at the Old Athens Foundry in the 1850s, the black, three-pillar construction was modeled after the Georgia State Seal. It was originally part of a larger iron fence designed to keep wandering livestock off campus. The three pillars represent the virtues of wisdom, justice, and moderation, and are intended as an entrance; the arch once had gates. Two white globe lights were added later. As we snapped shots of our crew, students' campus-bound streamed around the arch on both sides, but few walked under or through it.

This was not our imagination, but a tradition started in 1905 by a freshman named Daniel H. Redfearn, who reportedly vowed not to pass through it until he had a diploma in his hand. At the time, this was a much more difficult vow to keep as Redfearn had to hop over the connected iron fence. One young man's vow has morphed into a tradition wrapped in various myths. Not only are students fearful of not graduating, but also of going bald, never marrying, or being infertile. No wonder they steer clear of passing through the arch. Previously unaware of such risks, but with hardly a hair on my head, my list of arches is too numerous to pinpoint which one did me in.

While walking about in this southern gem, we came upon several *dawg sculptures* made of fiberglass and identical in height. First installed by the Athens-Oconee Junior Women's Club in 2003 as part of the *"We Let the Dawgs Out"* public art exhibit, each of the original thirty pups was painted by local artists with a clear local flavor. In 2010, the statues were auctioned off by the Club, generating over $25,000, which was donated to *AIDS Athens*. When we arrived in town, many of those same statues remained on display throughout Athens, complemented by the arrival of a new generation of bulldog statues. Finding all these dawgs and posing for a selfie might make for an enjoyable outing and could provide a real sense of accomplishment. Although we did not set out on such an adventure, we did manage to get a picture of Daniel riding atop what is now called *Truist Dawg*. With his red '01 jersey and leather helmet, the white bulldog is located just outside the Truist Bank downtown on E. Broad Street. This picture, which periodically appears on my phone as a memory, serves as a reminder of how quickly time passes and that we need to return to Athens.

A Grieving Mother and a Famous Father

Unbelievably, Georgia's first mascot was a goat and, believe it or not, the entire state of Georgia almost abolished football. Chartered in 1785 by the Georgia state legislature and set upon 40,000 acres, UGA is the first publicly funded institution of higher learning in the country. The school was originally named Franklin College in honor of Benjamin Franklin. The first university president, Abraham Baldwin, was a "*Yalie*" and modeled much of the campus after Yale College. However, he would not have known about Yale's mascot, a white English bulldog named *Handsome Dan* (he really is a handsome fellow), as the pooch did not arrive in New Haven, Connecticut, until 1892.

Starting in 1859, with the founding of the College of Law, the University of Georgia slowly replaced the name Franklin College. Throughout the years, the school was simply known as the *Red and Black*. According to newspaper articles, a goat was present at the Auburn game played on February 22, 1892. He wore a black coat, lettered with a red U.G. on each side and a hat with ribbons on his horns. Thankfully, there are no known pictures. Most unsportsmanlike, the

Auburn fans reportedly yelled throughout the game, "Shoot the Billy-Goat." The goat, who may have been more spectator than mascot, was ultimately replaced in 1894 by *Trilby*, a solid white female bull terrier, who attended games and served as the mascot for the Chi Phi fraternity. Legend has it that one late afternoon, *Trilby* attended a football workout along with her 13 children and as the puppies took total control of the practice with wagging tails and obligatory tummy rubs, one of the players reportedly said, "Well, Trilby has brought us a name, bulldogs."

Tragedy struck the Georgia football team on October 30, 1897, when a talented young athlete named Richard Von Albade Gammon died after suffering head injuries during a football game against the University of Virginia. The young man was just shy of his 18th birthday. With emotions running high and the public demanding action, the Georgia legislature passed a resolution 91-3 to ban football. In the wake of this tragedy and the resulting legislation, all three colleges that played football at the time—Georgia, Georgia Tech, and Mercer—voluntarily disbanded their teams. However, before Georgia Governor William Atkinson signed the resolution into law, he was given a letter written by Rosalind Burns Gammon, the mother of Von Gammon. Despite her obvious grief, she asked that her son's death not be used to defeat "the most cherished object of his life" and that "the University be trusted to make all needed changes for all possible consideration pertaining to the welfare of its students …" In the end, Governor Atkinson just couldn't sign the resolution into law, so he vetoed it, and Rosalind Gammon is widely credited with saving the sport in Georgia. Whether any university might be trusted to make *all* needed changes pertaining to the welfare of its students remains debatable.

A grieving mother may have saved football in the state of Georgia, but it was a famous father who is generally credited with saving the entire sport from abolition. Although Theodore Roosevelt never played football, he was a big fan. In many respects, it was tailor-made for him. Teddy had suffered from severe bronchial asthma as a child and after his father told him, "You must make your body," he had set out to do just that. He not only took up weightlifting and hiking as a youngster but also joined the Harvard Boxing Club during his college years. Mountain climbing and wilderness exploring, along with stints as a Dakota rancher, Rough Rider, and Police Commissioner of New York City, were proof that the President of the United States had indeed made his body.

Teddy Roosevelt was no stranger to the world of masculinity, and he undoubtedly believed that the physical nature of football helped build character. It was the ultimate manly game. However, he was also a father, and with his son, Theodore Jr., playing as a member of Harvard's freshman team, the President had an interest in the safety of players. At the turn of the 20th century, football had largely devolved into a brutal contest and gridirons were considered "killing fields." Players locked their arms in mass formations, and gang tackling ruled the day; in many ways, the game had lost any artistic ambitions. For instance, in 1904, there were an alarming 18 related football deaths and another 159 serious injuries. The following year, 19 young men perished, and 137 were left with lifelong injuries. Equally disturbing was the ineffectiveness of existing rules in protecting the players and the disregard for sportsmanship, as many injuries resulted from unfair play.

When newspaper editorials began calling for the sport to be banished, several schools—Stanford, California, Columbia, Northwestern, and Duke—would either drop their football programs or switch to rugby. All the while, Harvard teetered, as the school's president, Charles Eliot, described the sport as "more brutalizing than prizefighting, cockfighting or bullfighting." This ultimately caught the attention of the famous Harvard graduate who occupied the White House. Sensing things were coming to a head, the President called a meeting on October 9, 1905, with representatives from the three premier college powers of the time—Harvard, Yale, and Princeton. Roosevelt, who was known to "speak softly and carry a big stick," threatened to use executive action to abolish the game if they did not clean up their act. The violence had to be curtailed. Quite frankly, he did not have the authority to take such action, nor do presidents have the authority to render many of their so-called "executive orders," as Article II of the Constitution gives the President little authority beyond being the Commander-in-Chief. However, the public is generally unaware and, apparently, so were the representatives from the Ivy League schools present.

In response to Teddy Roosevelt's nudging, the schools issued a statement condemning the unnecessary violence and pledging to "clean up" the game. However, they did not make any specific changes to the rules of the game. Several weeks after the impromptu summit at the White House, Theodore, Jr. sustained injuries to his ribs and nose in a freshman game against rival Yale. The following week, the Harvard-Yale game was almost cut short when Harvard threatened to walk off the field after their captain suffered a broken nose when he was leveled after calling for a fair catch on a punt. The same afternoon, Union College halfback Harold Moore died of a cerebral hemorrhage after being kicked in the head while attempting a tackle in a game against New York University (NYU).

Following the utterly appalling season—bordering on a version of the futuristic death sport known as *Rollerball*—Roosevelt again called upon his alma mater and others to make radical changes to the sport. Meanwhile, NYU's chancellor—Henry McCracken—called for a nationwide meeting to either abolish the game or reform it. In all, sixty-two schools participated in the meetings that led to the formation of the Intercollegiate Athletic Association of the United States (IAAUS), which was renamed the National Collegiate Athletic Association (NCAA) in 1910. Changes agreed upon included abolishing mass formations, creating a neutral zone between offense and defense, doubling the first-down distance to 10 yards, to be gained in three downs and giving officials the authority to disqualify players for unnecessary roughness. Oh, and they agreed on one other little thing. The new rules would officially allow the forward pass. Not only was football saved, but the last of these changes was truly revolutionary and would set the sport on a trajectory toward total dominance.

As for head injuries and helmets, much has since been written. Much has been learned, and there remains much more to figure out. The first known football helmet was worn in an *Army-Navy* game in 1893. Admiral Joseph Mason Reeve, who had been hit in the head so many times that his doctor warned him the next blow might cause permanent damage, went to his shoemaker and had him fashion a hat with flaps. Hardly a helmet by today's standards, the shoemaker's creation was taken by Reeve back to the Navy, where it was used by paratroopers in World War I.

Starting in the early 1900s, soft leather caps were worn as optional headgear, and by the 1920s and 1930s, hardened leather helmets emerged. However, headgear remained a personal decision. The next big breakthrough occurred in 1939 when John T. Riddell introduced a hard plastic helmet. That same year, the NCAA made helmets mandatory in college football. Four years later, helmets became mandatory in professional football, although at this point, they were still open-faced. In 1955, a single-bar face mask, improvised by coach Paul Brown and an equipment manager on the sideline to help keep quarterback Otto Graham in the game following a whack to the mouth, made its way onto the field. Brown's creation, like almost everything he did in the football world, was a success, earning him a patent known as BT-5. By the early 1960s, facemasks were worn by every player in the game, leading to the adoption of a new rule prohibiting the grabbing of this bar, a violation referred to as "face masking." In time, the single-bar face mask was replaced by more elaborate forms of protection, with kickers and punters being the last holdouts as they were initially allowed to retain the single bar to promote "better visibility." In 2004, the single bar was banned in the NFL. Fittingly, the last football player to wear the single bar, under a grandfather clause, was Scott Darwin Player, an emergency replacement punter for the Cleveland *Browns* in 2007. You can't make this stuff up!

George Barclay was nicknamed "The Rose" for his dashing good looks. Not surprisingly, he was also known to have an eye for the ladies. Barclay played halfback for Lafayette College in Easton, Pennsylvania, and much like a wrestler or rugby player, he became concerned about being grabbed by his ears. With a face like his, the last thing he wanted was "cauliflower ears." At some point in the 1890s, with the assistance of an Easton saddle-maker, he designed a head harness consisting of three leather straps to protect those precious ears.

It should be noted that Barclay was one heck of an athlete, as he not only captained the football team but also played professional baseball. However, it is his creation, and perhaps his vanity, that was a harbinger of future concerns about the safety of football. If being repeatedly grabbed by the ears can physically change their shape, what happens to the brain when it is repeatedly struck? Furthermore, what did Admiral Reeve's doctor stumble upon when he told him another blow to the head might cause permanent damage? More recently, doctors, engineers, and scientists have gone inside the helmet and inside the human body to better understand these questions, with satisfactory answers remaining in the shadows. The truth, it seems, much like the players themselves, is a moving target and remains poorly lit, even under the brightest stadium lights.

The Bulldogs

In 1920, Morgan Blake of the *Atlanta Journal* newspaper declared that the "Georgia Bulldogs" had a certain ring to it, carrying both dignity and ferocity. Three days later, following a game against the University of Virginia, *Atlanta Constitution* writer Cliff Wheatley used the term in print. Thereafter, live mascot bulldogs, including *Mr. Angel, Butch, Mike,* and *Otto,* have dutifully done their part in standing guard on the sideline of Georgia football games. However, one name and bloodline of the bulldog has become synonymous with the University of Georgia, and *Uga* is the name-o.

The story begins with the marriage of two University of Georgia students—Frank "Sonny" Seiler and Cecelia Gunn. In 1956, while Sonny was in law school at UGA, the couple received a white puppy as a belated wedding gift from Frank Heard, a family friend. The couple named their English Bulldog *Hood's Ole Dan.* Cecilia, who loved her pooch as much as she loved Georgia football, altered a red children's t-shirt to fit the puppy and sewed a "G" she cut out of black felt onto the garment. On September 19, 1956, the bulldog, dressed in his newly created game-day digs, was taken to a party at the Sigma Chi fraternity house, where Sonny had been president as an undergraduate. They never intended to take him to the game, but after a few "iced teas," he was taken to the *Bulldogs'* game against Florida State. By all accounts, the dog was an instant favorite, and soon, head coach Wally Butts asked the couple for permission to use the dog as Georgia's mascot. Billy Young, a fellow law student and friend, suggested the name *Uga* and, in time, a spiked collar became the finishing touch to the wardrobe.

Following graduation, Sonny and Cecilia moved to Sonny's hometown and, although they took their dog with them, every official *Uga* has been owned by and lived with the Seiler family in Savannah, Georgia. In total, there have been 11 *Ugas*—all descendants of *Hood's Ole Dan*—each making the 223-mile trip to Athens for all home games. Along the way, the dogs have become legendary, even making their way onto the big screen. The bulldog mascot appeared in the 1997 movie *Midnight in the Garden of Good and Evil,* directed and produced by Clint Eastwood and based on the book of the same name by John Berendt. *Uga V*, who was cast to play his father *Uga IV*, is seen several times in the movie walking with John Cusack through *Forsyth Park*. The filming truly was a family affair as Sonny Seiler was cast as Judge Samuel L. White, and Seiler's daughter, Bess Thompson, also made an appearance in the movie. As for Seiler, he was well-versed in the story as he served as lead defense counsel for Savannah antique dealer Jim Williams, who was tried four times in the 1981 slaying of his lover before finally being acquitted. The case served as the centerpiece of the book and movie.

When we made our visit to *The Peach State* in 2015, our *Uga* was *Uga IX,* a bulldog named *Russ*, who had replaced *Uga VIII* in 2012 after that bulldog, named *Big Bad Bruce,* unexpectedly passed away following a diagnosis of lymphoma. *Russ*, like the dogs that came before him, was officially made part of the team through a ceremony on the football field when the head coach welcomed the next *Uga* by placing the well-known spiked collar around his neck. His jersey, like all the others for the past twenty years, was custom-made at the start of the season from the same material used for the players' jerseys. Each dog is also awarded a varsity letter in the form of a plaque, identical to those presented to all *Bulldog* athletes who letter in their respective sports.

Several *Ugas* have retired in pre-game ceremonies, passing on the collar to the next bulldog. To close the ceremony, the fans chant "*Damn good dog,*" a tradition dating back to the first *Uga.* When *Uga VII*, named *Loran's Best*, passed away unexpectedly on November 19, 2009, it was the Thursday before the final home game of the 2009 season, leaving the *Bulldogs* with no live mascot for the contest. Instead, a wreath was placed on his doghouse and the players wore a special *Uga VII* decal on their helmets to honor the canine. He, like all *Ugas* before him, was buried within the confines of the stadium in a marble vault near the main gate in the embankment of the South stands. Each dog has a specific epitaph inscribed in bronze and before each home game, flowers are placed on their graves.

Russ, who compiled a record of 44-19 as the mascot, retired after the 2015 season and, upon his retirement, UGA director of Athletics Greg McGarity said, "Russ has endeared himself to the Georgia people over the last three years. His dedication to duty when called upon has been exemplary, and it's fitting that he takes his place in the official line of Georgia mascots." His replacement, *Que*, who would serve as Uga X, would be the mascot until the end of the 2022 season, compiling a record of 91-18 and overseeing two consecutive National Championships.

As for the Seiler couple, Cecelia passed away in 2014. She was 80. Her husband, Sonny, the trial lawyer, passed away in 2023. He was 90. Thankfully, they shared their adorable, if not unusual, wedding gift with us and thankfully, their son, Charles, is now in charge of the famous mascots. This year, at the beginning of the 2023 season, the collar has been passed to *Boom* as *Uga XI*. With a Nike logo nearly as big as the Georgia "G" on his red shirt, along with a permanent, air-conditioned doghouse located next to the cheerleaders' platform—big enough for the dog and handler—it is indeed a dog's life. Following in his family's paw steps, the 10-month-old pup has a mighty big collar to grow into. No doubt he is already well on his way to being a damn good dog and a damn cute one too.

Between the Hedges

Sanford Stadium is a truly unique on-campus stadium, with a view of nearby rolling hills on the open west end zone and Georgia's campus. The stadium is named after University of Georgia President Dr. Steadman V. Sanford, who, after a disappointing 12-0 loss to in-state rival Georgia Tech in Atlanta in 1927, vowed to build the biggest stadium in the south. Sanford was especially sour following the defeat, as starting in 1902, Georgia played Tech annually at Grant Field because it provided for a larger gate, and despite heavy rains all week, Tech would take no chances against the quick *Bulldog* backs and watered down the field on the eve of the big game essentially creating a quagmire. After coaxing 300 fans and supporters to sign banknotes for $1,000 each, Sanford was able to raise the $300,000 to build the new stadium in 1929, thus ending an annual away game against a bitter rival. Amazingly, despite the looming stock market crash, not a single banknote was called. The brilliance of crowdfunding was on full display nearly a century before the online craze.

Georgia's iconic shrubs, Chinese privet (*Ligustrum sinense*), planted in 1929 and dubbed "the most famous flora in football," are deeply rooted in *Bulldog* lore. Many, obviously not seeded in the region or bulldog fans, ponder at all this fuss over shrubbery. In 1926, before the stadium was built, Charlie Martin, a former Georgia business manager, had gone to the Rose Bowl in Pasadena and marveled at the nearby mountain ranges and the beautiful roses that circled the field. Since Sanford is built on two natural hillsides, with views of nearby rolling hills, Martin wanted to recreate the *Rose Bowl* in Athens. However, after it was learned that roses would not thrive in Georgia, hedges were installed instead. The original 5,000-square-foot rectangle of greenery planted in 1929 consisted of hedges approximately 3 feet in height. Trucked in from Atlanta the night before the christening of the new 30,000-seat stadium, the hedges were literally planted in the red Georgia soil by shovel and flashlight just hours before kick-off.

What many don't realize is that the hedges have been completely removed from the stadium, not once, but twice. First, when Atlanta was chosen to host the Summer Olympics in 1996, *Sanford Stadium* had been one of several venues dangled to lure the games to Georgia. Bill Payne, president and CEO of the Atlanta Committee for the Olympic Games, had approached the University of Georgia about using *Sanford Stadium* as a soccer venue. However, there was a catch. Because a regulation soccer field measures 115 yards by 74 yards, in other words, roughly 25% larger than a football field, the hedges and a concrete path around the field would need to be removed. At the time, this was going to create a PR nightmare, as Georgia was a football state, not a *football* state. Luckily, all involved received a gigantic lifeline when it was discovered the hedges were diseased, suffering from an infestation of parasitic nematodes, and needed to be removed anyway.

Two years before the Olympics, the University of Georgia identified and removed 2,100 healthy clippings, divided them equally, and sent them to Dudley Nursery in Thompson, Georgia, and Hackney Nursery in Quincy, Florida, both run by UGA alumni. There, they were propagated and nurtured, and later, after the conclusion of the Olympic games, replanted two feet apart at a ceremony at *Sanford Stadium* before a host of Georgia dignitaries. Considered offspring from the original hedges, these were and are lovingly referred to by the Georgia family as "Hedges II." The plants were dug up again in 2017 to make room for a new locker room and scoreboard. Tagged and numbered, the healthy shrubs were again transferred to three undisclosed locations, where they were lovingly cared for while the stadium construction was completed. Replanted just days before the first Georgia scrimmage in April, and with a fresh trim, the hedges were home again. Astonishingly, of the three hundred or so plants that had been removed and replanted, only two or three were lost.

Every fall, the hedges are seemingly pummeled. They are, after all, in a football stadium with thousands of rabid fans and world-class competitors. When a parent tells a child to go outside and play, they don't usually mean to go out and roughhouse in the garden. Some of the abuse is accidental, such as when a player, perhaps pushed or just otherwise unable to stop, crashes into the hedges. Television crews have also been known to cover the hedges with wires and equipment. In the early days for *Uga*, before he had an air-conditioned doghouse, the bulldog would find shelter in the shrubs, especially during the sweltering heat of the early fall games. In the process, a few branches might be damaged, although, quite frankly, more damage was inevitably done to his wardrobe as he often emerged with a torn shirt. Still, another form of abuse is intentional, as hometown fans have been known to snip off a small piece as a memento. Additionally, when fans rush the field following a victory, some have gone through or over the hedges to do so. Visiting fans have also been known to lose control. When Georgia Tech beat Georgia, the away fans celebrated by tearing off pieces of the shrub and putting them in their mouths, much like players clinching a berth to the Rose Bowl or winning it.

The iconic phrase *"between the hedges"* was reportedly coined by legendary sportswriter Grantland Rice in the 1930s, when he first described how Georgia would "have their opponent between the hedges." Today, the phrase is used every Saturday in the fall when football is played in *Sanford Stadium*. For nearly 100 years, long before the renowned ivy began creeping along the brick walls of Wrigley Field and decades before any azaleas were planted in Augusta, these hedges have lined the field at Sanford, bearing witness to decades of both thrilling victories and heartbreaking defeats. Standing 5 feet tall and 5 feet wide, this shrubbery keeps guard over Athens' most sacred ground.

About two hours before kickoff, we, along with thousands of other fans dressed in red and black, lined the main entrance to *Sanford Stadium* to welcome the players and coaches on the traditional *Dawg Walk* before the game. As the *Georgia Redcoat Band* banged out tunes and the cheerleaders led the rally, we were given up-close contact with the Georgia football team and though they might seem mighty when on the field, the walk revealed the faces of boys, not men. It was a stark reminder that yelling should be in support of a player rather than against him, as he really is somebody's youngster. Besides the players, coaches, cheerleaders, and the band, fans were also warmly greeted by *Hairy Dawg*—the official costumed mascot for the University of Georgia. This dog made his debut at the 1981 Sugar Bowl, where Georgia defeated Notre Dame to win the 1980 National Championship. *Hairy*, who is one of the most recognizable mascots in all of college football, has become a staple for University of Georgia festivities. This Modern-day *Dawg Walk* is a relatively new tradition that started in 2001 when head football Coach Mark Richt appointed a spirit committee to build fan enthusiasm. The committee did well as enthusiasm for the Georgia football team saturates the walk and just about everything else in its wake.

After catching a glimpse of the team, we decided to head back over to the car. It was, after all, parked right outside the stadium, and we had a cooler full of tailgating goodies stashed in the trunk, as earlier in the day we had stopped at a grocery store, bought a Styrofoam cooler, and filled it with meats, cheeses, beers, waters, and sodas. Daniel had also loaded our grocery cart with chips, crackers, and an assortment of sweets, including oversized cookies. This parking spot, literally 15 yards (at most) from a stadium entrance, would become legendary in our family. But first, a little back story about how we got there.

When my dad had purchased tickets to the game, he had, in his words, also "splurged on a parking pass." He was initially quite proud of his purchase and talked about it throughout the entire drive from Atlanta to Athens, as well as again in the morning before the game. "There will be no long walk back to the car after the game," he told us. Visions of the aftermath of the LSU game, with our long walk on empty stomachs, still loomed large in our minds, as did the crazed van driver from years before.

Once we loaded the car for the final drive to campus before the game, we hung the prized parking pass on the rental car's front mirror and took the printed instructions and stick map along for the ride. Well, things got crazy in a hurry. First, the map appeared to be missing major landmarks, and the instructions were largely ineffective. This was compounded by the heavy traffic, roadblocks, and those inevitable turns that needed to be made from the furthest lane away. Eventually, we found a parking lot that was on our map, but as we approached, my dad's initial delight wilted like a week-old flower in a dry vase, as the stadium was barely visible on the horizon. However, we were waved through the parking lot to yet another. My dad's emotions were like a roller coaster: happy, then sad, then happy again. Much like a scene from a movie, we kept passing checkpoints and roadblocks and, at one point, as the road snaked around, it felt like we were going away from the stadium again. Around this time, my dad, clearly frustrated, said, "Are you kidding me? I've been ripped off. I can't believe it. How stupid of me." Finally, we approached a much steeper hill that was completely shut off. "Now what do we do?" we wondered. A police officer motioned us forward, asked us to roll down the window again and instructed us to park as close to the curb as possible, just up the hill on the right, to allow traffic to pass by. He then removed the roadblock, and as we climbed this final hill, we could see the outside wall of the stadium just a half dozen yards to our right. My dad had not been ripped off at all and we all said in unison, "Are you kidding me?"

As for Dad's health, it was no joking matter. John and I knew he had recently had some wonky bloodwork, but we had no idea just how bad it was. Dad had gone back to his oncologist, and after he got home, he was especially quiet and seemed distracted. Mom later told us that when she asked him if everything went alright, he just shook his head and put four of his fingers on top of the kitchen table. Without a word spoken, she knew exactly what it meant. Right there and then, Dad decided any word of his Stage IV cancer diagnosis would not leave that same kitchen table.

There are four acknowledged stages of cancer. Stage I is the first stage when the cancer is small and only in one area. This is followed by Stage II and Stage III, when the cancer is larger and has grown into nearby tissues or lymph nodes. In retrospect, when Dad was initially diagnosed with prostate cancer, he was in Stage II or Stage III. This is consistent with the surgery, followed by radiation, and the comments made by his surgeon that "there may have been a little bit that got away." The most severe stage is Stage IV, when cancer has spread to other parts of the body and is often diagnosed years after the initial cancer diagnosis and/or after the initial cancer has been treated or removed. Again, in retrospect, this fits my father's cancer trajectory. Contrary to popular belief, Stage IV cancer is not always terminal, but it is not curable either. Dad's cancer had metastasized, which meant more aggressive treatments would be required, and his five-year survival rate was a paltry 30%. Knowing Dad, he did not want to worry us, and he most certainly never wanted anyone to feel sorry for him. This, I suppose, is why he initially decided to keep us in the dark about his updated diagnosis and why he never showed us the four fingers he had shown Mom at the kitchen table.

The Problem of going 9-3

On October 17, 2015, we watched from "Between the Hedges" as Georgia battled Missouri. As for the actual game, it was a *dawg*. Even *Uga* gave up on the game, choosing instead to settle into the back of his sideline doghouse for a nice, long nap. There were no touchdowns and, although Georgia won the game 9-6 and ultimately finished 16th in the country, a palpable unrest could be felt throughout the stadium, wafting from the field seats to the rafters. Both teams, following *Uga's* lead, figuratively took a squat on the field. However, unlike *Uga's* handlers, who raced out to clean up any "number 2" he may have left on the field, nobody raced onto the field to clean up the mess left between the teams. The week before, things had been equally dreadful for the Georgia *Bulldogs* as they lost in Knoxville to the Tennessee *Volunteers*, and in that loss, sophomore running back Nick Chubb had sustained a season-ending left knee injury. Up to that point, Chubb had rushed for over 100 yards in 13 straight games and was ranked third in the nation with 801 yards rushing on 91 carries. Hauntingly, Chubb would sustain another season-ending injury to the same knee while playing in the NFL for the Cleveland *Browns* in a game against the Pittsburgh *Steelers*. Both injuries were deemed too gruesome to be shown on television. Hopefully, Chubb, with hard work and a little luck, can return to running again, as he is truly majestic with the ball in his hands.

In any event, Marshall Morgan, who had missed a chip shot from 26 yards about four minutes earlier, kicked the game-winner from 34 yards with 1:44 remaining. Indeed, a happy story for the Special Teams Unit. However, hardly anyone seemed to notice. Instead, many of the 93,000 cell phones on hand were locked into a remarkable ending to a game taking place 729 miles north in Ann Arbor, Michigan. The *Wolverines*, on the final play, flubbed a punt, which was ultimately scooped up by the *Spartans* for a touchdown, giving Michigan State an improbable 27-23 win over their cross-state rival. As an Ohio State guy, my phone was blowing up with fellow *Buckeye* alums asking me if I had watched the play and if I had seen the now-infamous *Wolverine* fan's reaction to the debacle. At the time, I had not. Now, like almost everyone who follows college football, I have seen it literally a hundred times. As for the Georgia coach, although he had not experienced similar punting woes and probably did not much care about the goings on up north, even though he won the game, things would soon blow up for him as well.

Mark Richt coached the Georgia *Bulldogs* for 15 years. By all rational metrics, he was a winner. In fact, with his 145-51 record, he won nearly 75% of all the games he coached at UGA. He also managed to win two *SEC* Championships and snagged five *SEC* Eastern Division titles. He also makes a cameo in one of my favorite faith-based football movies of all time—*Facing the Giants*. However, Richt did not give the *Bulldog* family the prize they sought. What they wanted was to beat Alabama and LSU. What they also wanted was a return to the glory days of Hershel Walker and the undefeated 1980 National Championship team. As a *Buckeye*, I cannot pass judgment. John Cooper, known in *Buckeye Nation* as "9-3," was the head coach at Ohio State from 1988 to 2000. By all rational metrics, he was a winner. He compiled a record of 111-43-4, and the 111 wins made him the second-winningest coach in Ohio State history, behind only Woody Hayes. However, his record against *That Team up North* was a paltry 2-10-1 and, although his team was inevitably invited to a bowl game nearly every year, *Buckeye* fans usually found themselves wishing we had declined the invitation as the team went 3-11 in those games. Cooper did not give the *Buckeye* faithful the prize they sought. What they wanted was to beat Michigan, return to the glory days of Woody Hayes, and garner additional National Championships.

On November 29, 2015, the day after Georgia beat Georgia Tech 13-7 in the final game of the season, UGA and Mark Richt parted ways. The *Bulldogs* finished with an all-too-familiar 9-3 record. If Richt had coached the winning *Bulldogs* in the *TaxSlayer Bowl* in Jacksonville against Penn State, it would have been his 10th double-digit-win season at Georgia. A week later, Kirby Smart became the 26th head coach of the University of Georgia football team. As a former all-*SEC* safety for the *Bulldogs* and a Georgia native, the defensive coordinator from Alabama brought with him homegrown credentials and just shy of a decade of side-by-side coaching with the master—Nick Saban.

More than a decade before, John Cooper and Ohio State had parted ways on January 2, 2001. In his place, the *Buckeyes* hired Jim Tressel, a beloved head coach from Youngstown State. Born in Mentor, Ohio, Tressel was a former quarterback at Baldwin-Wallace and later coached as an assistant at Akron, Miami (OH), and Ohio State, making him an Ohio favorite. Both Smart and Tressel would manage to please their faithful by besting their dreaded rivals and winning National Championships. Mark Richt was from Nebraska and played for the Miami *Hurricanes*, while John Cooper was born in Tennessee and played football for Iowa State. Had these gentlemen beaten their rivals, nobody would have ever considered them outsiders. After all, in most worlds, 9-3 is still pretty darn good.

"Holy Buckeye"

Ohio State and football Saturdays have been part of Daniel's life from the very beginning. When not attending a game, the family always gathered to watch the *Buckeyes* on TV, generally without exception. Usually, his grandparents would stop by the house and with 12:00 p.m. kickoffs, dinner out or something grilled was sure to follow. If my brother were in town, his family would always be part of such festivities as well. One year, when Dan was two or three years old, my brother, my father, and I went to a football game in Columbus while our wives and my mom went shopping. When we met up for dinner following the game, we learned that Dan had pouted the entire afternoon since he had not been included in going with the guys. It was the last time we ever attended an Ohio State football game without him.

The following season, Dad snatched great sideline tickets for the *Buckeyes'* home opener against Texas Tech. My brother, Daniel, my father, and I stopped to pose for a group picture outside the *Horseshoe* and just minutes after we found our seats, a freshman tailback named Maurice Clarett rumbled around the corner and broke free along the sideline for a 50-yard touchdown. My father, as if sensing the action was coming our way, picked Dan up and held him high above his shoulders so that he would not miss the action and while Dad could not see a thing, Dan saw every bit of it. Clarett became the first-ever freshman to start at tailback for Ohio State and finished with 175 yards on his debut. Quarterback Craig Krenzel, a Michigan native, was only 11 of 14 for 118 yards, but with Clarett, it hardly mattered. While Kliff Kingsbury threw for 341 yards and three touchdowns for Texas Tech—including two in the fourth quarter to Wes Welker—it was not nearly enough as the *Buckeyes* won the game handily, 45-21.

We knew we had seen a good team, but we had no idea just how good they really were. It was Jim Tressel's second season as head coach, and he had already gotten off to a good start in our minds as he had beaten the *Wolverines* in his inaugural season. Each week, we were treated to improbable wins, coach Tressel in his sweater vest and vanilla press conferences. After the *Buckeyes* beat Michigan in a slugfest, the team sat undefeated at 13-0. Following the win, coach Tressel accepted the invitation to play the Miami *Hurricanes* for the National Championship. Since Miami was also undefeated for its second straight season, ranked number one, and the reigning national champions, it set up a classic David vs. Goliath matchup. In Ohio, we can still remember the football prognosticators telling the world we had no business being on the same field as Miami and that Jim Tressel, to avoid embarrassing our school, should have rejected the invitation. Thankfully, he did not and, as you know, the experts were wrong. In a thrilling, double-overtime game, Ohio State won 31-24. I watched the game in the family room of my parents' house, along with my wife and dad. My kids, as well as my mother, were sound asleep upstairs, while the three of us hugged and high-fived following the crazy ending. I still remember my wife jumping into my arms and saying, "I can't believe it." Within seconds of the final whistle, Dad's phone rang. It was my brother calling from Virginia.

As for the *Hurricane* fans, I know we will never agree on the interference call in overtime, despite the still photographs showing the helmet tug before the ball's arrival. It is difficult to catch a pass while trying to see through the ear hole of a helmet. However, to ease your pain,

I'd like to take you back to regulation, or about 20 minutes before that play, as that is when the real controversy occurred. Do you remember? It was late in the fourth quarter, and Ohio State was leading 17-14. There was 2:24 left on the clock and Miami only had one timeout left. The *Buckeyes* were on their own 32-yard line. It was third down with six yards to go. Here, in Ohio, and truthfully throughout much of the nation, we were thinking one first down, and we'd clinch the victory as Miami would not be able to get the ball back with enough time left. Do you remember what happened next? We do, and we are more than happy to remind anyone who will listen. Krenzel took the snap from a shotgun formation, rolled to his right and threw a pass to Chris Gamble. The pass was perfect—right between the numbers—and thrown to where only the receiver could catch it. Gamble secured the ball and was clearly inbounds. Awesome, first down! That should end the game. But wait, there was more. Although the catch was made on the Ohio State sideline, the referee inexplicably called it an incomplete pass. The sideline could not believe it, and I know we could not believe it, nor could Dan Fouts, who was broadcasting the game. The replay showed not only was he in bounds, but he also got both feet down, making it a catch in the NFL as well. Watch it. You can find it online. Unlike the interference call, it is indisputable. But in a world before instant replay, the call could not be reviewed. Yes, the game has controversy, as it should never have even gone to overtime. That's our story, *Hurricane* fans, and we're sticking to it.

The Knauer Case

Sometime in the Spring of 1939, a baby's father met with the Director of the Leipzig University Children's Clinic in Leipzig, Germany. He made an unimaginable and, in hindsight, a most haunting request. He asked that the clinic's physicians kill his baby. When the physicians refused to do so, he reportedly appealed directly to Adolf Hitler to intervene. Born in a tiny village southwest of Berlin in the Fall of 1938, the infant had been born blind and deformed and was otherwise diagnosed as an "idiot." After receiving the appeal, Hitler purportedly ordered his personal physician, Karl Brandt, to meet with the Leipzig physicians to see if the baby's father was correct in describing his child's disabilities. Brandt personally examined the infant and, after confirming the original diagnosis, he ordered the murder of the child—later described by Brandt at the Nuremberg Trials as a "creature"—by way of a lethal injection when the hospital nurses were on a break.

Known as the "Knauer Case," this represented the beginning of a children's killing program. By the summer of 1939, Theo Morell, another Hitler physician, had written a lengthy memorandum about the need for a law authorizing the "Destruction of Life Unworthy of Life." Morell proposed killing people who suffered from congenital mental or physical malformations. The Reich Committee for the Scientific

Registration of Severe Heredity Ailments quickly followed suit with a decree on August 18, 1939, that called for the compulsory registration of all "malformed" newborn children, and as a further sickening gesture, in return for a small payment, obliged German doctors and midwives to report all children under their care who had been born with Down syndrome, microcephaly, paralysis, congenital deafness, blindness, and neurological disorders. Once reported, a panel of three "medical experts" in Berlin would review these registration forms and mark them with a red plus sign if the child should be killed or a blue minus sign if they believed the child should live. A question mark indicated further investigation was needed. Initially, these registration reports applied only to children aged 3 years or younger, but the reporting was later expanded to include older children and young adults.

By 1940, the first pediatric killing wards had been established to carry out these heinous crimes. However, citizen cooperation was still needed. How did this ever happen? Who would possibly go along with the mass murder of children? First, the program itself was shrouded in secrecy. Those involved were required to sign loyalty oaths, and if they did not comply, a visit from the Gestapo would follow, along with imprisonment or death. As for parental consent, it was either forged or obtained by outright fraud. Some children, if already institutionalized, were simply moved to the killing wards without explanation and "implied consent" was regularly assumed to have been given. Local health authorities also assured parents that their children would receive better and more specialized treatment and might even be cured of their disabilities. Lastly, if parents offered resistance or hid their children, threats of revoking custodial rights were used to achieve compliance.

The first children selected for extermination were taken from their homes in large grey buses with darkened windows. Weeks later, those same homes might receive official letters informing them of their child's death—usually from "influenza." Along with sincere condolences, parents were further advised that to protect the country from the further spread of infectious disease—especially in a time of war—an immediate cremation of the child had been performed. Although promised an urn could be delivered at "no charge," these same letters reminded parents that if a reply were not received within a fortnight, the urn would be buried. Regardless of the specifics of each letter, they all ended the exact same way—"Heil Hitler."

Murdering these children, especially in the early days of the program, was usually by medication in tablet form. However, if a child was unable to swallow medication, a lethal injection was used instead. Far from "mercy killings," many children suffered from lingering illness before death. Some were starved to death. Shockingly, these doctors of death were rewarded with bonuses for reaching established quotas. Equally appalling, children with cerebral palsy and Down syndrome were often subjected to experimentation, often while still living. Many of the specifics of these experiments were revealed at the Nuremberg trials but are too gruesome for this father of a special needs child to repeat and, as such, I will spare the reader the same. The exact number of disabled children exterminated will never be known, but scholars believe as many as 25,000 young, innocent lives were lost.

Encouraged by the success of the children's killing program, Adolf Hitler ordered the expansion of a "euthanasia" program to exterminate all adults with disabilities. Hitler remarked, "Worthless lives of such creatures should be gotten rid of," and "This will result in certain savings in terms of hospitals, doctors, and nursing staff." Military authorities echoed this justification by inferring that Germany would soon require additional hospital space to accommodate the anticipated wartime casualties. Such space should not be wasted on the worthless. This secret program became known as the T4 program, and it is estimated that as many as 275,000 disabled adults were systematically killed by 1941. Given these larger numbers, a more efficient killing method was needed, and these atrocities were soon carried out by poison gas. Hundreds were gassed at a time and body parts were collected and sold to researchers and institutions. Again, specifics shall be purposely avoided. Much like the children, death certificates were falsified. Infectious disease, it seemed, ran rampant in the region, as did strokes and heart attacks.

Killing became easy and those who questioned the wisdom or morality of such behavior soon went missing themselves. Many do not realize that the first Jewish people to be systematically killed were disabled Jews. These programs, their physicians and facilities, along with the streamlined killing techniques honed through the children's killing program and the T4 program, would, unfortunately, be used to implement the *Final Solution of the Jewish Question.* A monument commemorating the killing of the disabled was unveiled in Berlin, Germany, in 2014, thus ending the silence surrounding the first souls singled out for systematic murder. Unfortunately, many physicians, nurses, and health officials involved in these programs escaped penalty for their crimes.

Those Pesky Eugenics

Long before the killings in Germany, the United States also had a hand in discriminating against the disabled. Beginning with the Immigration Act of 1882 and continuing through the Immigration Act of 1924, restrictions barred entry by immigrants deemed morally, *physically,* or *intellectually* defective. Inspectors at Ellis Island, using chalk, marked the backs of potential immigrants needing further examination. The inspectors were instructed to keep a lookout for individuals with insufficient mental capacity or those unable to walk without assistance. For the Republic to stand strong, its citizens, it seemed, must at least be able to stand up.

It was also in the United States that compulsory sterilization of persons with disabilities was first legalized. Starting with Indiana in 1907, followed by a handful of others before World War I, by the 1920s, over half of the states enacted legislation authorizing forced sterilization. It is estimated that by 1939, more than thirty thousand Americans were sterilized. While some were severely disabled, others were diagnosed as only being blind or deaf. Surprisingly, in 1927, the

United States Supreme Court in *Buck v. Bell* upheld a Virginia statute that authorized sterilization. Ms. Carrie Buck, described as being of "low intelligence" and having an "illegitimate child" in 1924, was ordered sterilized. Justice Oliver Wendell Holmes's majority opinion, which obliterates the 14th Amendment equal protection clause and includes his highly provocative, if not outright snobbish, Ivy League statement, "Three generations of imbeciles is enough," has technically never been overturned.

Where did such thinking come from? Rummaging through history, much like looking through bargain items in a yard sale, you can't help but stumble upon eugenics—an outgrowth of the progressive era. Stuck in an old, dust-covered cardboard box—marked with a black Sharpie as being "half-off"—many, rightfully, walk on by. Some stop to peek. Picking through the box just to browse can be illuminating for the curious. However, others, unable to help themselves, are still buying. In fact, some, as if making a weekend run to *Sam's Club* or *Costco*, are buying such shenanigans in bulk. This social movement, which flourished in the United States and Western Europe in the early 20th century, is based on the belief that the genetic quality of humanity can be improved using selective breeding. The word eugenics literally means "good creation." Francis Galton, whose cousin was Charles Darwin, is generally considered the founder of this movement as he hoped to better mankind through the propagation of the British elite. Ah, yes, just the world needs—more elites.

Eugenics had (and still has) many famous advocates, including George Bernard Shaw. When not writing novels or plays, he was an occasional lecturer for the Eugenics Education Society and even reportedly told the *Daily Express*, "A great many people would have to be put out of existence simply because it wastes other people's time to look after them." Political leaders, including President Woodrow Wilson and Prime Minister Winston Churchill, also danced with eugenics, with Wilson using it as a justification for his beliefs that Black Americans were inferior to whites and Churchill presenting his concerns to the House of Commons pertaining to the multiplication and perpetuation of the mentally deficient. Not surprisingly, award-winning scientists—many with a god complex—are also knee-deep in eugenics. Consider Francis Crick, the co-discoverer of DNA and a winner of the Nobel Prize for medicine, who once blithely declared, "No newborn infant should be declared human until it has passed certain tests regarding its genetic endowment. If it fails these tests, it forfeits the right to live."

Lastly, Margaret Sanger—of Planned Parenthood fame—in her *The Pivot of Civilization* wrote, "Every single case of inherited defect, every malformed child, every congenitally tainted human being brought into this world is of infinite importance to that poor individual; but it is of scarcely less importance to the rest of us and to all of our children who must pay in one way or another for these biological and racial mistakes." Mistakes? Wow! Based on her own words, we can easily conclude she must have had a raging disdain for disabled minorities, and persons who continue to justify those words as an inartful defense of birth control play the willing role of composition contortionists.

In the eugenics world, social control bested individual choice and ironically ignored another pillar of their own sacred belief system—Social Darwinism. The elites, sensing their self-deserved head start might not be large enough, looked to further tip the scales by simply eliminating the other runners in the race of life. It all smacks of ugly elitism, unbridled paternalism and obvious hypocrisy. Who among us shall sit as judge and jury of who is unworthy of life? It also serves as a reminder that individuals are often sacrificed on the altar to please the democracy god and its insatiable appetite for "the public good." In a utopian society, how else can we protect our crops and make it rain, if not by the occasional forced sterilization and those generational rolling waves of fashionable murder?

Today, as previously stated, eugenics survives, but in a more subtle form. In fact, advocates for the disabled call this "silent eugenics." Following the discovery of chromosomes and the subsequent detection of chromosomal variations in adults and children, the quest for an even earlier detection of potential aberrations in utero began. First performed in the 1930s—as management for a condition involving excess amniotic fluid and otherwise known now as hydramnios—an amniocentesis is a medical procedure that involves removing and testing a small sample of amniotic fluid from the uterus. This fluid surrounds and protects the developing baby during pregnancy. In 1955, researchers discovered amniotic fluid might be used to accurately predict the sex of an unborn baby. Ultrasound joined the prenatal diagnostic toolbox the following year. As for amniocentesis, it was soon used to detect Down syndrome (in 1968), spina bifida, and other chromosomal abnormalities and, not surprisingly, the first abortions based on a prenatal diagnosis were performed shortly thereafter.

Amniocentesis is usually done between the 15th and 20th week of gestation and is typically recommended for women over 35 years of age, for women who have had abnormal screening tests, or for those with a family history of specific birth defects, including a previous pregnancy or child. These criteria are no doubt based on a solid medical foundation. However, they might also be based in part on a court case from the mid-1970s when a 37-year-old New Yorker sued her doctors after giving birth to a child with Down syndrome. The new mother alleged that her doctors had not made her aware of an amniocentesis and if they had, she would have terminated the pregnancy. Her case was what might be called a "wrongful life" case, and despite being awarded the child's medical costs for life, the couple put their daughter up for adoption the following year.

Following the discovery of trisomy 21 in the late 1950s, Jérôme Lejeune set out to find a cure for what he initially surmised was a curable disease. However, none was forthcoming. His studies of cancer were also at a standstill. Years before, as a young man living in the suburbs of Paris under Nazi occupation and riding his bicycle 68 miles round trip to take his examinations, he had no idea his medical path would eventually lead him to become a crusader for the disabled after his own discovery would put so many in danger. Born three years after Lejeune in 1929, Sir Albert William Liley was a New Zealand medical doctor who worked most of his life in Auckland and maintained a 200-acre forest in nearby King County. In 1963, after three unsuccessful attempts, Liley successfully performed the first-ever intrauterine blood transfusion. It was a truly miraculous merger of science and medicine. At the time, Liley had no idea he would one day join up with Lejeune in a frantic race to save lives from a world he had helped create. Lejeune was a devout Catholic, whereas Liley was purported to be an atheist. However, both understood the long-term ramifications of their achievements, and both had noticed in international scientific circles the emergence of ideas they found alarming.

Jérôme Lejeune—with his thick white hair, matching mustache, and infectious smile—was under no illusion about those diagnosed with Down syndrome or related malformations before birth, stating, "Either we will cure them of their innocence, or else it will be a massacre of the innocents." He also believed doctors would ultimately be asked to play the role of Pontius Pilate and recalled that Hippocrates had lived four hundred years before Jesus Christ or Saint Luke—the physician turned apostle and bestselling author in the Gospels—and therefore, human life was commanded by natural law prior to the Christian Law. In other words, his oath would not have allowed him to do harm to one person to relieve the suffering of another, regardless of his religious convictions. By 1971, having taken up a pro-life mantle, Lejeune was asked to speak at a public gathering to discuss new proposed abortion laws in France. However, when he went to speak, shouts of "Bastard Lejeune" rang out and projectiles soon flew about the place. Jérôme dodged a piece of meat, supposedly representing an aborted fetus, which was thrown at his head. In the back of the hall were truly horrible signs, with drawings of children with tongues sticking out and one with the inscription: "Death to Papa Lejeune and his little monsters!" Later, in 1973, the walls of his office were vandalized in red letters: "Kill Lejeune and his little monsters."

Rather than cower, the doctor essentially doubled down on his beliefs and labeled this hatred as *chromosomal racism*. For this, he paid a steep professional price, as he was no longer asked to speak at scientific conferences or at public gatherings. Shockingly, he was also the subject of a deliberate smear campaign implying he was a Nazi sympathizer or a communist and was part of the KGB. Others with similar beliefs were also implicated around the same time. Unfortunately, we have seen this playbook again and again, especially in the political arena. If you don't agree with someone, call them a Nazi or concoct a purported Russian connection.

As for Liley, he cared for infants endangered by Rh-factor incompatibility, resulting from the mother producing antibodies capable of injuring the infant's cells, especially the red blood cells. He would use a large needle to perforate the mother's abdominal wall, go through the uterine wall and remove a sample of amniotic fluid to examine the infant's condition. It was daring stuff, as was inducing early labor in the seventh month to save the baby. Based on his heroics, in 1967, Liley was appointed a Companion of the Order of St. Michael and St. George for valuable services to medicine, and in 1973, he was promoted to Knight Commander. Two years earlier, Liley had co-founded the Protection of the Unborn Child (now Voice for Life). Married with five children, he also adopted a child with Down syndrome. In 1977, he joined Jérôme Lejeune for a series of interviews titled *The Tiniest Humans*. Unfortunately, Liley committed suicide in 1983. Today, the Health Research Council of New Zealand annually awards the Liley Medal in recognition of an outstanding contribution to medical research.

While Jérôme Lejeune angered many on the scientific banquet circuit, he also found many new allies along the way. First, on December 6, 1962, during a dinner at the White House—amid the popping of flash bulbs in the Oval Office—Lejeune was presented the Kennedy Foundation award for his medical research and President John F. Kennedy himself presented the accompanying crystal trophy. Lejeune's primary contribution was to make faith an ally of science and not surprisingly, he soon gained the attention of the church. In 1974, he was appointed by His Holiness Pope Paul VI as a member of the Pontifical Academy of Sciences. Established in 1604, it was the first scientific academy in the world and with his appointment, Lejeune joined—despite the ongoing atheist fable—the likes of Galileo.

One day in December 1993, after returning from Rome and a meeting with His Holiness John Paul II, Jérôme developed a heavy cough. When it would not abate, he sought medical attention, was diagnosed with lung cancer, and was given only a few months to live. Between treatments and hospital visits, his final days were spent working at the Pontifical Academy for Life in conjunction with Pope John Paul II. After entering hospice care and with his family gathered on Good Friday, Lejeune confided, "My children, if I can leave you with just one message, the most important of all, it is this: we are in the hand of God. I have had proof of this several times over the course of my life. The details are not important." Jérôme Lejeune died on Easter Morning—April 3, 1994. His funeral was held three days later at Notre Dame Cathedral, where crowds of academics and government dignitaries mingled with the disabled and their families and where hope outshone sadness.

Following his death, Jérôme's family created the Foundation Lejeune, which provides research, care, and advocacy for those affected by genetic disorders, including Down syndrome, Williams-Beuren syndrome, fragile X syndrome, and other explained and unexplained intellectual disabilities. For his advocacy on behalf of the voiceless, the cause for the beatification and canonization of the Servant of God Jérôme Lejeune was initiated on June 28, 2007. In 2021, he took a major step toward sainthood when His Holiness Pope Francis approved the "heroic virtues" of the doctor. The papal recognition of Jérôme Lejeune's virtues means he is considered "venerable" by the Catholic Church. If the Vatican confirms a miracle attributed to his intercession, he will be beatified, and a second one would result in his joining Mother Teresa in being declared a saint. Two such miracles are seemingly a drop in the bucket, especially since there are thousands born each year.

Today, Down syndrome remains incurable, and the condition can only be eradicated by abortion. Each year, around 6,000 babies in the United States are born with Down syndrome, and although there is thankfully no population-based registry, as of 2010, it was estimated that 206,366 Americans were living with Down syndrome. This number is largely due to a rising life expectancy. In the 1960s, the average life expectancy for a person with Down syndrome was a paltry 10 years, with more than half of all deaths occurring in children under the age of two, whereas life expectancy jumped to a more robust 52 years as of 2020. Before the 1980s, most people with Down syndrome were institutionalized, which resulted in a life that was both shorter and of poorer quality. Medical advances, including heart surgeries and related treatments, have also played an enormous role in this remarkable turnaround.

Due in part to an increase in prenatal testing, including amniocentesis, approximately 67% of babies diagnosed with Down syndrome are selectively aborted each year in the United States. In this regard, the United States is not alone. In Iceland, which gained notoriety following a CBS report in 2017 describing a Country "where Down syndrome is *disappearing,*" the abortion rate is much higher and in Denmark, the rate is an unfathomable 98%. By comparison, 3 out of 10 pregnancies worldwide are terminated by induced abortion and in the United States, that number stands at approximately 18% as of 2020. In England, Scotland, and Wales, there is a 24-week time limit to have an abortion, but the law allows for terminations well beyond that window if there is "a substantial risk that if a child were born, it would suffer from such physical and mental abnormalities as to be seriously handicapped," which includes Down syndrome. In 2022, a decision from the English Court of Appeal—as if borrowed from the pages of a dystopian novel—rejected an appeal to this legislation filed by Heidi Crowter, a disability rights advocate with Down syndrome from Coventry, England. The result upheld legislation that allows the abortion of babies with Down syndrome up until birth. Forget about silent eugenics, as this would be better described as screaming eugenics. As for Ms. Crowter, undeterred by this inexplicable setback, she has decided to take her case to the European Court of Human Rights. You go, girl! Let me know how or where I can contribute.

As if this is not enough, there are actual documented cases of children born with developmental disabilities being denied life-saving medical treatments. One such case took place in the United States in the early 1970s when a baby was born with a repairable intestinal constriction that prevented normal feeding. The baby was also born with Down syndrome. Eerily like the "Knauer case," it was the parents, and not the medical providers, who refused to authorize medical treatment, which resulted in the death of the baby. Unfortunately, in a slew of cases that followed, parents alone were not to blame, as medical professionals advocated for the refusal of life-saving treatment as well. In 1982, parents relying in part on their pediatrician's advice refused to allow lifesaving surgery to correct an esophageal defect, even though the surgery was relatively routine and had a high rate of success. The baby, of course, was also born with Down syndrome. Nurses at the Indiana hospital where the baby was born filed an action to save the child, but a judge refused to intervene. Six days later, the baby died, having been denied intravenous feeding, reminiscent of the killing programs in Nazi Germany.

With most pregnancies involving a Down syndrome diagnosis ending in termination, there must be a plausible explanation. Life must be horrible for children and parents alike. Well, not exactly. A recent survey of Americans with Down syndrome ages 12 and over found that 99% indicated they are happy with their lives. Furthermore, 97% report liking who they are, and 96% report liking their appearance. What about the parents? Are they as happy? Apparently so. For instance, in one survey, 99% of parents report they love their child with Down syndrome, and 97% are proud of them. Alright, but most parents genuinely love their children and take pride in them. How many have struggled and become discouraged by their situation? Surprisingly, especially given the number of pregnancies ending in termination, 79% report that their outlook on life is more positive because of their child with Down syndrome. As for siblings, the numbers are similar to those for parents, with 96% reporting affection towards their brother or sister with Down syndrome, and 94% expressing feelings of pride towards their siblings.

Wading into the pool of a highly charged political issue is fraught with danger, as you need to look no further than the horrific treatment received by Jérôme Lejeune and the unbearable burden carried by Sir Albert William Liley. However, regardless of one's personal beliefs, clearly, these numbers don't add up. The disconnect must lie at the feet of expecting parents, the media, and the medical profession. What we do know is that prenatal testing in the modern world is not only recommended but is now expected. This is especially true, given the prior litigation mentioned earlier. As a result, an increasing number of chromosomal aberrations will be detected. This will inevitably occur and will only intensify over time as testing becomes more accurate and comprehensive.

Historically, medical instruction clearly counseled parents to end such pregnancies, especially with anticipated early childhood mortality and inevitable institutionalization. However, those 1970s recommendations are grossly outdated, as are the materials still being provided. Any cursory review of the information provided to an expecting parent reveals a clear bias and a focus on the negative rather than accentuating the positive. This is now clearly out of step with reality. Today, the quality of life for those with disabilities continues to grow exponentially, as does the length of life. The resources and opportunities for parents with children with disabilities also continue to grow exponentially. In other words, the quality of life has improved for the entire family. Of course, life is filled with heartache for the healthy and disabled alike, but not terminating a pregnancy based on antiquated rationales might just be the greatest decision one can make. Just ask those 99%, as I'm sure those parents would be willing to share their own personal life experiences with you. I know I would. Lastly, my only unsolicited advice would be to make a fully informed decision, as true family planning should require nothing less. Slogans aside, on this we can all agree.

Toomer's Corner

"Auf Wiedersehen, Mr. Wiest." Most everyone was happy to see him go. After entering a guilty plea to felony first-degree criminal mischief and receiving an agreed-upon three-year suspended sentence, the 29-year-old German, through his attorney, informed the court that he intended to return to Germany upon receiving his passport. Jochen Wiest was also ordered to pay $20,807 in restitution to Auburn University, a $1,000 fine, and court costs. For setting fire to a live oak tree with his black lighter, he was also given a campus trespassing ban.

The scene of the crime was at the intersection of Magnolia Avenue and College Street, at the northeastern-most reach of the campus of Auburn University and at the starting point of downtown Auburn, Alabama. Better known as *Toomer's Corner*, this sacred spot has been home to two large Live Oak—*Quercus Virginiana*—trees for quite some time. While many believe the trees were certainly planted there by the 1930s, many, including the University, suggest that the trees were likely planted as early as 1880, possibly by Auburn city founder Judge John Harper. Regardless, by all rights, they should never have been there, as the Live Oak is a coastal species, typically found in sandy soils and more prevalent in Mobile than in Auburn.

Live Oaks might live for centuries and can grow to monstrous proportions. While the trees at *Toomer's Corner* never came to match the size of such kin, these twins still provided large limbs hanging over the corner of the intersection and perfect for a rolling tradition. *Toomer's Corner* is also home to *Toomer's Drugs*, originally started in 1896 by Sheldon Toomer. Better known as "Shel," the former half-back on Auburn's first football team graduated from Auburn with a degree in Agriculture and Pharmacy and opened the store with a $500 loan from a gentleman named John Reese. Many believe the tradition of rolling the corner with toilet paper, also known as "TP-Ing," following an Auburn victory, began with *Toomer's Drugs* employees throwing ticker tape from their telegraph onto the power lines outside the store. As for "Rolling the Corner," it originated as a student celebration in the early 1960s and after the city removed all power lines and transitioned to underground utilities, tree rolling, without the wires, remained.

Jochen's inexplicable actions took place hours after an inexplicable Auburn victory over LSU. Our guy trip crew, who had witnessed the wild ending, was sound asleep back at a hotel when the tree was set ablaze. But more about that later. On September 24, 2016, several hours before kickoff, we strolled through *Toomer's Corner*, stopping at *Toomer's Drugs* for their world-famous fresh-squeezed lemonade. The corner building—painted white with blue trim—sports a long soda counter on one side and a store with mounds of Auburn *Tiger* merchandise on the other. Like many others, we also stopped to gaze at the oaks, pose for pictures, and inquire with locals about the health of these splendid trees. You see, Mr. Wiest was not the first to do them harm.

On January 10, 2011, an undefeated Auburn football team defeated Oregon, 22-19, in Glendale, Arizona, to win their second consensus National Championship in school history. A half dozen weeks before, in the Iron Bowl in hostile Tuscaloosa, Cam Newton threw for three touchdowns and ran for another, leading Auburn back from a 24-point deficit for a stunning 28-27 victory over Alabama. This unlikely series of events was simply too much for Harvey Updyke, Jr., a "self-proclaimed" Alabama fan, so he set out to do something about it. One day, after buying a four-pound bag of herbicide called Spike 80DF from an agricultural products store under false pretense, he hopped in his car then drove to Auburn, Alabama, where the "herbicidal maniac" poisoned the oak trees at *Toomer's Corner* by pouring 500 times the amount needed to kill the trees. It is unclear exactly when the dastardly deed took place, but Updyke planned the crime for a month and later stated, "Every night I'd stay up all night long, and they used cameras on the trees, and I figured out when the slowest time, what day of the week and what...night was the slowest around those oak trees, so I could go in there at that time and not get caught."

Whether he would have ever been caught remains unknown. However, when he called the wildly popular and incredibly entertaining *Paul Finebaum Radio Show* on January 27, 2011, claiming to be "Al from Dadeville, Alabama," he set in motion his ultimate undoing. That's what happens when you confess your crimes to the entire nation. After taking the call, Finebaum, who is an *SEC* icon and a legendary journalist in all things pertaining to college football, questioned the wildly unsubstantiated claims made by Updyke about Auburn students celebrating the death of Paul "Bear" Bryant. "Al from Dadeville," calm but angry, just had to respond to Finebaum's apparent dismissiveness, stating, "Well, let me tell you what I did. The weekend after the Iron Bowl, I went to Auburn, Alabama, because I live thirty miles away, and I poisoned the two Toomer's trees."

For many, including me, Finebaum is a way of life even when he is, or I should say was, bashing my conference as not being as good as his. Regardless of which conference is best, at the time, it is undisputed that nearly every person in Alabama tuned in daily. As it turned out, the sales manager and the warehouse salesperson of the agricultural products store were listening to "Al from Dadeville," and what they heard spooked them. The next day, the police and the State

Department of Agriculture were in their office tracking down the purchase. Not surprisingly, an Auburn student who was also listening called the campus police, who, in turn, called Gary Keever, a horticulture professor. When early tests were negative, many hoped the whole thing was a prank, but later tests confirmed the worst—the trees were indeed poisoned, and their chance of survival was slim.

In the end, good-old fashion detective work, along with a little luck, ultimately led the police to Harvey Albert *"Al"* Updyke, who later pleaded guilty to a Class C felony of criminal damage of an agricultural facility and was ordered to serve six months in jail, spend five years on supervised probation, and pay $800,000 in restitution. Given the delayed decline in tree health and the initial promising test results, although Updyke told the truth about poisoning the trees, he most likely lied about when he did it. Experts believe he most likely committed the heinous act after the National Championship and not the *Iron Bowl*.

Why did these men do such things? In the case of *Toomer's Corner*, did these guys just hate those trees? Pouring poison near the base of the Oaks was surely no gesture of affection, nor was setting one ablaze. How could one have such contempt for other people, many of whom were his neighbors, while the other was so oblivious to the safety of those around him? Upon closer examination, it is likely that these two men had completely different motives; however, their actions are clearly intertwined with fandom, crowd behavior, and a lurking ugliness that percolates up every now and then in the sporting world.

The word *fan* comes from the Latin term *fanaticus* and was originally used to describe a religious devotee. Today, our modern English vocabulary uses phrases such as "sports fan" or "sports fanatic" to describe a person who enjoys watching or attending sports. However, this is by no means a new phenomenon, as large crowds of supporters have been gathering at sporting events for at least the last couple of thousand years. Consider, for example, the ancient Greeks, Romans, and Byzantines' love for chariot racing and gladiator matches. These devotees have been around for quite a while and there have been plenty of them. History also reveals riots in ancient Pompeii in 59 A.D. during a gladiator match, and in Constantinople, race fans set the city's hippodrome on fire multiple times in the fifth and sixth centuries. When they were not lighting things on fire, they were literally killing each other by the thousands. It turns out that bad behavior from sports fans is nothing new.

The *Circus Maximus* is an ancient Roman chariot-racing stadium and mass entertainment venue located in Rome, Italy, dating back to the 6th century BCE. The place was huge—nearly three times larger than the Roman Colosseum—and could accommodate 150,000 spectators dressed in the colors of their favorite racers. Fans took great pride in their chariot teams and not only cheered for them but also purposely and enthusiastically placed curses on rival charioteers in the form of "curse tablets." Not only did they "pray" in writing for chariot malfunctions, but also for illness to racers and even death to the rival horses. Justine Gubar, in her book, *Fanaticus-Mischief and Madness in the Modern Sports Fan* (which she wrote primarily as a response to the atrocious behavior directed at her by some *Buckeye* fans following her reporting of the "gear sale and subsequent cover-up scandal" at Ohio State), describes this as "mid-fourth-century trash talking in a book." It makes me wonder what one might dig up near *The Horseshoe* or *The Big House* if these curse tablets were still in use during the last century, and I shudder to think what one might have wished upon *inedible raw nuts* or certain *unnamed vermin*.

Being a fan is both physical and emotional, psychological and social, personal and communal. When you sign up for fandom, you agree to sweaty palms, butterflies in your stomach, and a racing heart. Uncontrollable mood swings are also part of the deal, along with irrational feelings of loyalty and devotion to a team or town that can inevitably break your heart. Can anyone say Cleveland sports team fans? From the outside, it looks like an abusive relationship, and that's all I'll say on the matter. This whole thing has been bothering non-sports fans for millennia, as Greek philosophers as early as the sixth century BC lamented the acclaim and public commemoration of useless skills such as running or wrestling. Of course, there is true value to be found in outrunning a charging bear or being able to repel an attack from an assassin, and, on such matters, Aristotle, Plato, and Socrates would be bound to heartily agree.

Granted, none of it is rational, but still, why do a handful of fans engage in such bad behavior? Clues might be found in the ashes of the Hippodrome and those early documented riots in Rome and Constantinople. The anger of the mob—much like the destructive path of a storm—leads us directly to the incredible power wielded by a crowd. A crowd, it seems, can put a spell on an individual, causing them to engage in actions they would otherwise never have considered. Fans riot when their teams lose but also riot when their teams win. What? When they win? Yep, strange, right? Being together in large numbers, especially when wearing similar markings such as team apparel, can also create a false sense of anonymity. However, those pesky security cameras can easily remove that cloak of invisibility. Some fans simply crave attention and involvement outside their normal lives. Much like a superhero, it gives them a second—often more exciting, even if ultimately more expensive—alter ego. To be clear, not all sports riots involve sports fans, as many are sports agnostics at best. A tiny fraction of the population just likes to break things and set them on fire, but that's another drive for another day.

The greatest spell, cooked up in the witch's cauldron, is a desire to belong to something bigger than yourself, even if it is ultimately destructive. For years, European soccer (football), especially in England, faced terrible violence at the hands of hooligans. Bands of these team supporters, usually made up of impressionable youth or, inexplicitly, middle-aged men, would take to the streets and stadiums before, during, and after matches with the sole aim of creating chaos. For a while, they were pretty darn good at it. Imagine a group of lily-white rioters with matching soccer tattoos and buzz cuts. Over time, as financial investments in clubs by owners, boards of directors, and nearby neighborhoods increased, pressure grew for a more favorable stadium experience, and the hooligans eventually got the big squeeze. It turns out money, at least in this case, was not the root of all evil but the cure for bad fan behavior, even if curtailing the hooligans' unlawful behavior squeezed some families out with exorbitant ticket prices.

A final, and what I believe to be the most obvious piece of the bad behavior puzzle, is the excessive consumption of alcohol by some sports fans, whether watching sporting events in person or at a bar or restaurant. This might also go a long way in explaining the many bad tattoos brandished by some hooligans and rioters alike. Getting back to college football, I've been quite surprised by how few times our paths have crossed with grossly inebriated fans. In fact, the only one I can recall involved an off-duty police officer sitting in front of us at a game, and the neighboring fans apologized on his behalf after he left the game at halftime, telling us, "He is normally a great guy, who is known for his charity work around town." So, how have we otherwise escaped watching liquid belligerency in action? There are a few plausible explanations. First, we seldom sit anywhere near the student sections at these games, and we are never way back up in the rafters. In other words, we have good seats around other families and alumni. Second, our trips surround pre-game festivities on campus rather than frat row or other off-campus "activities." Lastly, following the games, we seldom stick around. As I said, when Mr. Wiest set the tree on fire, we were sound asleep back at the hotel—hours removed from any campus revelry.

Sports are a human creation revealing beauty, grace, and perseverance while also revealing our crack lines and faults. Sports fandom is a uniquely human undertaking, so why would it be any different from other aspects of life, flashing an occasional ugliness? This is especially true when considering other areas of human competition outside of sports. In the end, the desire to have fun and the desire to belong may have been behind each unfortunate case and these, too, are human cravings. However, to be clear, these are isolated incidents in sports-fan socialization. As a rule, trees, animals, and opposing fans are usually left unharmed, and the benefits of being a sports fan far outweigh the dangers.

In fact, since sports tend to be consumed in a group, being a fan fulfills another human desire—to spend time with others. By providing a sense of belonging, sports consumption fulfills the human need for social interaction. Being a fan provides an opportunity to spend time with close friends and family members. As much as I enjoy gardening, it just doesn't bring the family together like sitting down to watch an Ohio State football game. Furthermore, the level of communication between individuals is often greater when watching a sporting event than going to a museum or a theatre. If you don't believe me, consider the fact that there is no need to whisper; nobody worries about whether they silenced their cell phone, and when was the last time you were "shushed" by somebody nearby when you were watching a college football game? As a *bonus*, the commercials can drag the games out for hours—as my wife and daughter are more than happy to remind us—giving everyone plenty of time to chat and to break open more chip dip.

Long after Greek philosophers lamented the existence of sports fandom, many social scientists have continued a chorus of condemnation, with one comment going so far as to suggest "no human being on this Earth has to or needs to attend sports events." The usual concerns include that fans are lazy and aggressive, have adopted negative behaviors, and have poor interpersonal relationships. But is any of this true? Probably not. Given the number of steps taken on game day for those attending sporting events, it can be analogous to a long hike in the woods. As for those watching at home, there is very little activity except a few trips to the refrigerator, but then again, few people jog in place while reading a book either.

In *Sport Fans-The Psychology and Social Impact of Spectators*, the authors explore these notions of laziness along with a slew of other concerns expressed by critics of sports spectators. First, if sports fans are lazy, why does research reveal they perform better in college than non-fans and are more involved with and have better impressions of their universities? Regarding aggression, research reveals no difference between individuals attending sporting events and those with no interest in sports. What about those perceived negative behaviors? We've touched upon the connection between alcohol and sports, but research has failed to reveal any ongoing relationship between sports fandom and alcohol consumption. What happens at a game may be a bit like Vegas in that it stays at the game. It is also worth noting that, alongside any negative behaviors, sports teach a multitude of positive behaviors, including the importance of a strong work ethic, the value of perseverance, and the importance of fair play. Lastly, research failed to reveal any support for the notion that conflict over sports has a negative impact on relational quality. In *Fever Pitch*—both the original English *Arsenal* story and the subsequent American Boston *Red Sox* story—the obsessed fan finds a way to put their love of the local team in perspective, and they both end up with the girl by the end of the story. Just saying.

It turns out that being a sports fan also creates a positive correlation between levels of identification and self-esteem and a negative correlation with the frequency of depression. Hello, Cleveland sports fans! Good to know, right? Furthermore, psychological health was related to a high level of team identification with a local university sports team. Hello, *SEC* fans! Good to know, right? Studies further suggest that the geographically closer the team is to the sports fan, the better for overall psychological health. Much like the theatre, sports provide a level of escapism, while drama, ritual, and excitement in the arena allow "unfettered expression to sports fans' feelings." However, the research did further reveal that fans might experience negative effects and depression after watching their team lose. This is not surprising as disappointment is also a very human experience and helps explain Mondays in Northeast Ohio.

It has also been noted that in the modern world of increasing fragmentation and the paradoxical isolation created by social media, sports fandom provides society with a common language. It fosters a common identity or an overall sense of community, and this is especially true in "college towns" across the country. The authors in *Sport Fans-The Psychology and Social Impact on Spectators* conclude with the following thoughts on sports fans: "Maybe we should view sport fandom as a natural supplement, a tropical spice, a spiritual, emotional substitute. In the same way that herbs and spices can improve the taste of a bland main dish, sports fandom can add a dash of eustress, excitement, thrill, and wonder to our lives and society as a whole." A tasty thought, indeed.

Ultimately deemed unrecoverable, Auburn fans gathered around the original oak trees in 2013 for a commemorative block party, giving the familiar vegetation "one last roll." Thousands gathered in this celebration of remembrance, burying their beloved friends under a white canopy in a final gesture of love and admiration. By the following year, in 2014, the university announced it had rid the soil of any traces of poison and the first replacement trees were planted at *Toomer's Corner* on the frigid morning of February 14, 2015. While the tree closest to College Street adapted to its new home, the tree closer to Magnolia Avenue failed to thrive and was ultimately replaced on July 21st with a third tree of the same height that had been planted on campus as a spare. In 2016, during our visit to Auburn, these two trees from a nursery in Ehrhardt, South Carolina, finally began to take root, thereby allowing for rolling during the season and on the night following Auburn's victory over LSU.

The tree closest to Magnolia Avenue—the replacement for the replacement—was set ablaze hours after our visit to *Toomer's Corner* and damage caused by the fire necessitated its removal. Later, the tree closest to College Street was also removed, as it had failed to become fully established for unknown reasons. The following February, while we trudged through another Ohio winter, two fully grown trees, with seemingly far less fanfare, were again planted at *Toomer's Corner*. This is what fans do. They are unrelenting in preserving community and tradition. At Auburn, on a corner, Live Oaks will remain no matter what is thrown at them or their school. Six years later, in 2023, under a closely monitored growth program including weekly health assessments, one of college football's most unique and iconic traditions finally returned. Let the good times roll!

Growing Pains

For the most part, Daniel's school experiences were largely positive. However, we did have our fair share of negative experiences. The same is true for my daughter, and as I'm sure all parents can attest, for any child. While Daniel attended special education classes, we made every effort to integrate him into a typical class setting. My daughter, on the other hand, was designated as a "gifted student." Imagining any bell curve, we initially resisted this designation. The term seemed loose and woefully overused. Besides, aren't all kids gifted in some way? Regardless, we did ultimately relent after her teachers outlined the benefits of such a designation, especially in terms of her college trajectory. So, with one child in special education and another in the gifted program, we lived in two separate worlds. Then one day, quite unexpectedly, these worlds collided when some concerned parents formed a group to discuss issues facing gifted students and to express concerns surrounding the current curriculum options. My wife and I showed up at a meeting at a neighborhood library, believing discussions would center around Latin, physics and, if time permitted, the formation of a chess club. Unfortunately, as parents expressed frustrations, it soon turned into a gripe session surrounding classroom integration. I can still hear one mom, with glasses and hair pinned back unnaturally tight, saying, "My kid's job is not to teach some other kid," while another chimed in, "Yeah, my kid should be focused on their own education." Heavily outnumbered, my wife and I did not utter a single word. Nor did we ever say that teaching is the best way to learn, even if now we wish we had. We did get up to leave. And we never went back.

When Daniel was in 8th grade, his school class went to Washington, D.C. This is essentially a rite of passage for many students throughout the country and if you have ever been there, you know that at any given time, the place is literally crawling with both bureaucrats and young teenagers dressed in matching-colored T-shirts. Early on, my wife and I decided Dan should go and after discussing the matter with his teachers, it was agreed that he would be more than welcome if a parent accompanied him. I'd like to say we flipped a coin, but given my love of history, I was always the designated choice. The night before we were to depart by bus, and after packing our set of four matching T-shirts—powder blue, maroon, lime green, and yellow (which we both still have)—Daniel began to complain about his stomach and by the following morning, he was doubled over in pain. Instead of boarding a bus, we found ourselves at the local children's hospital emergency room. Thankfully, Dan's issue was ultimately resolved with a little help from a laxative, but by then, we had missed our ride. After texting his teachers, we raced off in my car across Pennsylvania and Maryland, meeting up with his classmates at the Smithsonian.

In the end, it was a wonderful few days and it gave me a great insight into how hard teachers work. Looking back on it now, I was able to share an experience no other parent had the chance to have. While I was annoyed at the snarky and downright rude treatment the kids received when visiting the capital building, I was left heartened by the interaction between Daniel and his classmates. By nature, they are more inclusive than those generations who came before them, which makes us happy. As for those joggers in the National Mall, maybe practice a little more patience or pick a different route, as you're likely to come upon large groups of pimple-faced, braces-wearing kids regularly. Or feel free to ease up on the shaking of heads and the audible sighs. Who knows, one day, that kid might be yours and if not, they will still, one day, help pay your salary. I know their parents already do. Now, in all fairness, I had my own elitist longings as food courts were our daily staple, which was made more difficult with so many wonderful restaurants nearby. More than once, I daydreamed of grabbing Dan and going over to the *Old Ebbitt Grill* or hopping into my car for a quick run to just about anywhere in Georgetown. Two years later, my wife agreed to chaperone the band/choir trip to New York City with both our kids, and, like me, they mainly dined on food court "cuisine." However, unlike me, she rode on the bus and after hearing about their overnight drive, maybe I lucked out with our late start.

Being a parent of a disabled child carries a certain level of loneliness. Your experiences put you on a path shared by scant others, and, for the most part, you must walk alone (unless it is a Saturday afternoon in Anfield, where nobody ever walks alone). Paradoxically, you are never able to travel incognito. Every get-together, party, or school function feels like walking into a cocktail party naked. There is always a peering eye, and the music—like a needle being abruptly lifted from a record—always seems to come to a scratching stop or at least an awkward pause before restarting. My wife and I call it "living out loud." While many friends, neighbors, and family members are empathetic, they can never truly understand your situation. How could they, as they have their own issues? As the saying goes, "Walk a mile in my shoes."

Our victories have typically come from within rather than from without, as the macro world has, for the most part, been disappointing. Case in point, when Daniel was 10 years old, we had our first national political spotlight moment when, during the 2008 presidential campaign, John McCain picked Sarah Palin as his running mate. Many were drawn to her folksy demeanor as the governor of Alaska, while others were concerned about her lack of experience on a national stage. Republicans seemed to like her, while Democrats did not. Big surprise, right? However, my wife and I, for a fleeting moment, finally had someone who understood our situation, as her youngest child—Trig—was born with Down syndrome. We were so excited. Unfortunately, our excitement soon turned to disgust as one demeaning comment after another was thrown the governor's way, and her son was the brunt of unsubstantiated innuendo and ugly vulgarity. Now, to be fair, this inevitably happens on both sides in every political cycle (just ask Governor Walz about the internet trolls who attacked his son in the most recent election cycle), but this felt different. This was personal for us and revealed truths we had previously dared not contemplate—the world at large simply didn't care about us. And perhaps more alarming, many disliked our son and those like him—without any reason. Again, we felt alone.

While many people are just mean, others—on both a macro and micro level—seem reckless or, at best, sloppy. Whether it be a late-night host, a beloved comedian, or even an old family favorite movie, the insults are seemingly hurled without warning. Heck, even former president Barack Obama once joked on the *Jay Leno Show* that when he bowled, "it was like the Special Olympics or something." Perceived or real, words hurt and, occasionally, those words have also come from some of our closest friends. "Little yellow buses," "being special," the "R" word—or any word purposely changed to end in "tard"—need to be taken to the nearest back-alley dumpster or office shredder. Going one step further, "trophies for everyone," though it seems well-intentioned as a metaphor for life's lessons of winning and losing, probably needs to be reined in a bit as well. Coach a group of disabled children, many of whom struggle just to walk or talk, and then tell me who should or should not get a trophy. Much like the "N" word and other racial, ethnic, gender, or sexual orientation slurs, it would surely be a more perfect world without them, in this father's humble opinion. In a world teeming with perceived grievances and a relentless orchestration of feigned outrage, it is also understood that a certain level of societal fatigue has set in. Our family shares it with you. Lest we seem thin-skinned or an enemy of free speech, we do not advocate any formal abridgment of speech or thought. Recently, a good friend and mentor told my wife and I about a book by John Bevere entitled *The Bait of Satan: Living Free from the Deadly Trap of Offense*, and while we intend to read it, learn from it, and try to live by it, I would also offer to others a lesson my mother taught me when I was just a little boy—"Maybe think before you say something."

War Eagle

"Sweet Auburn! Loveliest village on the plain." These words are taken from a poem called *The Deserted Village,* written by Oliver Goldsmith in 1770 and although referring to a town in Ireland, the description was embraced by Auburn fans and made their own. So, it was that our first night on "the Plains" had us dining at a former train station, now a restaurant fittingly named *The Depot.* Once an integral part of the Confederate war efforts, the Depot's tracks were ravaged in a series of attacks led by Major General Lovell Harrison Rousseau and his "Rousseau's Raiders" in 1864. The damage inflicted was substantial, with the existing depot incinerated, the cross ties burned, and the rails twisted and otherwise mangled into what came to be called "Sherman's neckties." The raid, which disrupted the transportation of military supplies to the rebels, struck another major blow to the life of the Confederacy. In 1870, following the war, the depot was rebuilt, and, in 1896, this train station was where university students greased the tracks with pig grease, lard, and soap when Georgia Tech came to town to play the first Auburn football game of the season. Locally referred to as the "Wreck Tech Pajama Parade," after skidding down 400 yards of greased tracks, the train reportedly missed the station by over a mile, causing a dumbfounded and weary *Yellow Jacket* team to walk

back to town, all while lugging their equipment. In retrospect, fortunately, the train did not jump the tracks, and nobody was hurt, except perhaps for a few blistered feet from the long walk back to town. Not surprisingly, Auburn won the game 45-0.

The train station was struck by lightning in 1904 and again burned to the ground. From the second round of ashes, the depot was rebuilt yet again, based on a Victorian design by Auburn University engineering/architecture student Ralph Dudley and, for decades, there were eight trains stopping in Auburn each day. However, in 1970, the Auburn depot sold its last passenger ticket. Thankfully, by the time we came to town, the building had been renovated and converted into a wonderful restaurant serving seafood and steak. The outside brick is coated in dark grey, while the inside brick is painted white, featuring black trim and exposed wood and steel beams. Along the outer edge are black button tufted booths, accompanied by black wooden chairs and lamps dangling from wheel and wire along the outer walls. In the middle of the restaurant are larger tables illuminated by several ornate chandeliers. As expected, dinner was delicious and included a spicy blue crab dip, blackened redfish, shrimp and grits, and crab-stuffed rainbow trout. We topped off our gorging with helpings of coconut and almond rice pudding and vanilla New York-style cheesecake in a mason jar. Yum!

Earlier that day, we had flown into *Hartsfield-Jackson Atlanta International Airport*, grabbed a rental car, and driven the 101 miles to Auburn, Alabama. The drive, although originally dreaded, was quite smooth as the infamous Atlanta traffic that we had encountered the year before when traveling to Athens was largely avoided since the airport sits to the south of downtown and the 285 beltway. Given our late-afternoon arrival, we decided to head straight to dinner and check in at our hotel afterward. As such, we arrived at the restaurant thirty-five minutes prior to our reservation and were informed that we would be given a table as soon as one became available. Or so we thought. Our gang found the perfect spot to wait, leaning against a wooden rail below a set of large bay windows and, with a drink in hand, it was especially fun when a train rumbled through the station without slowing. The trains were literally several yards away from our perch. However, after the second round of drinks, we began to wonder about our reservation. Where was our table? When we finally inquired, we were told that we would be seated ten to fifteen minutes early, but that was the best they could do. Somewhere along the way, we forgot that Auburn, Alabama, is on Central Standard Time and not Eastern Standard Time. I guess we could have checked into the hotel before dinner, after all.

Before the game, after strolling through campus, with our obligatory stop at the campus bookstore for additional "merch," we came upon a white signpost with a miniature tiger at the top. At the top of the post, and pointing left, a smaller sign shaped like an arrow, also painted white, read, "Heaven on Earth 0 mi." We knew we must be close to the center of the Auburn universe. Another sign further down on the post, painted orange, also pointing to the left, read, "Tiger Walk 1.1 mi." Good to know, as we would be heading there at some point before the game. Just below, at the very bottom of the post, was a red arrow-shaped sign facing down towards the ground. It read, "Hell (Tuscaloosa) not far enough." Chuckling about the sign, we asked several nearby Auburn fans where we should go for lunch, and in unison, from different corners of the intersection, we heard, "Momma Goldberg's."

Momma Goldberg's Deli, which originally opened its doors in 1976, was packed. Apparently, word has gotten out about "*Momma's Love, All the Way.*" This sandwich includes roast beef, ham, smoked turkey, and muenster cheese on a steamed-seeded bun, and when you say, "all the way," you just agreed to mayo, brown mustard, lettuce, tomato, and Momma's sauce. Yes, of course, that's what we ordered. Duh! Founder Don Dement, an Auburn graduate from the class of 1963, set out to create an old-school deli and with the help of family, including his wife, the place is still going strong 37 years later. When we could not find a place to sit after ordering our sandwiches, a young couple invited us to join them at their table. The only thing as good as *Momma Goldberg's* food is good old Southern hospitality.

Dressed in burnt orange and navy blue, colors used for Auburn's first football game in 1892 (and what I personally believe to be one of the sharpest color combinations in all of college football), we joined thousands of *Tiger* fans for the pre-game festivities, including the *Tiger Walk*. Starting back in the 1960s, on game day and two hours before the game, the players walk from the Athletics Complex down Donahue Drive to *Jordan-Hare Stadium*. The passion and commitment of players and fans create an amazing scene, and Daniel always enjoys getting near the players to get high-fives, wish them "good luck," and tell them to "try your best."

Long before we are out of bed on a Saturday morning—apart from my brother, who is always up early—the Auburn band typically goes through their two-hour rehearsal starting at 7 a.m. Thereafter, they usually take a break for food before changing into their uniform to report to the *Tiger Walk*, followed by the *Four Corners Pep Rally*. Then it's showtime—The Game. Next time you see a band member, wherever you are, make sure to thank them for their hard work, as, by all accounts, it is a gruelingly long day. Not only do they perform and march at pep rallies long before kick-off, but they also bang out fight songs for hours during the contest. Beloved half-time shows constitute a significant part of the fan experience, as do the closing numbers played after the final whistle has blown. This they do, dressed head to toe in full uniform, while carrying their instruments. We knew nothing about the *Four Corners Pep Rally*, but after speaking with the parents of a drum major and a cheerleader, we learned that the band, which is partitioned into sections, marches down from Donahue and Heisman Drives and converges just outside the stadium for a pep rally before the gates open. It was fun to watch the band come together in an intersection under a traffic light and whip the crowd into a frenzy. It was also fun to watch the parents, or more specifically, the "momma tigers" we had met earlier, during breaks, run water bottles out to their "little pride and joy."

Once inside the stadium, we were seated a few rows up from the field level, near the corner of the end zone by hedges and rows of beautiful orange flowers. We also had a bird's eye view of the most beautiful and majestic creature, *War Eagle VII*. Before setting foot on this campus on the plains, we shared a general level of confusion as to why Auburn had two mascots. The fans, including their human mascot dressed as a tiger, yell *War Eagle*. So, are they Tigers or Eagles? Or both?

Aubie, Auburn's costumed tiger mascot, was originally a cartoon character created by *Birmingham Post-Herald* artist Phil Neel that first appeared on a football program in 1959. In 1962, *Aubie* began to stand upright, and the following year, he started wearing a blue tie and a straw hat. The cartoon became a costumed mascot in the late 1970s after the University approached *Brooks-Van Horn Costumes* in New York to assist in making this transformation. The firm, known for designing theatrical attire for Broadway and Walt Disney, was given football programs from the early 1960s, along with $1,350.00. Their creation has been a spirit leader and goodwill ambassador for Auburn University ever since.

Now, what about the eagle? The University's motto, *War Eagle,* originated during the Civil War with a legendary tale of a soldier from Alabama who came across a wounded young eagle during the Battle of the Wilderness. The soldier, who was a former Auburn student, named the eagle *Anvre* and nursed it back to health. After the war, the soldier returned to campus as a faculty member and brought the eagle with him. For years, the two could be seen together on campus and the eagle became a symbol of the school's fighting spirit. Legend has it that at an Auburn football game in 1892 against Georgia, the elderly eagle broke free from his owner during the game and circled the field overhead, much to the excitement of the fans. Although Auburn won the game, *Anvre* did not fare as well, as he fell to the ground and died. So, Auburn is known as the *Tigers*, but their battle cry is *War Eagle*. Got it? I hope so.

War Eagle VI, also named *Tiger*, arrived at Auburn on October 8, 1986, and like the two eagles before her, she was cared for by members of the Alpha Phi Omega fraternity. She was six years old and originally from St. Louis, Missouri, where Federal agents seized her as part of an illegal breeding operation. In 2000, after forty years of fraternity oversight, she was transferred to the Auburn University Raptor Center. During the 2000 football season, she began the tradition of flying around the stadium before home games.

Perched near us, on his trainer's arm, at the back of the end zone, was *War Eagle VII*. Breaking with tradition, his name was not *Tiger*, but *Nova*, in part to avoid confusion, since *Tiger*, although retired, was still alive. *Nova* made his first flight at a Kentucky game in 2004 but would not officially become *War Eagle VII* until 2006. With a 6-foot wingspan and weighing in at 6.5 pounds, he was smaller than some of his predecessors. "Our War Eagle" was hatched in 1999 at the Montgomery Zoo and, after being deemed non-releasable due to human imprinting, came to Auburn in 2000.

On September 24, 2016, as we settled into our seats to watch a battle between dueling tigers, it was the eagle that took our breath away. Just prior to kickoff, *Nova* took to the skies over the stadium. It gives me goosebumps just thinking about it. Soaring majestically, the eagle gracefully glided above 87,000 fans, making a giant arcing loop as the crowd shouted, "*War Eagle, Hey*," and then, with precision beyond apprehension, landed in the middle of the 50-yard line. It was, quite simply, marvelous and surely ranks among the best pre-game rituals we have ever seen. The following year, after 58 such virtuoso performances, *Nova* was sidelined due to a diagnosis of cardiomyopathy—a chronic disease of the heart. However, *Nova*, as of this writing, is still serving as *War Eagle VII* and continues to make guest appearances for thousands of adoring fans.

Aurea is currently *War Eagle VIII*. The golden eagle arrived at the Auburn University Raptor Center in 2016 by way of Selma, Alabama, where she was found with an injury to her right wing. Although she made a remarkable recovery, it was decided, given the drag in her flight, that she was non-releasable. With a 6.5-foot wingspan and weighing 7.7 pounds, *Aurea* made her first stadium flight on November 17, 2018, and was officially named *War Eagle VIII* the following year. She is also joined by a bald eagle named *Spirit*, who, on occasion, will make the flight before the games. With the blessings of the U.S. Fish and Wildlife Service, the Auburn University Raptor Center, as part of the Auburn College of Veterinary Medicine, houses and cares for these beautiful creatures.

As for the football game, it was a wild ride, made crazier by the embattled *Tiger* coaches on each side. Auburn, coached by Arthur Gustavo "Gus" Malzahn III, came into the game at 1-2, with losses to both Clemson and Texas A&M. Malzahn, who had been the head coach since 2013, was better known for being Auburn's offensive coordinator for the 2010 National Championship Auburn team with Cam Newton at quarterback. Auburn fans were hoping he could repeat the magic. On the other sideline, coaching the LSU Tigers, was Les Miles, a coach who won the National Championship at LSU in 2007 and who makes nearly any press conference an adventure. Part coach, part quirky late-night comedian, with a splash of philosopher and theologian thrown in, he is an interesting cat, so to speak. He played football at Michigan, and for the longest time, the rumor mill churned out story after story about his inevitable return to coach *That Team Up North*. However, it never happened, and as an Ohio State guy, I'm left to ponder what that might have looked like for the *Buckeyes* and *Wolverines* alike. Anyway, his *Tigers*, who had opened the season ranked 5th in the nation, were 2-1 but had suffered a shocking loss to the Wisconsin *Badgers* in the season opener and had been wobbling since. Some say LSU is the best coaching job in the *SEC*, as there is no instate rival to compete with for recruits or glory. However, the fans are demanding, believing they belong right alongside Alabama with a ring on every finger. When Les showed up at Auburn that day, it had been nearly a decade since his National Championship and his seat, if not red hot, was smoldering.

After Auburn kicked a field goal in the first quarter, LSU answered with a touchdown. This was followed by two Auburn field goals in the second quarter, so that Auburn took a 9-7 lead into halftime. Following his daughter's advice, Malzahn's decision to trade his usual game-day visor for a cap appeared to be working. As for his relinquishing the offensive play-calling duties, the verdict was still out. At the end of the third quarter, things were tight as Auburn clung to a 13-12 lead.

Auburn, literally on the foot of Daniel Carlson's six field goals, led the game 18-13 with 2:56 remaining in the fourth quarter. At one point, my brother and I wondered if Carlson might be a number one draft pick, even as a kicker, as it was obvious his leg was, in actuality, a howitzer. After yet another kickoff through the endzone for a touchback, LSU started their final drive on the 25-yard line. Although quarterback Danny Etling had Leonard Fournette in the backfield, given little time on the clock, he proceeded to march the team down the field with pass after pass. With 1:17 remaining, he had managed to get his *Tigers* down to the other *Tigers'* 27-yard-line and then, with 28 seconds remaining, secured another first down at the Auburn 14-yard-line. After an incomplete pass on first down, Etling was sacked on second down, putting the ball back at the 20. LSU quickly called a timeout with 24 ticks remaining. On third and sixteen, Etling completed a 10-yard pass to the Auburn 10-yard line.

What happened next was surreal. LSU was called for an illegal shift, which resulted in the ball being placed at the 15-yard line and the clock stopping with 1 second remaining in the game. This made it fourth and 11 and created a situation where the clock would start once the teams were set. After the ball was placed on the field by the referee,

LSU scrambled quickly to the line of scrimmage. Etling took the snap and avoided the rush by scrambling to his right and throwing to DJ Chark in the corner of the endzone for an apparent game-winning touchdown. Chark, who seemingly dragged his toes in bounds, was mobbed by the entire LSU football team, along with *Mike*, the LSU Tiger mascot. For those watching at home, the television announcers cried out, "The Tigers roar. Ball game." As dejected Auburn players walked off the field, coach Malzahn could be seen motioning to the referees about something, all while Les Miles was pointing his team to the exits. At that point, we heard the referees announce that "the previous play is under review." The play was like a giant suitcase with a lot to unpack. Did the receiver make a clean catch? Was the LSU team set when the ball was snapped? Did the quarterback cross the line of scrimmage before he threw the pass? Did Leonard Fournette, running out as a receiver in the same corner of the endzone, and throwing a defender out of bounds, commit offensive interference? Would that even be reviewable?

None of the above. Within mere moments, the hometown *Tigers* roared as the referee announced, "After review, the ruling is that the offense did not get the snap off prior to the clock going to zero." He kept talking, but nobody could hear a thing as the place went crazy, with the Auburn team running to the opposite end zone and jumping into the stands. We were jumping up and down and hugging everyone around us while those watching at home heard the game announcers bark, "We have had a cataclysmic reversal on the field. Auburn is the victor. Have you ever seen such a swing of emotion?" Our answer is a resounding no!

After the game, the Auburn coach stated, "I was pretty confident time had expired." We concurred as the scoreboard was at "0.00" when the ball was snapped. Our questions, we dared not ask aloud, were why there was only 1 second to begin with and why did the clock start so fast? We will never know. These might not seem important, but in football and in life, mere seconds or inches can change the course of history. Less than 24 hours later, on Sunday afternoon, while we were heading home from another wonderful guy trip, Les Miles was fired as the head football coach at LSU. His offensive coordinator, Cam Cameron, was sent packing as well. Even though Miles had won 10 or more games in seven of his eleven full seasons and won 77% of his games, Baton Rouge had finally grown tired of his quirkiness and stubbornness. Yes, he won a National Championship, but in football, as in life, the question remains—what have you done for me lately? LSU announced that defensive line coach Ed Orgeron, a man now known and loved for his deep voice and mighty Cajun accent, would take over as the interim head coach for the remainder of the season. In time, Orgeron would be named head coach, meet a kid named Joe Burrow and win a National Championship in 2019.

Two weeks after our return from *the loveliest village on the Plain*, Daniel, my wife, and I gathered on the far sideline of the Woodridge High School football field. Dan was dressed in a blue blazer, button-down, dress shoes, and a pair of khakis. Maybe proper Southern football attire was finally wearing off on us—or at least on him. Of course, his mother had also insisted that we all be dressed appropriately for Daniel's introduction as part of the 2016 Homecoming Court. Our daughter was near the end zone and was dressed in her snappy—and incredibly suffocating—marching band uniform. My parents sat high atop the home bleachers. The weather felt borrowed from somewhere south of the Mason-Dixon line, as it was a hot, muggy evening, with dark, menacing clouds sketched along the horizon. As the three of us walked across the field, we basked in the glow of the setting sun.

The night before, we had asked Daniel if he had voted for himself and he said, "No." When we asked him who he had voted for, he said, "Jacob Malley. He's a great guy." We both chuckled and nodded our heads in agreement. Many of Daniel's senior classmates were incredibly good kids. There are too many to name and if I were to try, I would inadvertently forget one. Overall, the whole class had a special feel and when Dan was named the 2016 Woodridge Homecoming King, we were shocked but not surprised. He was given a green silk crown, which he proudly wore all night. Dan still has it. He is fond of reminding locals and strangers alike that the coveted crown was once his. The town paper acknowledged his victory, and the mayor sent him a congratulatory letter. However, later that same evening, as my wife worked in the concession stand during the game, she overheard a conversation regarding our son's victory. Apparently, the cheerleading squad had campaigned for Daniel to be the King. As several women discussed these events, one of them, while shaking her head and rolling her eyes, said, "Why do kids do things like that? How unfair to all the others on the Homecoming Court."

These are snapshots from the life of a parent of a disabled child. Any sweet bite is inevitably followed by a shot of vinegar, and had we known about Dad's summer visit to his oncologist, it would have been downright bitter. Although he kept the news to himself, he was told he had at most one to two years left to live. Earlier, before the school year had begun in earnest and before our trip to Auburn, our daughter had performed at a local band show at a nearby high school. These typically included a dozen or so bands, who ferociously supported each other with wild cheering during every single performance. These shows also included plenty of snacks, countless pin-wearing parents, and a flurry of supportive messages read over a loudspeaker by a commentator in the stadium press box. At one point, between performances and during a cloudless sunset, a voice called out from high atop the stadium for all to hear, "Claire, good luck this year. We love you. Granny and Grandpa." Those sweet words overpower any tart utterance, even in the twilight.

Tuscaloosa, Alabama

One solitary grey cloud—smallish but thick and defined—seemed to stop, then hover near the rim of the stadium before discreetly dipping out of sight forever. Otherwise, the untouched sky had turned the purest blue, orange, and yellow as we slumped into our early evening seats in the lower bowl of *Bryant-Denny Stadium*. The past week, to our chagrin, had brought about unexpected turbulence. Perhaps we had been naïve, as we had been warned we were in for a bumpy flight. Things had initially gone smoothly and, until now, tomorrow had always been tomorrow. The past week had changed all that. The empty seat was our reminder. Tomorrow had finally reached the shores of today, and we were all about to have to fasten our seatbelts.

Dad had always talked about seeing a game in Tuscaloosa. We all had. It was on our radar from the very beginning of the guy trips, but until this year, it had remained elusive for a host of reasons. First, the *Buckeyes* had duked it out with Alabama in 2015, and though we had finally gotten the better of the *Crimson Tide*, that Sugar Bowl battle still felt a little too fresh. Second, further clashes had initially felt inevitable given the two captains—Urban Meyer and Nick Saban—at the helm of their respective ships. Did we really want to cheer for a team that might very well break our hearts come playoff time? Lastly, up until now, the stars had not aligned as Alabama's home schedule had not overlapped with ours. But, make no mistake, Alabama was on our bucket list as it is synonymous with college football itself. Much like the Willie Nelson song goes, "It was always on our mind." A trip to see an Alabama game was not only desirable but inevitable. If you count their National Championships, you run out of fingers and must use your toes. You do! With 18 in total, they probably needed to build a separate museum just to store all those trophies. Saban is a household name, but then again, so are Paul "Bear" Bryant and Joe Namath. If you made a list of star football players who played for the University of Alabama, you would need to bring a banker's box of notebook paper. A quick glance in any NFL locker room is a testament to this statement. Championships are, after all, won by great players, not shabby ones. Heck, even *Forrest Gump* suited up for the *Crimson Tide*. Need we say more?

Finally, the stars had aligned, or so we thought. On October 14, 2017, we would see Alabama play Arkansas in an *SEC* clash in Tuscaloosa. No more excuses, and if Alabama steamrolled our *Buckeyes* later in the season, so be it. Obviously, the *Tide* dynasty was not fading any time soon, and a "rebuilding phase" might not happen until Nick Saban retired, which did not seem to be even remotely on the horizon. Then, several days before the game, as I was driving back to my office after an afternoon in court, I noticed I had several messages from my parents. Although things have loosened up a bit, especially since the Covid-19 pandemic, back in 2017, and not so long ago, you dared not have your phone go off when in court. This was bad for the client but considered an intolerable act by the lawyer. As such, I always tried to silence my phone once I retrieved it on the other side of the court's metal detector. In any event, the messages were cryptic but otherwise clear—please call right away.

Sitting in the parking lot outside my office, I nervously dialed my dad's number. Deep in my heart, I knew something bad must have happened, as multiple calls of an urgent nature are never good, right? Unless, by chance, someone in the family won the lottery! I still remember the first thing he said when he picked up: "Hey Jim, how was court? Did everything go alright?" After assuring him things had gone well, he then told me, "I'm sorry, I've got some bad news. I am down at the hospital. There is a great deal of blood in my urine, and I could barely walk, so your mom brought me down to have it checked out." Suddenly, I felt flushed. "Should I come down?" I asked. "No, no, please don't. There is nothing you could do anyway," he responded. My dad then continued, "The real reason I called was to tell you I'm probably not going to be able to make it to the Alabama game this weekend." At first, he chuckled, and then, growing more somber, he said, "I got so close, but it doesn't look like it's in the cards, especially with all the walking. Anyway, you need to promise me you will go and have a wonderful time with Daniel and your brother." Suddenly, I felt a level of sadness sweeping over me. I wanted to cry but dared not. Instead, I managed to respond in a quiet voice, "Dad, I don't know, the guy trips are the four of us, not the three of us." My father then switched gears and played the money angle, "No, you should go. I'd hate to see all the money go to waste. We already have the airline tickets, the hotel is booked, as is the rental car and, of course, the tickets to the game. I even purchased another parking pass this time." Reluctantly, I told him I would think about it and would call John after he had done so. Before hanging up, I asked him one last question, "Dad, is the blood related to your cancer?" I had no idea if it was a silly question, but, in retrospect, I suppose it was. His initial silence was followed by, "I think so. But right now, let's make sure you get to that Alabama game. I can't wait to hear all about it."

A nickname for the University of Alabama is *"The Capstone,"* derived from a speech given by then-President George H. Denny in 1913. A capstone is the top stone or high point, and Denny, who had become president the year prior, believed the school represented the capstone of public education for the state. Established in 1820 and opened to students in 1831, the campus was designed by architect William Nichols and, in 1838, the University became one of the first five universities in the United States to offer engineering classes. In 1865, on April 4th—my son's birthday—Union soldiers set the school ablaze, with only seven buildings being spared. The President's Mansion—a classic example of Greek Revival architecture in the South, which still serves as the president's on-campus residence today—was one of the buildings saved from destruction. Following the war, during the Reconstruction Era, a reorganized school was opened again to students in 1871. A great deal has happened on this campus and not all of it is pretty.

After flying to Birmingham, Alabama, we made the 58-mile drive to Tuscaloosa and our hotel just off campus. It was a cloudy and incredibly muggy evening, and after settling into our rooms, we set out for our annual Friday night dinner. Unfortunately, nobody in our family can remember the name of the place, as I'd love to give it more attention. We do recall that it was highly recommended, and the décor was beautiful, but that's about it. I also recall we just sat there dumbfounded at what had happened during the week leading up to the game. John kept repeating, "I can't believe Dad is not here." Trying to put a happy face on the situation felt forced, but we forged ahead for him and Daniel. At one point, we thought about calling Dad but decided against it. When the waiter arrived, things initially got worse, as when we tried to engage him in conversation about the *Crimson Tide* and the University of Alabama, he told us he knew little, having just moved from Ann Arbor and being a lifelong Michigan fan. Wow, what were the odds!? He was a good guy, and we all had a good laugh after we told him he was stuck with a table full of *Buckeyes.* He promised not to ignore us, and we promised to give him a good tip. Both sides lived up to their end of the bargain.

Following dinner, which was cut short by our low-level brooding, we went back to the hotel and chatted about Dad and our plans for the next day. We all had another good laugh when I pulled out the parking pass, recalling the Georgia parking pass and wondering if Dad had pulled off another coup. If nothing else, laughter does seem to help create a wonderful distraction, and we were happy for these momentary interruptions. Daniel was especially quiet most of the evening, but after seeing a smattering of Alabama fans and Arkansas fans in the hotel lobby, he told us he was ready to watch a little football, and he would tell his grandpa all about it when we got home. My brother, who Dan adores, also did his best to cheer him up.

Our parking pass placed us seemingly in the heart of Greek Row near campus, and, quite frankly, we were left stupefied by the size and the opulence of the houses. In fact, so impressive are these homes, *House Beautiful* featured a photo shoot in the May 23, 2023, issue with the deserving headline: *The 15 Most Outrageous University of Alabama Sorority Houses—These aren't your average college dorms."* Seriously, put down this book (I know it is hard), and look this up on the internet. For example, the *Phi Mu* house cost $13 million to build and is a 40,000-square-foot Neoclassical-style mansion. These structures are truly princess material and clearly magazine-worthy. I'm just wondering how they get anyone to leave after graduation! The University of Alabama boasts one of the largest networks of sororities and fraternities in the entire country. In fact, approximately 12,000 students, or 36% of the undergraduate body, are engaged in Greek life, and the school is home to 71 social Greek-letter organizations. Dan, my brother, and I were half-tempted to visit my old fraternity, just to peek, but we thought better of it, as we didn't want some young chap to feel obligated to give us a tour, all while his fraternity brothers were shooting hoops or diving into a swimming pool.

It just so happened to be homecoming weekend, and we, along with thousands of others, lined up along University Boulevard to watch the Homecoming Parade. This was when we got our first glimpse of *Big Al*, the costumed elephant mascot for the University of Alabama. The story of this pachyderm begins in 1930 when sportswriter Everett

Strupper, writing for the *Atlanta Journal* after watching the Alabama-Ole Miss game, noted the incredible size of the *Crimson Tide*. He described the scene as follows, "*... At the end of the quarter, the earth started to tremble, there was a distant rumble that continued to grow. Some excited fan in the stands bellowed, 'Hold your horses, the elephants are coming,' and out stamped this Alabama varsity.*" Other writers soon joined in by referring to the offensive lineman as "red elephants." Still, although the undefeated 1930 team was declared the national champions after a 24-0 win over Washington in the Rose Bowl, the elephant did not become the official mascot until *Big Al* made his debut in the 1979 Sugar Bowl.

Like many schools, Alabama's first known mascots appear to have been dogs. The first pooch, dating back to 1894, appears to have been a stray that was taken in by students. Where have we heard this story before? In 1921, a sad story appeared in the *Tuscaloosa News*, describing the death of the school mascot "*Pat,*" a "fine English bulldog," who "gave so much pleasure to the students at the University." In 1931, despite being referred to as elephants, several Alabama alumni from Phoenix presented the school with a little burro during the team's visit to the Rose Bowl. The donkey was purportedly named *Poison*. Later, starting in the 1940s, the school acquired a live elephant, which was housed on campus and originally named *Alamite*. The elephant would lead the homecoming parade, and later, the queen would ride into the stadium on the head of *Alamite*. Housing the large animal proved costly and impractical, and starting in the mid-1950s, the school began to rent the animal—presumably from a nearby circus or zoo—for game days.

After several failed attempts to secure another live elephant to reside on campus, a group of students created a costumed mascot. The first to don a giant fiberglass pink head was Melford Espey, Jr., but by most accounts, it was not well received. In fact, the costume bordered on the bizarre, and when the University of Alabama squared up against the University of Miami for an away game, a local paper referred to the mascot as a weird pink elephant "if that's what you can call it." The poor creature was the stuff of nightmares, and barely a child would be brave enough to wander near it. To make matters worse, the new coach, Paul "Bear" Bryant, is said to have told Espey, "never to let that big red rat anywhere near (him)." Besides the creepy factor, Bryant and past coaches had never been overly enamored with an elephant as a mascot anyway, as most thought it would result in the team being portrayed as big, slow, and clumsy. Nobody wanted to cross a coach, especially the Bear, so the mascot often stayed far away from the coach, the team, and those frightened children.

Creating lovable and, yes, quite approachable characters is how the Walt Disney Company has built an empire. *Big Al*, the elephant mascot we saw leading the Homecoming Parade, was originally the brainchild of University of Alabama student Walt Tart, who, as a member of Tau Kappa Epsilon fraternity, met with chairwoman Ann Paige to come up with something different for the 1979 Homecoming. Thereafter, he reached out to other schools in the *SEC* and discovered several mascots had been designed and constructed with the help of a little Disney magic. Tart and Paige then worked up their courage to approach Bryant, who was not only the head football coach but also the athletic director for the University, who had the final say. The coach readily approved of the lovable pachyderm, if anything, to be done with the predecessor's fiberglass pink head. The name was chosen through a student vote, in honor of the original *Alamite* and a popular local DJ on campus, Al Brown. *Alamite* would be glad to learn that *Tide for Tusks* was established as a student organization and a non-profit to raise awareness of the poaching of African elephants and fund efforts for elephant conservation in partnership with conservation groups in Africa. The organization also supports scholarly research in undergraduate, graduate, and post-graduate studies at the University of Alabama.

Marching behind *Big Al* and the Alabama Cheerleaders—with the Dance Team and Spirit Squad—was the 400-member *Million Dollar*

Band from the University of Alabama. Although the band was founded in 1912 with just 14 members, the legendary name is believed to have originated in 1922 following a *Crimson Tide* loss to the Georgia Tech *Yellow Jackets*, 33-7. After the game, a reporter asked a prominent Alabama supporter, "What does Alabama have?" His response was, apparently, "A Million Dollar Band." Hearing this story is reminiscent of when Ohio State won the National Championship against the University of Miami in January of 2003. After the game, when asked to comment about the win, Coach Tressel responded by saying, "We always had the best damn band in the land. Now we've got the best damn team in the land." Bands are indeed a source of great pride at most universities.

Behind Alabama's band was the homecoming court, followed by a barrage of elaborate floats, one after another, from sororities, fraternities, and university clubs. The parade was truly a spectacle rivaling any St. Patrick's or Thanksgiving Day parade. Dan loved it, mainly due to his front-row seat and plenty of attention from the sorority floats.

Earlier that same day, we had dined at a local establishment for lunch. Although I cannot recall the name of the restaurant, I most certainly remember the patrons. We had struck up a conversation with a few locals, and once they learned we were visitors, suggestions for how we should spend the afternoon flowed like beer from the taps behind the bar. At one point, after our new friends asked the bartender for a pen and a sheet of paper, maps were drawn for us with times and locations for pre-game activities. These moments might seem insignificant, but they are the essence of what we believe makes the games so special. That is, experiences are most enjoyed when shared with others, and community is never finite. It is also how we learned the parade was a "must-see."

Following our freshly drawn maps, much like pirates searching for buried treasure, we eventually made our way into *The Quad* for a little tailgating and window shopping. We also managed to purchase bags full of local merchandise, including a khaki-colored baseball cap for

Dad with the classic crimson *"A"* on the front. Next, about an hour before kickoff, we made our way over to the Gorgas Library, also located in *The Quad*, to hear the *Million Dollar Band* perform "*Yea, Alabama*" and "*Rammer Jammer*" in a spirited performance generally known as *"The Elephant Stomp."* Dan loved it, as he not only got to hear the band but, along the way, managed to pose in a few pictures with a few of its tender-hearted members. He also managed to get front and center in a picture with a dozen or so cheer squad members. Dan really is "*The Man.*" Lastly, we enjoyed several sightings of a large mechanical elephant operated by the university's theatre department meandering through campus and resembling a Broadway contraption—in look and movement—from *The Lion King*. It was a rather elegant elephant, to be sure, but aren't they all?

Bryant-Denny Stadium stands like a European castle. As you approach this behemoth structure, you cannot help but feel a sense of wonder, especially knowing all that has taken place inside this southern cathedral. Opened in 1929, it was originally named *Denny Stadium* in honor of George H. Denny, the school's president from 1912 to 1932, and later, in 1975, the state legislature added longtime coach and alumnus Paul "Bear" Bryant to the stadium's name. Interestingly, Bryant continued with the Alabama football program through 1982, making him one of only a handful of Division I coaches to have coached in a stadium bearing his name. From 1929 to 1945, the stadium had a capacity of only 12,000, and when Bryant retired as head coach, the capacity stood at 59,000. When we entered the stadium in 2017, the capacity stood at 101,821, but following renovations in 2020, the capacity shrank slightly to 100,077. Surprisingly, it is only the fourth-largest stadium in the *SEC*, but as a testament to the popularity of football in the South, it is still the eighth-largest stadium in the United States and the tenth-largest stadium in the world.

Roll Tide

No other state has been maligned like Alabama, with maybe the exception of Arkansas, West Virginia, and Mississippi. Remember when Bill Clinton ran for President and in the early Democratic primary debate, was made out to be a total hick? I do. Remember, more recently, when discussing border security and national politics, certain political pundits and talk show hosts joked about a wall being needed to keep West Virginians out of northern Virginia? Funny how they mixed up who was who during the Civil War, but, hey, whatever. As for Mississippi, much was discussed about this previously during our visit to Oxford, Mississippi, and Ole Miss, but it is no secret that the *Magnolia State* has long been the punchline in nearly every clichéd joke. For whatever reason, many self-professed elites have also taken specific aim at Alabama as being particularly isolated, poor, and otherwise backward. It holds a special disdain that goes way back. In fact, in 1900, a journalist for the *New York Journal* wrote the following, "A *Hill-Billie* is a free and untrammeled white citizen of *Alabama*, who lives in the hills, has no means to speak of, dresses as he can, talks as he pleases, drinks whiskey when he gets it, and fires off his revolver as the fancy takes him." There you have it. The first known use of the phrase "hillbilly" took specific aim at the citizens of Alabama.

Southerners are acutely aware of these attitudes. How could they not be? It permeates nearly everything in our national discourse, and there is no better place to feel and hear their response—loud and clear—than by attending an *SEC* football game where music and ritual seamlessly blend with a sense of pride. The result is a series of Southern anthems sung with gusto by her faithful parishioners. For example, during a typical home game at the University of Tennessee in Knoxville, you will hear the Osborne Brothers classic, "*Rocky Top,*" sung no less than 100 times. At least! We know, as we eventually got there for a game. Listen to the lyrics, and you understand the pride they feel for where they live, along with the final verse which takes a parting shot at life elsewhere: *"I've had years of cramped-up city life / Trapped like a duck in a pen; / All I know is it's a pity life / Can't be simple again / Rocky Top, you'll always be / home sweet home to me; / Good ol' Rocky Top; / Rocky Top, Tennessee / Rocky Top, Tennessee."* I swear I still hear it in my head when I doze off to sleep. Thanks, Todd! Author Eric Bain-Selbo explores these themes in greater detail in *Game Day and God-Football, Faith, and Politics in the American South,* which makes for a fascinating read.

In Tuscaloosa, they have their own Southern anthem—*Lynyrd Skynyrd's* classic and equally out-of-this-world catchy— "*Sweet Home Alabama.*" It seems an obvious choice, especially since the chorus is tailor-made for home games at the University of Alabama. However, if you listen beyond the chorus and delve further into the lyrics, there is much more going on than originally meets the ear. This song is a bone-crunching uppercut landing squarely on the jaw of fellow musicians who just so happened to have thrown the first swing. Beware of the counterpunch, as in this case, it may just become a never-ending mega-hit.

To further explain, especially for those who are younger, Neil Young wrote a song in 1970 called "*Southern Man.*" For those not old enough to recall this tune or who have never even heard it, Young wrote it as a condemnation of bigotry in the Southern United States.

However, the song's title paints with an overly broad brush—while inexplicably excluding Southern women from condemnation, and the lyrics—meant to show hypocrisy among Southern whites—take a gratuitous shot at persons of faith with the line: "*Don't forget / what* ***your*** *good book said*."

First recorded in 1974, Lynyrd Skynyrd's *"Sweet Home Alabama"* is a musical reply to Neil Young and others and the relentless criticism of the entire region and all her folk. Although Young was by no means the first to offer condemnation, his song was seen as another example of piling on after the whistle had blown. In response, the lines, *"In Birmingham they love the governor / Now we all did what we could do,"* acknowledge the political shortcomings in Alabama and with segregationist George Wallace, while pointing out that many people did not agree and acted against bigotry. The song also makes clear that hypocrisy and immorality run throughout humanity and are not unique to the South: "*Now Watergate does not bother me / Does your conscience bother you? / Tell the truth?"* Lastly, the song strikes a defiant note: "*Well I heard Mister Young sing about her / Well, I heard ol' Neil put her down / Well, I hope Neil Young will remember / A southern man don't need him around anyhow."* Ouch! Now, to be fair, Neil Young—who has long woven social issues into his craft—has declared the song was meant to be about the civil rights movement and has otherwise apologized by stating, "I don't like my words when I listen to it."

Regardless of how it came to be, *Sweet Home Alabama* is now a classic southern anthem regularly played at *Bryant-Denny* stadium, with the fans joyfully singing: *"Sweet home Alabama (ROLL TIDE ROLL) / Where the skies are so blue / Sweet home Alabama (ROLL TIDE ROLL) / Lord, I'm coming home to you."* Speaking of *Roll Tide Roll*, it is said more often than "hello" during a football Saturday in Tuscaloosa. It is relentless and, not surprisingly, utterly despised outside of Tuscaloosa, but what does it signify? The rallying cry is believed to have started in 1907 by journalist Hugh Roberts from the Birmingham Age-Herald, who, during awful weather conditions, described the field in a game against Auburn as a *"crimson tide."* The mud on the field had apparently turned the white Alabama uniforms crimson due to the iron-rich soil in Alabama, and when the team ran together back onto the field, it was said the team looked like the tide rolling in. In the end, the team got a new name, and the fans were given a new cheer. Before then, the team was known as *The Thin Red Line*. We can all agree the powerful Alabama team would not be the same with a constant chant of *Roll Thin Red,* right?

On the first offensive play of the game, Damien Harris rumbled down the field for a 75-yard touchdown run. It was quite a start to our Saturday night and for the *Crimson Tide*. The Alabama football team, which entered *Bryant-Denny Stadium* 6-0 and ranked #1 in the country, steamrolled the Arkansas *Razorbacks* 41-9 to remain perfect for the 2017 season. The rushing game and the overall physicality of the *Crimson Tide* created a world of hurt for the *Razorbacks*, and nearly all the 101,821 on hand loved it. While Alabama rushed for over 300 yards, Arkansas could only manage to eke out a paltry 27 yards for the entire game. Before the game, we had gotten close to the field and had watched the Arkansas team as they went through their warm-ups. At one point, my brother looked at me and said, "They look terrified." Simultaneously, we both chuckled and said, "Wouldn't you?" Here they were, playing away from home in an enormous stadium—akin to the Roman Coliseum—before one hundred thousand fans and against a beast of a team. Furthermore, there was no quick way out, as, unlike a prize fight that can be called at any time, the *Razorbacks* could not simply lie on the canvas and hope to hear the bell. No, they would have to go the full 60 minutes before being allowed to escape the Roman Empire. If the stadium did not intimidate every Arkansas player, Alabama's entrance most certainly did. As a *Buckeye*, I know it sure scared the heck out of me. At the opposite tunnel, the *Crimson*

Tide did not run onto the field; instead, in a sign of total confidence, they walked out onto the field together, many with arms folded.

Starting at quarterback for Alabama was Jalen Hurts. His backup, Tua Tagovailoa, got in at the end of the game and managed to complete one of two passes in mop-up duty. Hurts completed 12 of 19 passes for 155 yards, with one touchdown and one interception that came in the third quarter. It was his first pick in 206 consecutive passes and was Alabama's second-longest streak without such a mishap. He also ran the ball for 41 yards on 10 carries. At the time, we had no idea that these two quarterbacks were on a collision course with destiny that would unfold before the entire country in just a few short months.

The Alabama team we saw that night was one year removed from a heart-wrenching 35-31 loss to Clemson in the National Championship. Trailing by 10 points going into the fourth quarter, Clemson scored three touchdowns in the final fifteen minutes, including a 2-yard winning touchdown pass from Deshaun Watson to Hunter Renfrow with one second left in the game. Jalen Hurts had thrown for 131 yards, including one touchdown pass, and 63 yards rushing on 10 carries. However, his biggest run came on a 30-yard scamper, which momentarily was the go-ahead touchdown with 2:07 remaining. Hurts had put in a workman-like performance for Alabama, but all the glory that night belonged to Watson, who threw for 420 yards, including a clutch throw in the final moments to win the game. Interestingly, Clemson's coach Dabo Swinney, whose team had suffered a stunning loss to Syracuse the night before, was on hand at our game with other members of Alabama's 1992 championship team. Although Dabo received a warm reception, especially given the heartbreaking loss he inflicted upon the Alabama faithful the year before, the biggest applause was reserved for former head coach and apprentice to Paul "Bear" Bryant—Gene Stallings. We stood for the former coach, who is a hero in our family, but more about that later.

Despite losing the National Championship, Jalen Hurts completed a historic freshman season with the *Crimson Tide*, throwing for

2,780 yards and 23 touchdowns with only nine interceptions. He also rushed for 954 yards and 13 touchdowns, and after completing 75% of his passes in the Iron Bowl against Auburn, he ultimately took an undefeated team to the big dance. Coming into the 2017 season, as just a sophomore, he was in complete command of the team. After Alabama dismantled Arkansas, they rattled off another four straight wins, upping their record to 11-0. This was followed by a disappointing loss to Auburn in the Iron Bowl, but after Georgia returned the favor by defeating Auburn in the *SEC* Championship, Alabama squeaked into the College Football Playoff (CFP) as the number 4 seed. Their first opponent, as fate would have it, would be the number one-ranked Clemson *Tigers*. This time, Jalen Hurts would not have to duel with Deshaun Watson, and after going 16-24 for 120 yards and throwing a pair of touchdowns, the sophomore took his team to back-to-back National Championship games with a convincing 24-6 win. Their opponent would be the Georgia *Bulldogs*.

Jalen Hurts entered the National Championship game against the *Bulldogs* with an impressive 26-2 record and was the reigning *SEC* Offensive Player of the Year. As for Alabama, it was their third straight appearance on the biggest stage. However, after Hurts went just 3 of 8 in passing for a meager 21 yards, the mighty Alabama team we had watched earlier in the season found themselves trailing Georgia 13-0 at the end of the first half. Head coach Nick Saban, after conferring with his staff, including offensive coordinator Mike Locksley, did the seemingly unthinkable by pulling Hurts and replacing him with freshman phenom Tua Tagovailoa. Although the quarterbacks were informed in the locker room, many players were unaware until the Crimson Tide took the field for their first offensive series.

The freshman, who up to that point had only seen mop-up duty at the end of games, already settled as Alabama victories, entered the National Championship, and played like a senior captain, showing no signs of any freshman jitters. Tua went 14 of 24, but more importantly, threw three touchdowns, including a game-winning 41-yard dart in overtime on 2nd and 26 to fellow freshman Devonta Smith. One year after a crushing defeat on the last play of the game, Alabama won the National Championship 26-23 on the final play. In the process, the coaching staff had set in motion a quarterback controversy that would put two teammates on divergent paths. After being benched in the National Championship, Hurts lost the starting job to Tagovailoa the following season. Then, in a reversal of fortunes, after Tua exited the *SEC* Championship with an ankle injury, Hurts was given the chance to attempt a come-from-behind win against the Georgia *Bulldogs*. With the script reversed, Hurts tied the game with a touchdown pass to Jerry Jeudy and then scored the go-ahead touchdown on a 15-yard run to lift the *Tide* to a 35-28 victory. However, after sitting on the bench for most of the pummeling inflicted upon Alabama by the Clemson *Tigers* in Alabama's fourth consecutive National Championship appearance, Jalen Hurts announced his transfer to Oklahoma, where he would ultimately finish second to Joe Burrow in the Heisman trophy balloting the following year. Today, Jalen Hurts is the starting quarterback for the Philadelphia Eagles, while Tua Tagovailoa is the starting quarterback for the Miami Dolphins. In retrospect, Saban benched one NFL quarterback for another. These are the difficult decisions faced at an elite football program, such as the University of Alabama. Some might call it "first-world problems."

The Trifecta

At some point during our game, we decided to take a stroll around *Bryant-Denny Stadium,* and surprisingly, we were able to walk at field level behind the Alabama football team. For obvious reasons, the team and benches were roped off from our path, but it was fun to be so close to the players and the action. And then, that's when we saw him. Dressed in a white long-sleeve collared *Nike* shirt with a crimson "A" on the left breast, pleated khaki pants, a big black watch on his left hand, and a headset, he was the head coach of the Alabama football team. Short by football standards, with brown hair combed straight back, he paced back and forth with folded arms. Alabama was up big, but Nick Saban, in full-blown teacher-coach mode, still looked agitated. In two weeks, the legendary coach we gawked at would turn 66 years old, and just months after that, he would win, in part by his bold decision to switch quarterbacks, his fifth National Championship for the *Crimson Tide.*

Nick Saban was born in Fairmont, West Virginia, on October 31, 1951. Fairmont sits just southwest of Morgantown and the Pennsylvania border, in a region—parts of Ohio, Pennsylvania, and West Virginia—generally considered the geographical cradle of American football coaches. The lines drawn to demarcate such a region, if it really exists beyond imagination, might need to be redrawn using a mechanical compass, with Fairmont in the dead center of it, as Saban not only chased the Bear but caught him and then passed him, at least in my humble opinion. If any college football fan disagrees, including Florida State fans who must surely have Bobby Bowden on the tip of their tongue or Nebraska fans who love Tom Osborne, let me ask one simple question. If your team could have Nick Saban as the head coach in the modern world of college football as it exists today, rather than in the past, especially in his prime, would you take him? If you're still undecided, let me put this into perspective. As an Ohio State football fan and alumnus, I generally believe that the *Buckeyes* have won nine National Championships. Now, consider who some of our coaches were over this nearly one-hundred-year period: Paul Brown, Woody Hayes, Jim Tressel, Urban Meyer, and Ryan Day. In case you are wondering, Woody won 5 of those nine championships in his 28 years as head coach at Ohio State. Nick Saban, on the other hand, has 7 in total, with 6 of those at the University of Alabama. This he did in a fraction of the time.

For those who do not agree, I get it. You don't believe Saban caught the Bear or passed him. I respect the holdouts. But let's all agree on at least one thing: it really is a two-horse race between Nick Saban and Paul "Bear" Bryant as the best college football coach of all time. No disrespect to Woody, Bobby, or Tom, but these two legendary Alabama coaches not only brought a dozen National Championships to Tuscaloosa but also made it the center of the college football universe. Bryant, who was born in Moro Bottom, Arkansas, on September 11, 1913, became the head coach at Alabama in 1958. Fresh off a successful campaign as the head football coach at Texas A&M, Bryant returned to Tuscaloosa, where he had been an end for the *Tide* from 1933 to 1935. When asked about the abrupt decision that quite frankly left the *Aggies* more than a little stunned, Paul Bryant said, "The only reason I'm going back, is because ...Momma called. And when Momma calls, you have to come runnin."

While Paul Bryant rolled into town in a white Cadillac, dust-covered from the 650-mile trek from College Station, Nick Saban arrived at the Tuscaloosa Regional Airport on January 3, 2007, via a private jet. Forty-eight hours before, Mal Moore—Alabama's athletic director—had embarked on a stealth flight to southern Florida with the mission of convincing Saban to become the head football coach for the *Crimson Tide*. Less than two weeks before, Saban, who was the head football coach at the Miami *Dolphins*, made no mention of "momma" calling, and when asked if he had any comment about his rumored departure to Alabama, he said, "I guess I have to say it. I'm not going to be the coach at Alabama..." He would soon regret this statement, and it would take years for many fans to forgive him. Many still have not. The thing is, he may have really meant it when he said it.

Mal Moore had previously struck out luring Steve Spurrier to Alabama, and when he thought he had crafted a deal with Rich Rodriguez at West Virginia, the *Mountaineer* coach backed out in the 11th hour. Moore was reeling and needed a splash hire, and although he was not "momma," he happened upon another weapon to make Nick come "running" to Alabama—Nick's wife—Terry. As luck would have it, Saban was at the *Dolphins* headquarters when Moore came a-calling at the Saban home. By the time Nick showed up, Terry and Mal had chatted for over an hour, and the former Alabama quarterback and Bear Bryant recruit had already formed a solid bond with the coach's wife. Moore wanted to hire a new big-name coach, whereas Terry just wanted her husband to be happy. Both agreed to do everything possible to ensure he was on the flight to Tuscaloosa.

Paul "Bear" Bryant and Nick Saban are seemingly opposites. Saban, usually dressed in sportswear and khakis, looks nothing like his predecessor, whose suits and trademark hat are still worn by faithful fans to this day. When you think about Alabama fashion, you can't help but see houndstooth, but it is doubtful that you imagine a windbreaker and khakis. Bryant was over six feet tall, even without the hat. Nick, not so much. Saban can certainly be intimidating, but

Bryant was one tough son of a gun. In fact, one afternoon, Paul and his teenage friends found themselves at the *Lyric Theatre* in downtown Fordyce, where a traveling carnival had set up nearby. One attraction featured a black bear in a cage, and the owner was offering a dollar a minute to anyone willing to wrestle the bear on the *Lyric Stage*. At the urging of his friends but also hoping to impress a reddish-blond girl named Drucilla Smith, Paul agreed to the fight. In front of a packed 200-seat theatre, the young man was alone on stage with the muzzled bear, and after charging the bear and pinning the animal to the ground, the owner entered the fracas and removed the muzzle. The teenager managed to pin the bear a second time, but after the bear escaped his clutches, he felt a burning sensation on the back of his ear. The bear had finally fought back by biting the young Bryant on the back of his ear. The bear then became much more menacing, flashing his teeth and growling. Paul knew his time on stage was over, so he jumped into the first row of seats, much to the delight of the crowd. Paul never got paid, as the owner skipped town following the theatrics. However, Paul Bryant had earned much more than a dollar. He had earned a lifelong nickname—*Bear*.

Both men had one unexpected thing in common. Both inherited, perhaps surprisingly, lethargic *Crimson Tide* football programs. The Bear's predecessor, J.B. Whitworth, who coached the team from 1955 to 1957, had an abysmally poor record of 4-24-2 during his tenure. Saban's predecessor, Mike Shula, finished the 2006 season with a 6-6 record, and although his overall record was 26-23, he had been on the sideline for five consecutive losses to Auburn. Furthermore, since the Bear's retirement in 1982, Alabama secured just one National Championship in 1992 under coach Gene Stallings. In both instances, the school was seeking a significant turnaround in its fortunes, and ultimately, both men delivered. All coaches like winning, but Bryant and Saban shared another characteristic—they both despised losing.

They also knew how to recruit players. Bryant, known for his folksy style, was beloved by the parents of recruits and soon developed one of the most comprehensive recruiting programs in the nation. Bryant preached the importance of character building and education to the parents, promising a winning football team to the lads. This would be accomplished the old-fashioned way—through hard work and relentless, if not brutal, practice. Saban, although not known for smoking cigarettes or shouting instructions from a bullhorn atop a tower, shared another commonality with the Bear. Practice for his players was not meant to be easy, either. Although not as gut-wrenchingly hard as the Bear's workouts, Saban demanded players surrender entirely to detail and process. This might be equally exhausting in its own way and, although Saban may not have made the same impression on the parents of recruits as Bryant did by doing dishes or helping to straighten a kitchen after dinner at a recruit's home, his recruiting mastery is equally legendary. Besides winning college football games, Saban could offer young athletes something the Bear never could—the chance to become filthy rich.

In the end, Paul "Bear" Bryant finished his career with an overall record of 323-85-17. This record also includes stints at the helm of Maryland, Kentucky, and Texas A&M. At Alabama, his record was 232-46-9. He helped bring seven National Championships to the university, as he played in one and was the head coach for six more. In the end, Nick Saban has seemingly finished his college football career with an overall record of 292-71-1. This record includes stints at the helm of the University of Toledo, Michigan State, and LSU. At Alabama, his record was 206-29. Although he never won a National Championship as a player, like the Bear, he won 6 for the University of Alabama as the head football coach. He also won 1 National Championship as head coach at LSU. On second thought, maybe it comes down to a coin toss between the two, and for Woody, Bobby, Walter, Tom, Frank, Knute, John, Bernie, Bo, Fielding, Pop, Urban, Jim, Pete, Lou, Bud, Eddie, Ken, Larry, Steve, Dabo, Barry, Mike, Don, LaVell, Amos, Hayden, Mack, Bill or even Joe supporters, who believe I might have spoken rashly, tell me what you got!

If Alabama does not surely have the two greatest coaches of all time, they still have my family's absolute favorite. In our world, the *Crimson Tide* hit the trifecta, with Gene Stallings sitting alone at the top. As a talented player and a great coach, his personal story makes him a rock star in our eyes. In fact, the same goes for his entire family and, although we have never met, we consider them part of our own.

Long before my son was born, Gene Stallings became part of football lore when, along with a band of college teammates from Texas A&M, he attended a camp in 1954 in the small Hill Country town of Junction, Texas. Later known as *the Junction Boys,* these players endured a grueling 10-day boot camp with daily temperatures topping 100 degrees. The new coach at Texas A&M was Paul "Bear" Bryant, and he had set out to "separate the quitters from the keepers." The result of this experiment is now the stuff of legends. Although many players did not finish camp, Stallings did, and when his new coach discussed football techniques, he would write down everything Bryant said with a stub of a pencil on a small notepad that he stuck in the waistband of his football pants.

Later, and long before my son was born, Gene Stallings became a part of coaching lore when he became the Head Coach at Texas A&M and later won two National Championships as an assistant coach at Alabama in 1961 and 1964. He also won the Super Bowl as an assistant for the Dallas Cowboys under head coach Tom Landry. Lastly, he further solidified his Alabama lore when, as head coach, he led the *Crimson Tide* to another National Championship in the 1992 season. This team, along with their coach, was the team we saw honored at halftime of the Arkansas game, and I just wish I could have found a way to sneak onto the field to shake his hand, or, given the way we were all feeling, wrap him in a big old hug.

For you see, long before my son was born, Gene Stallings and his family became a part of advocacy lore. Their journey on this most noble front began on June 11, 1962, with the birth of their son, John Mark. Shortly after his birth, Gene and his wife, Ruth Ann, were told by a doctor at the hospital their son was a "mongoloid," and the couple should consider having him institutionalized. Professionals and friends alike told them it would be "easier on the family" and that "the baby will become such a burden to (their) girls." Many families at the time, overwhelmed, either had their disabled children institutionalized or otherwise kept out of the public eye, and as for Down syndrome, it remained taboo. Flooded with feelings of guilt, shame, and isolation, the couple did not know what to do or where to turn. Quite frankly, and speaking from personal experience, those feelings of isolation never truly subside. In 1962, resources were limited, and guidance was hard to find. To make matters worse, Johnny was born with a congenital heart defect known as "Eisenmenger's syndrome," and the couple was told he probably would not survive long.

Based on our own previously mentioned experiences following the birth of our son in 1998, the medical profession still has plenty of room for improvement in the handling of parents and children born with disabilities such as Down syndrome. However, nobody ever told us our son was a "mongoloid" and should be institutionalized, and unlike the Stallings, we were never told our son would never walk or talk. We were just told, "He would never achieve any higher education," while we endured a "teardrop" sign placed on the door of the delivery room. Whatever, and really? But, unlike the coach, I was never told my son would hinder my chances of being a successful lawyer. Many others, throughout the first half of the 20th century, having been given horrible advice and having no other place to turn, did what they were told was best for the child and parent. For those countless parents, you are without blame.

Thankfully, the Stallings—along with many other unnamed parents across the country—stood firm. An institution was not an option, and slowly, in time, these children would no longer remain hidden from the public. Isolation would be replaced with stimulation, and exclusion would be replaced with inclusion. Around this same time, a national spotlight was aimed at the deplorable conditions of many institutions and into the longing eyes of those previously forgotten souls.

As for Johnny, he learned to walk and talk, and while his heart condition would forever terrify his parents, he became an otherwise healthy and productive young man. Not surprisingly, he also became his father's best friend. Johnny also found work, including a stint as a tour guide at the *Bear Bryant Museum* on the University of Alabama campus, where he no doubt shared many "inside" stories of the *Crimson Tide* and his other favorite coach. In time, Gene Stallings became an outspoken advocate for individuals with special needs and filmed a public service announcement for the United Way in 1987 alongside his son. *The Stallings Center*, as part of the *RISE* program, opened on November 20, 1994, on campus and is dedicated to early childhood education for children with varying abilities, including traditional learners. In 1997, the year before my son was born, Stallings wrote *Another Season-A Coach's Story of Raising an Exceptional Son.* Penned as a love story from a father to his son, the parallels between his experiences and ours are uncanny, and his book is, in part, a further inspiration for this writing.

Returning Home

Following a game or in the waning moments of the contest, we typically pose for a stadium picture with all the guys. Not only are they "proof of game," but they make for great mementos and *Facebook* post material. Even though I do not always manage to get one, my brother has usually managed to enlist a neighboring fan in this endeavor. After the Alabama game, we did our obligatory shot from the sideline. After assuring an unknown fan—turned—volunteer photographer that the shot "looked great," we turned to each other in a group mope. The image was woefully incomplete without Dad. Moments later, Daniel decided to call his grandfather, and, although cell phone reception is typically horrible inside stadiums, we were able to FaceTime him. My brother, thinking quickly on his feet, realized that if we turned his phone towards us in a selfie, we could also capture our dad in the stadium shot if my son kept him on FaceTime and faced his phone towards the camera. The picture is far from perfect, but we managed to get all of us in the shot, and it is one of our all-time favorite pictures from the guy trips. Dad may not have made the game, but through the power of technology, he did manage to join us inside the stadium.

Getting home from Tuscaloosa was bittersweet. Although sad about our dad's absence, the three of us managed to soak up the

Alabama football experience as best we could under the circumstances. My brother and I will always remember the wonderful hospitality the local fans showed us. As a father who was hurting, I am especially indebted to all the kind acts and tender gestures directed towards Daniel. There was so much our dad would have enjoyed about the trip and, although it provided us with a fleeting distraction, we could not help but feel guilty for going without him. Yet, on the other hand, we knew he would love to hear our stories and to see our pictures. It seemed doubly unfair to him if we downplayed the whole thing. So, we played it up as best we could without overdoing it. When we got home, Daniel told his grandfather, "It was the best guy trip ever," although we all knew—including my son—that it wasn't. How could it be? My mom later told me Dad was devastated about not being able to go. Later, he had considered flying down to surprise us, but he knew he couldn't possibly make it work. For the first time, a twinge of resignation had crept into his mind.

Dad was ultimately diagnosed with bladder cancer, in addition to his prostate cancer and metastatic bone cancer. A month after our Alabama trip, he was given a nephrostomy tube, which is essentially a "thin" catheter going directly from one's kidneys to a bag. In time, he would be given a second tube. The dressings needed to be changed frequently, which required a weekly visit to yet another medical provider, in addition to his oncologist. While some patients find little discomfort with the nephrostomy apparatus, these suckers gave my dad fits. One day, he told my mother that when he felt better, he was going to "figure out a way to fix these blasted tubes." Always an engineer! He was so clever that nobody doubted him. In fact, another day, around the same time, I noticed he was staring at the ceiling, so I asked him what he was thinking about. He told me he was trying to visualize a pulley system to run along the top of his office, which would help make it easier for him to get around. He said his arms still felt fine, so why not put them to use?

Since my father had received radiation treatment previously, it was no longer an arrow in his quiver against cancer. Accordingly, his oncologist referred him to a specialist to discuss bladder surgery. This was sometime in November. I accompanied my parents to Dad's appointment and was reminded of my own aging, as the doctor was at least ten years my junior. He was also a very confident young man as well. He assured my father he could successfully do bladder surgery, but then he said something I was not prepared to hear. First, he said, "The bladder cancer is behind the other cancers in development and will probably never catch up." Initially, I saw the sense in this comment and nodded in agreement with my parents. However, he then continued, "Although I can do it, do you really want to spend your last days recuperating from surgery?" Speaking like a young guy with plenty of time hopefully ahead of him, not only was it bleak, but for the first time, it sounded like cancer had the upper hand, and it was the latter stage of the war. Later that night, "Your Last Days" played over and over in my head. Suddenly, I was afraid, and that night, as I lay in bed, I openly wept and begged God to give Dad a cure.

Three weeks after we had returned from Alabama—on November 4, 2017—our family gathered on a couch in the great room of my house to watch the #3 Ohio State *Buckeyes* battle the Iowa *Hawkeyes* in Iowa City, Iowa. Gathering at the house on Ohio State football Saturdays was a regular occurrence with cut-out cookies, chicken wings, and whatever else Daniel and his mother had cooked up during the days before. It was a cloudy day, and most of the leaves on the nearby trees had turned brown or had already littered my yard. At one point, as we watched the game, the cameras panned up from field level at *Kinnick Stadium* to reveal the *University of Iowa Stead Family Children's Hospital*, which directly overlooks the stadium. It was then, like much of the nation, that we were first introduced to a new tradition where fans, players, and coaches stop at the end of the first quarter and wave at children and their parents, who wave back from their hospital windows. Some had signs, and many had little shaved heads. Before the game, Urban Meyer and the Ohio State team had indicated their desire to participate in this wonderful new tradition. Although the game was tied 10-10 at the time, my dad, with tear-filled eyes, looked over at me and said, "Oh boy, we're screwed, and maybe that is alright." Several hours later, after Ohio State had been pummeled 55-24, we talked about going to an Iowa game when he felt better. We both instinctively recognized the *Hawkeye* faithful had not only created a beautiful football tradition but also had constructed a large window looking straight into our very souls. It was also obvious Texas A&M and *the 12th Man* now had some serious competition as to the best tradition in college football, and had we known about Boston College and the *Red Bandana* Game, which celebrates the life of Boston College graduate Welles Crowther—a hero of 9/11 who lost his life-saving people trapped in the World Trade Center—declaring a clear winner would have been like searching for a teardrop in a pouring rain.

Dan's grandpa continued to battle cancer throughout late November and early December with several rounds of traditional chemotherapy treatments. It made him terribly sick, and it was around this time the entire family surmised Dad's cancer was more serious than he had let on. The enemy is a relentless foe, and we were all beginning to take notice. One night, shortly after a treatment, he attended a musical performance at my daughter's high school. By now, he had gotten into a pattern of wearing dressy sweatpants and bringing a pillow with him any time he was out. Given the hard metal auditorium seats, this is a good idea even if you don't have cancer. In any event, before the performance began, he leaned over to my wife and said to her that when he was in his last treatment, he had been thinking about her mom. He then said, "Judi, I want you to know just how brave your mother was. What I'm doing is easy in comparison. She must have been a remarkable woman. I wish I could have met her." That simple moment, with those beautiful words, summed up my dad. Even in a dark place, he found a way to make a positive comment while deflecting attention away from himself.

Around this same time, I can recall meeting my parents for dinner at a nearby restaurant that just happened to be one of their favorite

Friday night hangouts. It must have been following another school function, as my wife and kids were there as well. We were seated at a high-top table on the bar side as the place was packed. While we waited for our dinner order to arrive, my father kept putting his head down on the table. We all knew he felt horrible, and when I asked him if he wanted me to drive him home, he said, "Please." As I drove towards the house, he said to me, "I'm so tired. I'm just so tired." In response, I told him we would be home in five minutes and that he could get some rest soon. He then said, "No, I'm so tired of fighting. I'm just so tired of fighting. Do you think your and John's kids will understand? I think they will, don't you?" There are moments that change your life forever, and for me, this was one of them. I was tired as well. I was tired of being selfish. I was tired of acting spoiled and cowardly, even as I, along with friends and family, regularly told him to "be strong" and "you can beat this." So, as much as it pained me, I said to him, "Dad, you don't need to keep fighting this for us. You can put this down when you are ready to do so. The kids will be alright. We will all be alright, including Mom." As we rode in silence, I think we both felt relieved to have had our conversation. When I finally got back to the restaurant, I dared not repeat a word of our talk, especially in front of my kids. They were already visibly shaken. Instead, I hugged my wife, and we cried together as a family right in the middle of the crowded restaurant. As for dinner, I cannot remember if anyone even took a bite of their food.

Following the drive and our chat, Dad slowly seemed to rebound from his low. This was no doubt, in part, from his taking a break from traditional chemotherapy, even though he was still receiving Zometa infusions and a cocktail of other medications including, at various times, abiraterone, amlodipine, aspirin, atenolol, atorvastatin, Caltrate, ferrous sulfate, isosorbide mononitrate, Lupron, Nitrostat, prednisone, Simethicone, Xtandi, and Zytiga. Maybe the chat had also helped relieve the stress he had been feeling. Who knows. As we entered the holiday season, he had an extra spring in his step, especially with family in town. We spent Christmas Eve together at my childhood home, and the following day, everyone came to our house for Christmas dinner and what we called "second Christmas" when the kids opened the gifts from their grandparents. Daniel also made a point of showing his grandpa the framed Oklahoma print that Kasey and his brother had given him just a few days before. My son also donned his new Alabama pajamas and showed his grandparents the Alabama ornament that Santa had given him. When Dad saw the Oklahoma print, he just shook his head and said, "Dan, that is way cool. Maybe next year's guy trip?"

A week later, our entire family gathered for a formal dinner in a private room and wine cellar at one of his favorite restaurants—*Papa Joe's*—to celebrate the end of 2017 and the beginning of 2018. My brother was there, along with my sister-in-law Radlyn and my nieces Mia, Sami, and Rae. My dad's younger sister Jill was there along with her husband-Uncle Frank. From my mom's side of the family, my Uncle Ed was there along with my Aunt Ruth, as were my cousins and their families. My wife Judi was there, as were Dan and Claire. Dad's friend Brian was there. Dad was especially joyful. We all were.

“The Loneliest Words I Know”

The new year was, quite frankly, lousy from the start. On the first day, just hours after our fabulous dinner party with the entire family, we gathered at our house to watch Kasey and the Oklahoma *Sooners* battle it out with the Georgia *Bulldogs* in the Rose Bowl and for a chance to play in the National Championship. Although Kasey had been red-shirted, Daniel was dressed in a *Kasey K* Oklahoma football jersey as Santa had learned of Dan's friendship with the future *Sooner* long snapper. Strange how things had changed. Several months prior, we were horrified not only to watch the *Sooners* beat Ohio State in the *Horseshoe* but also to see Baker Mayfield plant an OU flag at the center of *our* field. Dang! Now, here we were, screaming for his success at every play. Unfortunately, Oklahoma lost a heartbreaker in overtime, and it seemed to set in motion a string of losses in our family. Several weeks later, given the late start time of the National Championship game between Alabama and Georgia, Dad rebuffed an offer to watch the game together. He felt whipped.

In the weeks that followed, Dad took a marked turn for the worse. He could barely eat, as his stomach was extremely swollen. His pain levels were clearly elevated as he winced with most movements, all while those dang tubes continued to give him fits. My brother called me around this time and asked how Dad was doing. For the first time, I told him he should try to spend as much time in town as possible. I had a sense that things were declining fast. I just didn't realize how fast it would happen, and little did my brother know he would soon be spending more time in Ohio than in Virginia.

On a dreary winter day, while I was in court for work, John and my mom accompanied my father to his scheduled visit with his oncologist. Until this point, tests were typically taken, medications regulated, and treatment options otherwise explored. Things started as they usually did and then, in an instant, everything changed. His oncologist entered the room, briefly greeted my family, and then told my father, "Things are bad. The last labs showed that the cancer has spread everywhere." He then said, "You should seriously consider hospice." As my mother and brother sat in stunned silence, my father stoically responded, "Doctor, is hospice what you would recommend?" His oncologist nodded and said, "Yes, it is." Without any hesitation, my dad indicated he would like home hospice instead of in a facility and then, as if he caught himself, stopped and looked at my mother and asked if that was alright with her.

Being an oncologist is tough stuff. Any victories are tempered with crushing defeats. Wins are never a cakewalk; even when they occur and are marked as such, it is best to use a pencil with an eraser. Every day is literally like stepping onto a battlefield, or using a football analogy, it's like stepping onto the sideline against a team whose sole purpose is to destroy yours. Imagine you're the coach of that scared and vulnerable team. Some players may be newbies, while others are seasoned veterans. Regardless, everything changes when the whistle blows, and the ball is kicked from a tee. Before the game, you sat the team down, gave them your strategy, suited them up with pads and helmets, and gave them a motivational speech. "Now, get out there and execute our plan, believe in yourself and win the game!" However, amid the battle, what do you tell your players? "Hey, these guys are formidable, don't take victory for granted." We know, coach. "You can do it. Be strong. Make them fight for every inch." We're trying, Coach, but we're playing hurt. Our roster is seriously depleted, remember? Or "Hey, keep your guard up; these guys play dirty." Yeah, we know; why are the referees letting them get away with this?

Granted, many doctors are required to have hard conversations with their patients and their families. Still, oncologists' communications surround an all-consuming disease that invades the imagination and occupies the memory. The language they speak is a stigma unto itself, and sometimes, the words expressed in this language surround death and dying. Again, using football as a metaphor, sometimes the coach must tell his players not to go back into the game, but instead to take the football and go home. At what point does the coach, after seeing the players looking over to the sideline for guidance, run onto the field and say, "No more. I've seen enough. We forfeit." There are some games when the score is out of reach, and, as they say, it is not how you start but how you finish. Fighting for the sake of fighting is no way to finish, as not every game can be won. If you must lose, do so with grace and honor. If you must lose, it is better to be surrounded by those you love than on a distant, unknown field surrounded by strangers. This must be a terrible burden to carry for any oncologist.

My mother and brother told me what happened next bordered on the surreal. My father and the oncologist stood up simultaneously, walked towards each other, and met in the center of the room, where they shook hands. They then thanked each other and said "goodbye." That was it. They would never see each other again. After the others exited, my brother went back to see the doctor alone. He told the doctor, "I want you to know a little about my dad. Not only is he a wonderful husband, father, brother, and grandfather, but he is a preeminent engineer. I thought you should know; you have been treating a great man, and he is my dad." The doctor thanked my brother and said, "I already knew he was a great family man, but I had no idea about what he did for a living. He never talked about it." As my brother turned to leave, Dad's oncologist said, "There's one more thing you should know. He was a great patient."

Hospice is defined as a specialized form of care that provides physical comfort and emotional support for individuals nearing the end of life. This care focuses on managing pain and symptoms to ensure the patient's final days are as comfortable as possible. Medical care at home typically includes a visiting nurse, prescription medications, and medical supplies, and in my dad's case, it would include a wheelchair and, later, a hospital bed. After getting the news of Dad's decision, my wife and I sat the kids down in the living room of our house and told them that their grandpa would be entering hospice at home. His cancer diagnosis was no secret, but this sudden turn of events required some further explanation. Before we could even explain what hospice was, our daughter, who was a senior in high school, burst into tears. Our son sat there quietly, fidgeting, but seemed more upset for his sister than for his grandfather. We decided to leave it at that for then, and I'm not sure we ever did tell him his grandpa was going to die. I suppose we didn't want him to be afraid or try to avoid spending time with his buddy, and we recognized that he would learn what was going on soon enough.

Our family experience with hospice can be divided into two parts, with the first part being unexpectedly liberating, while the second part was unimaginably difficult. We had been told in the first meeting with a hospice nurse that Dad would initially rebound as his body was able to finally recover from years of cancer treatment. This "honeymoon period" would be followed by a leveling off and then a quick decline as the cancer once again took control. When the time came, Morphine and anti-anxiety medications would become his final diet.

For the month of March, things did indeed get better. Dad had a constant stream of visitors, and he was largely able to participate in family functions. My daughter had landed the lead role in her high school musical, *School of Rock*, and we got Dad, in his wheelchair, a middle front-row seat. Not surprisingly, he loved it! We all did—she nailed it! Daniel, always nurturing and wanting to help, usually made himself the designated wheelchair pusher for his grandpa during this time, and even when he managed to hit a bump, the occupant hardly seemed to care. My daughter, who was heading off to Mount Union University in the fall, had a campus orientation around this same time. Since my dad did not attend with us, Claire used her cell phone to film herself going from her dorm to the student union, then to the cafeteria, and finally to the buildings where she would follow her grandpa in becoming a mechanical engineer. Later that same night, we all sat down near Dad's bed and watched the video streaming to a large TV while sipping smoothies. Her narration was beyond precious and brought a gigantic smile to her grandpa's face.

Some days were seemingly tougher for us than for him. I recall him sitting in the corner of his office with a cup of coffee and saying, "Jim, since I'm up and feeling good today, we need to do a few things, if you're up for it." After I responded, "Sure, Dad, what do you need?" he said, "In the top drawer is a group of papers, do you see them? Ok, the top one is the information for the cemetery in West Virginia. Below are the instructions for everything that needs to be done, along with the individuals who need to be contacted. Do you see those? When the day comes, I'll need you to find those." In that moment, when he was so gosh darn strong, how could I be weak? I'd like to think I stepped up for him, and although I could barely look at the documents, I made a mental note of where everything was and promised to do everything he'd asked, even if someone in the family disagreed. On another day, I can recall my dad and our pastor praying together while intermittently discussing his funeral arrangements. If he was afraid of dying, he never let on, but he was blatantly afraid of forgetting to do something to help us out when the time came. Throughout his entire journey with cancer, I never heard my father say one time, "Why me?" As I wrote in my first book, my dad remained optimistic throughout his ordeal. He was fond of telling the entire family that he had lived a fairytale life, having been born in America, coming of age in the 1950s, having married the most beautiful woman in the world—my mom—and having had children and grandchildren.

The summer before our trip to Alabama, Dad had set out to build up his endurance by going for daily walks with my mom. Some nights, they would walk several miles through the old neighborhoods nearby where I once delivered newspapers while in school. The kids and I joined them on more than one occasion, usually after dinner on Sunday evenings. That same summer, my father, who was finally in a "semi-retirement" stage at 73 years old, tackled several large projects around the house, including painting the entire exterior by himself. Additionally, he continued to travel regularly for his consulting work. His strength seemed exceptional, and his attitude remained upbeat. When not working on the house or traveling for work, he spent afternoons in a nearby garage with his friend Brian. After decades of tinkering, he was finally making great headway in restoring his Jaguar Mark IX. It was indeed finally taking shape, complete with wheels and everything.

One day in late March, Brian brought the finished car to the house. Although Dad had taken a test run in the car earlier in February, it was on a makeshift front seat, constructed from a milk crate. After walking several laps around the newly painted grey car—with a wood-paneled dash, cherry red leather seats and the distinctive silver "Jag-U-ar" ornament on the hood—he and Brian hopped in and took it for a spin. As the car pulled away, we saw the license plate, which read "Whynot," and could not help but smile.

A few weeks later, in early April, Daniel celebrated his twentieth birthday at his grandparents' house. He was joined by his mom, his sister, his grandmother, and me. His grandfather briefly joined the festivities to sing "Happy Birthday" with the family, and then, immediately following Dan's blowing out the candles on his birthday cake, literally crawled on all fours back upstairs to his bedroom. He would not let anyone help him, was visibly agitated by his condition and tried to leave the party without any fuss. In retrospect, he was trying to conceal his condition from his grandchildren, especially since it should have been a joyous occasion.

Although I cannot recall the day, there came a time when Dad became completely bedridden. Most of it remains a blur—except his pain. One day in April, after an especially horrible week for all of us, a hospice nurse, who I recall being a sweet middle-aged Black woman, gently grabbed me by my hand and told me, "Your dad is 'taking the turn.' If you need to say anything to him, you should do it soon." Moments before, I had watched her slowly and meticulously move my father from one side of his bed to the other. I thanked her for telling me and for taking such good care of him during her visits. Some other nurses might want to consider another line of work, but that is a story for another day. In any event, as I walked out to my car to return to work, I stopped, turned around, went straight back up to his room, grabbed him by his hand, and told him, "Dad, you are the best father a son could ever have. I love you so very much, and I want you to know that." He smiled and said, "I love you, too. I am so very proud of you and your brother. You boys have made me a very happy father. I hope you know that." We both then nodded our heads in unison. It was the last clear conversation I can ever remember having with him.

Dad drifted in and out of consciousness for what seemed like an eternity. It was tough, heart-wrenching stuff. We made a point of having the kids see him, when possible, but it was excruciatingly hard for anyone to see him in his condition. In honor of his memory and as a courtesy to my family, much of what transpired in those final days shall remain buried in our memories alone. We were witnesses to it and it will remain a scar across our hearts forever. However, in time, our prayers were answered. On a Thursday afternoon, as I sat in a chair next to my father's bed, I no longer prayed for Dad's recovery but for God to take him. "Please take him right now," I prayed. God did not. However, after this prayer, as I looked out the window into the woods behind my parents' house, I noticed it had started to snow. Being in late April, that was strange, even for Ohio. Then I saw a fox dancing atop a rock as it tried to capture floating snowflakes. It was whimsical, if not magical, to witness. Then the fox stopped and looked straight up at me before scampering off into the grove. Was I seeing things? None of us had had much sleep for nearly a week, so maybe it was a hallucination. I'm still not sure if any of it was real. However, as I turned back towards my dad, I noticed he was still breathing, but it was much less labored. He also seemed sweaty, like a fever had broken.

The next day, on Friday, I went to work and then had dinner with my wife and kids. Following our meal, and after discussing the matter with my family, I went back to my parents' house to spend the night there. My brother and sister-in-law had been essentially living at my parents' house for the past week and were at their wits' end as they had left their daughters back in Virginia and had no idea when they would return home. As I pulled up, I noticed the house seemed especially dark, given it was only about 9 p.m. Something told me to be quiet. I slinked about and saw my dad was still comfortably sleeping, and next to him, in a chair, my mom was also sound asleep. It was the first time I had seen her sleep in nearly a week. The love and devotion she had shown my father were truly incredible and beyond words. For much of the time, she had literally been a one-person hospice facility, especially when the rest of us had gone home or to work. Making sure not to wake her from her much-needed break, I covered her with a blanket, and, in an adjoining room, I noticed my brother and sister-in-law were also fast asleep. Silently, I went from room to room, turning off any remaining lights, then curled up in bed in my brother's old room, where, after saying "Goodnight, Dad," out loud to myself, I fell asleep almost immediately.

"Jim, it's your dad; I think you need to come here," my sister-in-law whispered as she awoke me from my slumber. On Saturday, April 21, 2018, in the early morning hours before the sun had risen and while we all quietly slept, Dad had passed away. After nearly two decades of fighting cancer, he had finally put down his burden. He was

74 years old. For him, I'm sure, it seemed a perfect time to say goodbye. Like in days of old, in our childhood home, he had his family together on a Friday night. As we gathered around him that morning, we did not cry but expressed relief that his suffering was finally over. As we shared stories, my brother said it reminded him of when we were younger and Dad would go on a business trip. By the time we woke up, he was already gone. For our entire lives, it seemed Dad was always going ahead with plans for us to meet him later, so it was not surprising he had gone ahead of us one more time.

Later that same morning, after sharing the somber news with family members, my Aunt Jill and Uncle Frank stopped by my mother's house to share in our grief. Much like my brother and sister-in-law, they had been far from their home in Miami, Florida, as they had essentially been living in Ohio for the past few weeks as well. Earlier, I had called my wife, shared the news, and given her permission to tell Daniel and Claire, as I wasn't sure I could do it at that moment anyway. I can recall my wife saying the sun was shining, but everything seemed a little less bright. I fully agreed as any relief we felt was coupled with an overall feeling of a washed-out blurriness. At some point, before the kids arrived, my brother and I, after huddling up together, approached Uncle Frank with a specific request. The guy trips needed a fourth person. We knew it, and we knew exactly what to do about it. There was no reason to wait for a "better time," and Dad would have been entirely on board with our snap decision, especially for Dan's sake. Would our uncle be willing to step in and serve as the fourth member? Without hesitation, he said, "Yes, it would be my honor."

The following weekend, my daughter attended her senior high school prom. She was driven to it in a snazzy, recently restored Jaguar Mark IX. Her date would one day be my son-in-law and, although he never met my father, Austin would one day join us on our guy trips.

Oklahoma

Our "guy trips" are always made up of a group of dudes on a mission to watch football, drink beer, and eat meat. Over the years, this has remained unchanged. Although tea, finger sandwiches, white doilies, and vegan dishes have their place, our trips are typically not one of them. However, we are always open to visiting a nearby museum, especially if it fits nicely into our overarching "guy trip' theme. After arriving in Oklahoma City, we went straight to the *National Cowboy & Western Heritage Museum*, effectively "killing two birds with one stone," as the museum is one of America's premier institutions for Western history, art, and culture. If the "guy trips" have ever visited a museum that cried out rough and tumble, this would be the one, and in case finger sandwiches are more your thing, the museum grill has not only brisket sandwiches and Frito chili pie but also an assortment of salads and even a veggie wrap.

In the entranceway of the museum stands a breathtaking white plaster sculpture, over eighteen feet tall and weighing thousands of pounds, entitled "The End of the Trail" by James Earle Fraser. Visitors, upon entering a glass atrium, gaze upon a lone weary warrior slumped atop his horse—spear by his side—frozen in time. First created as a small bronze sculpture in 1894, Fraser subsequently created replicas, including this final all-inspiring version, which made its debut in 1915 at the *Panama-Pacific International Expo* held in San Francisco. Fraser's creation is one of the most recognizable images in the United States, as it has spawned countless postcards and belt buckles, and the pose has often been recreated by performers at traveling shows and rodeos. The museum acquired the piece in 1968, and sitting near the entrance, the massive artwork offers the perfect welcome to the wonderful galleries that await exploration. The friendly staff, dressed in denim, leather, and rhinestones, also helps on that front as well.

Originally established in 1955, the 200,000-square-foot museum boasts over 28,000 Western and Native American artworks and artifacts and has the world's most extensive collection of American rodeo photographs, barbed wire, and saddlery. Once inside the confines of the museum, we began our exploration in a gallery devoted to the American cowboy, followed by a walk through an actual, recreated town called *Prosperity Junction.* The one-room schoolhouse and the jail were fascinating. Artwork is in great abundance throughout the museum, including countless works from Remington and Russell. In fact, they are more common than mosquitoes in a Canadian woodland. One could easily spend an entire day in the *Art of the American West* gallery, but with limited time, we moved through with lightning speed. If historic firearms are your thing, you are in for quite a treat as the collection is massive, as is the collection of Native American Art. One specific collection worth mentioning that caught us off guard was the ornate feathered Native American headdresses. Perhaps previously ignorant, we were stunned at their sheer size and intricacy. Lastly, the rodeo collection, including an actual rodeo arena that was boxed and fenced, was completely unexpected. In the end, the overall experience revealed a kaleidoscope of cultures that was and is the American West.

Truthfully, when I steered the party towards the *National Cowboy & Western Heritage Museum*, I had one thing on my mind—*Westerns.* More specifically—*John Wayne.* Again, the museum did not disappoint. The *Western Performers* Gallery explores the various ways the

American West has been portrayed in literature and film and, right as you enter this gallery, you come face to face with the Sunset movie theatre, which shows clips from all the classics. Tucked behind the theatre, we found the John Wayne display—complete with a timeline—containing artifacts and memorabilia from his roles stretching from the 1920s through the 1970s. Numerous other stars had equally impressive displays, and we quickly learned the museum is also home to the *Hall of Western Performers.* The list is extensive. A few names besides Wayne that caught our attention included Gary Cooper, James Stewart, Gene Autry, Barbara Stanwyck, Roy Rogers, Dale Evans, Gregory Peck, Ronald Reagan, Kirk Douglas, James Garner, Maureen O'Hara, Reba McEntire, Melissa Gilbert, Clint Eastwood, Steve McQueen, Sam Elliott, Robert Duvall, Charlton Heston, Tom Selleck, Kevin Costner, Kurt Russell, and Lou Diamond Phillips. And you say you're not a Western movie fan!

Three of the above-mentioned inductees and, perhaps others, share pivotal life experiences with our group. First, John Wayne, who is synonymous with the Western genre itself, was in part responsible for the creation of the museum, as not only did he provide seed money, but he also led a parade—along with members of various Native American tribes—for the public opening. Wayne also served on the museum's board of directors until his death in 1979 from stomach cancer. He was 72 years old. It was not his first brush with the dreaded disease. Born in 1907—long before much was known about certain causes of cancer— "*The Duke*" was a heavy smoker for much of his life. Fifteen years after he beat lung cancer, he faced a second fight with the terrible disease and, through his own ordeal, became a passionate advocate for others fighting cancer. To honor his memory, his family created the *John Wayne Cancer Foundation* in 1985 to lead the fight against cancer with courage, strength, and grit. The foundation provides funding for multidisciplinary basic, clinical, and translational research on many complex cancer problems. The *Block the Blaze* program also provides youth education about skin cancer protection and prevention. *Duke,* now that you've finally met our dad/grandpa in the grandest of all sweeping western landscapes, I'm sure you know you have one tough, patriotic guy by your side. Tell him we said "hello," that he would love the museum, that we miss him, and that we will see him soon. However, not yet, as we have a few more college football destinations to knock off first.

If John Wayne sits atop a western mountain range, he is further joined by two other twin peaks named Roy Rogers and Dale Evans. In fact, Rogers—a fellow *Buckeye* by birth—is nicknamed "*the King of the Cowboys*," and Evans—who co-starred in the highly successful television series *The Roy Rogers Show* with her husband from 1951 to 1957—wrote and sung (as a duet with her husband) the legendary song *"Happy Trails."* Both are legends to the world at large, but they also share a special and more personal bond with my family. Their daughter Robin, who was born in 1950, had Down syndrome and unfortunately passed away shortly before her second birthday from the mumps. Robin was also born with a congenital heart defect, and her parents were originally advised to have her institutionalized for what was certain to be a fleeting time on earth. Instead, they chose to take their daughter home. As previously mentioned, in the 1950s, most physicians recommended that children with Down syndrome be "put away" in an institution or home regardless of heart issues. In 1953, following her daughter's death, Dale Evans Rogers published *Angel Unaware* and, in doing so, blazed a new trail in the world of special needs. The touching story is told from Robin's point of view as she converses with God while waiting to get her wings during her brief life, and her mother—as an author—beautifully describes how Robin was a precious gift from God sent to strengthen her faith and draw their family closer together. *Angel Unaware* became a bestseller and changed the lives of millions. As for Roy Rogers and Dale Evans, our family would readily nominate you as inductees to our own personal hall of fame for trailblazing parents of children with special needs. Happy trails to you until we meet again!

Before our visit to the *National Cowboy & Western Heritage Museum*, we briefly contemplated a visit to the *Oklahoma City National Memorial & Museum*. More specifically, as we loaded up the rental car, I mentioned a visit as a starting point for the trip. Still, I quickly noticed my brother and uncle were both shaking their heads negatively in unison. Having visited this sacred and solemn location several years later, they made the right call. It was too soon, and it would have been too much. The museum and memorial, situated on the former site of the *Alfred P. Murrah* Federal Building, pay honor to the 168 individuals—many just toddlers in pre-school—who lost their lives on April 19, 1995, when Timothy McVeigh parked and detonated a Ryder rental truck filled with explosives. The resulting explosion further destroyed the entire north face of the building. Inside the museum is a Gallery of Honor for every person who was killed, and outside is a Memorial Field of empty chairs. By looking back at their stories and the families they left behind, it is hoped to better understand the impact of this unimaginable violence while offering comfort, strength, peace, hope, and serenity to visitors, a grieving community, and a wounded nation.

The museum further honors the survivors, rescuers, investigators, and all who were affected by the Oklahoma City bombing and, in doing so, indirectly honors my father. To further explain, in 1995, a day or two after the explosion, as Dad was walking through an airport when returning home from a business trip, he was approached by the FBI and asked if he would fly directly to Oklahoma City to assist with the investigation and be a part of the Oklahoma Bomb Task Force (known as "OKBOMB"). Doing so without hesitation and without a clean change of clothes, Dad, along with many other investigators, experts, and engineers, spent days meticulously combing through the remnants of the *Alfred P. Murrah* Federal Building to determine the exact cause for the unspeakable destruction, and as a result, helped build the case against McVeigh and his cohort—Terry Nichols.

When the FBI approached my father at the airport, he was recognized as a world-renowned mechanical engineer in the automotive and tire industry, specializing in accident reconstruction. He was also a known commodity, as the agency had turned to him previously. Two years before the Oklahoma tragedy, a terrorist attack was carried out when a bomb was detonated in the parking garage below the North Tower of the World Trade Center in New York City. On February 26, 1993, a massive eruption—caused by a 1,336 lb. urea nitrate-hydrogen gas device carried in a van—carved out a blast crater six stories high and 200 feet wide. Although it failed to make the North Tower collapse onto the South Tower, as dastardly intended, it nonetheless killed six people instantly and caused over a thousand injuries. Middle Eastern terrorism had finally arrived on American soil. Hundreds of agents descended on the site and, in the rubble, uncovered a vehicle identification number on a piece of wreckage that seemed suspiciously obliterated. This, they surmised, might be the source of the explosion. A few days later, Dad got the call. Would he be willing to help figuratively put the tires on the van back together? Although an enormous task, almost beyond comprehension, and analogous to putting together pieces of a severely burned and damaged puzzle scattered throughout a large burned-out parking lot—further mixed with countless other unrelated puzzle pieces—he did not hesitate to roll up his sleeves and get to work. As a kid, I recall him constantly telling my brother and me that all big projects or great achievements begin with small steps. He told us it is how everything gets done. Brick by brick, a building reaches for the sky, and word by word, a story is written.

Piece by piece, with the assistance of many fellow patriots, the van and its tires were reconstructed, thereby creating the linchpin in the prosecution of the al-Qaeda terrorists responsible for the heinous act. Later, in Dad's home office, along a back wall, he hung a framed chalk rendering created by a sketch artist during his testimony at the trial. However, he was most proud of the *New York Times* reporting that, during his testimony, which was described as clear and concise, he unabashedly placed the tire atop a table for all to see, literally right in front of the defendants. That tickled him. Dad despised those who harm others or destroy things. He also had a lifelong dislike for bullies. After he had passed away, my Uncle Ed—my mom's younger brother—shared a story at dinner one evening that I had never heard while growing up. It turns out that one night, while my grandparents were out of town, my mother and her sisters (my aunts) had a small get-together at their house. Things got out of hand, and several unsavory characters showed up. One guy was especially large and menacing, and when Mom asked everyone to either ratchet things back or go home, this guy saw it as an opportunity to become even more obnoxious. Mom was dating Dad at the time, and when Dad saw this guy's reaction, he told him it was time to go. The guy then proceeded to pummel my father. However, it was what my father did next that made a lasting impression on my uncle and everyone else who was present. He described how my dad got up from the floor, dusted himself off, and told the guy, "You still have to go." And leave he did, much to the relief of everyone.

Although called into duty worldwide for work, Dad always made it clear that we came first. It was another way he taught my brother and me how to be men. Your family always comes first. No matter where he might be, Dad always found a way to be home for weekends, important events, and our soccer games. Whenever my brother or I stepped onto a field, we knew he was on the sideline, even if it meant a redeye flight. At our father's funeral, a good friend and colleague—Hal—shared a few words about their business trips together and his relentless effort to get home. Hal quipped, "Who knew you could be in Japan and get back to Ohio the same day in time for dinner with the family? Well, Jim did, and he made it happen!"

Enter Francesco Gessino

Located on Ed Noble Parkway just off Main Street, tucked in a booth with the smell of a hickory-fired grill, the guys, along with countless *Sooner* fans, enjoyed our Friday night dinner at *Charleston's* in Norman, Oklahoma. It was our first football dinner since Dad's passing. However, it was also our first "guy trip dinner" with Uncle Frank and the first of many more to come! Established in 1993 and part of the Hal Smith family of restaurants, our dinner spot featured dark woods and gas lighting, serving traditional American classics, including oven-roasted chicken, grilled pork chops, barbecued baby-back ribs, and steaks. The meal was great, and as it turns out, this would not be our only visit to *Charleston's*. Several years later—following Covid-19—my wife and I traveled back to Oklahoma with Daniel to see the *Sooners* battle the West Virginia *Mountaineers* as guests with Kasey's parents. My wife, who has an aunt and uncle in nearby Mustang, Oklahoma, planned a visit over the weekend. Since we were staying in Oklahoma City, they told us to meet them at their favorite restaurant, *Charleston's* in the city. When we pulled up, Daniel and I, with mouths watering, grinned from ear to ear as we knew what we were about to experience. The following year, we repeated the experience during our stay for the Kent State *Golden Flashes* game. It has become part of our Oklahoma tradition, bringing together families that were otherwise divided by hundreds of miles. That's what football does.

Francesco Gessino is an original family name. However, like many Italian immigrants who came to America in the late 19th century and early 20th century, the name was shortened, cleaned up, and given an English varnish. The result—"Frank Jessie," or as our uncle likes to say, "instead of inheriting a beautiful Italian name, I'm named after two train robbers from Missouri." Regardless, our uncle, like our aunt, was born and raised in Akron, Ohio. Frank is not only a former college basketball player but also a coach at both the University of Akron and the University of Cincinnati, where both teams played in the NCAA tournament. In fact, the Cincinnati team made the Elite Eight. Our uncle also coached multiple high school teams and served as athletic director for several high schools in Northeast Ohio. One such school was his alma mater—St. Vincent-St. Mary—where he served as athletic director for Lebron's junior year, and when the high school star appeared on the cover of *Sports Illustrated*. By all accounts, it was a period of total mayhem.

However, the mayhem was nothing compared to the heartache our uncle had endured years before we ever knew him. Frank's only child—Scott—was smart, engaging, and admired by all who knew him. Like his father, he was also a great athlete, and like my brother and I, he shared a passion for soccer. Unfortunately, Scott Michael Jessie died suddenly from natural causes in 1994. He was only 19 years old. While I cannot possibly comprehend the grief or pain caused by the loss of a child, I can say with absolute certainty that we greatly admire the grace and strength shown by our uncle and probably do not tell him that enough. It is truly remarkable, but we also acknowledge the scars remain and the underlying wound will never fully heal. When Jill and Frank married in 2009, it was in Oxford, Ohio, near the University of Miami, where my aunt had attended college and Scott had spent a year. While the rest of the guys never got to meet Scott, we would no doubt have loved having him along with us on the "guy trips." As we like to say, he would have been a welcome addition and would have fit right in. In the meantime, we thank him for letting us borrow his father.

Following our inaugural Oklahoma dinner, we returned to the *Sooner Legends Inn & Suites*, where I had booked two adjoining rooms. The locally owned hotel was a quirky joint, regularly frequented by fans and former players, and with a ton of Oklahoma memorabilia. The 167 rooms, every hallway, and any other nook, for that matter, were dedicated to OU athletics history. Roaming through the hotel was akin to taking a stroll down an all-things *Sooner* memory lane, with the first two rooms off the lobby dedicated to Barry Switzer and Joe Washington. Unfortunately, the hotel was another victim of the dreaded Covid pandemic and permanently shut down operations in 2020. The memorabilia was auctioned off, and the hotel was slated for a rendezvous with a demolition crew and bulldozer. Nonetheless, many memories remain, as a wrecking ball cannot diminish them.

Art Imitates Life

One of the greatest joys of our guy trips has been when we have stumbled upon the completely unexpected. This happened in Norman, Oklahoma, and it was all because of where we parked our car. After grabbing breakfast at the hotel, we decided to head directly to the Oklahoma campus and spend the entire day exploring before the late-afternoon game. Daniel was completely "geeked up" to see Kasey, so it made no sense to have him bouncing off the hotel walls when we could unleash him on a sprawling university campus. When we arrived at the University of Oklahoma, we initially considered finding public parking, but because it was so early, we managed to find street parking in a nearby residential neighborhood. I guess it proves the early bird gets the worm, or at least, in our case, a great street parking spot. However, for full disclosure, although we scoured the sidewalk and nearby signposts for confirmation that we were parked legally, we were all noticeably relieved that the car was still there at the end of the evening and without any ticket atop the windshield.

Walking towards campus, with nothing but football and cheeseburgers on our minds, as we crossed the intersection of W. Boyd Street and Elm Avenue, we made a stunning discovery—the *Fred Jones Jr. Museum of Art.* Lucky for us, it was open. It turns out the museum is one of the finest university art museums in the United States. Just minutes earlier, we had no idea. Originally founded in 1936 by OU art professor Oscar Jacobson, the museum now holds over 20,000 objects in its permanent collection. In 1992, it was renamed the *Fred Jones Jr. Museum of Art* in honor of the prosperous Oklahoman, businessman, and ardent art collector. The industrialist-turned-civic leader assembled an impressive collection of Native American art and European paintings from the 19th and 20th centuries.

Thirteen years before our fateful discovery, the museum found itself "with art worthy of world-class architecture," so the school commissioned Hugh Newell Jacobsen to design the 34,000-square-foot *Mary and Howard Lester Wing* and to renovate and expand the original museum building. The resulting wing, which doubled the size of the original museum, is a sequential matrix of nine identical house-like pavilions ("huts") organized in a square configuration and connected by corridors. The tenth pavilion, extending from the square and acting as the main entrance, caught our eye, as did the Vermont slate and Texas limestone.

Surprised by stumbling upon an art museum on our way to a football game, we were equally unprepared for what our eyes would gaze upon once inside. In 2000, the University of Oklahoma received the single most important collection of French Impressionism ever given to an American public university. As part of the Aaron M. and Clara Weitzenhoffer collection, the gift included 22 paintings and 11 works on paper by Degas, Gauguin, Monet, Pissarro, Renoir, Toulouse-Lautrec, Van Gogh, Vuillard, and others. The collection, known by only a handful of scholars and virtually unexhibited for 50 years, was a donation made at the bequest of Clara, an art collector and long-time supporter of the University of Oklahoma. This truly magnificent collection is made even more remarkable by its intimate presentation. In addition to the works donated, the bequest included Mrs. Weitzenhoffer's 18th-century decorative arts, period furniture, porcelain, and silver. The masterworks are displayed just as they were in the wood-paneled rooms in the Weitzenhoffer Oklahoma City home. Imagine walking around inside someone's house and looking at their artwork in a study, hallway, or family room, except in this case, the art is worth millions, and there are museum attendants around every corner.

One piece, *Shepherdess Bringing in Sheep*, a painting by Camille Pissarro from 1886, was part of the collection donated to the museum in 2000. The painting was also one of many works stolen by the Nazis in 1941 during their occupation of France in the Second World War. After the war, the painting, originally owned by Raoul Meyer, came into the hands of a Swiss art dealer. Meyer attempted to retrieve the painting in 1953 but was informed that his claim was too late, and he later declined to purchase his own property back. In 1957, the Weitzenhoffer family acquired the painting in good faith from a New York art gallery. In 2012, Leone-Noelle Meyer emerged as the heir to Meyer and sought the return of the painting, which ultimately led to a series of legal battles spanning the Atlantic Ocean, from Paris to Oklahoma.

After much legal wrangling, an initial compromise was reached to rotate the painting between the university and a museum in France. However, the legal tug of war resumed anew when Meyer sought to void the agreement and have the work returned to France permanently. Part of her change of heart arose when the *Musée d'Orsay* in Paris got cold feet about returning the painting to Oklahoma. Citing insurance nightmares and other potential risks associated with loaning a multi-million-dollar piece of work, the museum refused to accept the painting as a gift. Finally, in 2021, after further negotiations, Meyer transferred the title to the OU Foundation. In return, the foundation will assume all costs and the painting will remain on permanent public display between the *Fred Jones Jr. Museum of Art* and a chosen museum institution in France.

It is often said that art imitates life. Art tells our story, and so doing inevitably reveals the history of those who are *different.* Dutch painter Jan Joest of Kalkar painted *The Adoration of the Christ Child* in 1515.

Doing quick math, that was more than 500 years ago and centuries before the founding of the United States. Although quintessentially Dutch and depicting the holiest of stories, the piece might otherwise be considered typical, especially for its time and subject matter. In fact, hanging on a museum wall today, one might walk right by it. However, for those who stop to examine the rendition of Jesus and the Mother Mary, two other participants are revealed to have Down syndrome or a related diagnosis. One is a shepherd looking down on the scene from behind a post at the center of the painting, and the other is an angel standing behind the Mother Mary. Both are situated in what would seem to be places of honor. It is unknown why the painter put them there or how Down syndrome impacted the artist's life. Regardless, he painted it into *the story*.

Andrea Mantegna, who was born in 1431, was an Italian Renaissance painter and a student of Roman archaeology. He experimented with perspective. He may very well have previously joined Jan Joest of Kalkar in including the disabled in his art. In 1982, Dr. Brian Stratford, a specialist in developmental disabilities at the University of Nottingham, posited Mantegna used a little boy with Down syndrome as the model for his Christ child. Initially, the distinctive facial features and shape of his hands and toes were dismissed in the elite art world as purely coincidental. However, the Gonzaga family of Mantua, Mantegna's sponsor, was known to have a boy with an unidentified "illness." Furthermore, the artist himself was known to have a child with a "similar illness." Regardless of whether the child model had Down syndrome or why the painting reflects characteristics similar thereto, both the painter and sponsor had children with a "similar illness." It was part of *their story*.

The rise of Christianity led to more public depictions of people with disabilities, in part because in the New Testament, Jesus shows kindness and forgiveness towards people who are lame, blind, and otherwise *different*. The early church, contrary to many modern misguided notions, often welcomed those who were disabled, even when nobody else would. For example, in 1287, a nobleman and his wife—living in a castle called Metola near what is now Florence, Italy—hoped for the birth of a boy to continue the family legacy. Instead, they had a baby girl. As the countryside eagerly awaited the announcement, silence fell upon the land. There was no ringing of bells or celebrations. Not only was the baby a girl, but the baby was also *different*. Their daughter was born blind, unusually small, and with a hunched back. She would never be able to see or stand up straight. Embarrassed and ashamed, the parents hid their baby girl in the castle and did not even give her a name. A servant took the baby to a nearby church where she was baptized and given the name Margaret, meaning "Beautiful Pearl." A name her parents, along with much of the world, would surely have rejected. Fearing the family might be discovered to have a child, her father had a room built alongside a small church in the forest where he sent her to live when she was six or seven years old. She would live there for the next thirteen years, during which she learned scripture and developed a love for God.

Eventually, her parents took Margaret to a shrine in the town of Castella and ordered her to stay there all day and pray to God for a cure so she might be able to go home and live with them. Without even saying "goodbye," her parents left and never returned. In the years that followed, Margaret became a beggar. Essentially homeless and without family, the disabled woman also became known for her cheerful disposition and willingness to preach *the word* to anyone who would listen. In time, she was taken in by a group of women dedicated to prayer and good works and later by a wealthy family. Margaret died on April 13, 1320. She was only thirty-three years old. Today, she is known as Blessed Margaret of Castello, Patron of People Who Are Blind, Deformed, Hunchbacked, or Unwanted. She is forever part of *our story*.

Those who are *different* make up a rich and diverse tapestry in our story. While some are born with physical and intellectual disabilities, others acquire their disabilities through life experiences, including accidents, disease, exposure, age, and war. Smallpox and polio have cut a wide swath, as have malaria, HIV, and Covid 19. Multiple sclerosis and Parkinson's are joined by dementia and cancer in altering normal lives. Workplace injuries are all too frequent, as are injuries at home and while driving—not to mention the casualties of war, including missing limbs, lost eyes, and other disfigurements. Psychological injuries, although not as immediately recognizable, are also hovering and ever-present, and if left unchecked, a virtual powder keg. Noticeably *different,* all these people have been called, at one point or another, lame, crippled, handicapped, senile, slow, special, retarded, idiot, insane, stupid, crazy, freak, lunatic, and feeble. They are also referred to as being disabled or *different.*

Families historically bore responsibility for the disabled, and when there was no family, the community was expected to step in and help care for them. The brutality of the early-primitive world seems to have been somewhat accommodating to those who were disabled. Perhaps, more likely, there was little choice, for every hand—diminished or not—was needed for sheer survival. Modernity, preoccupied with groups and categorization, upended this natural order, as did its obsession with work and productivity. The new world also turned more and more towards medicine, physicians, and a previously unexplored word—*diagnosis.* While the church continued its mission of good works, including caring for the needy, the public sector entered the fray. Soon, insane asylums, community hospitals, and special schools popped up across the country and in Europe. The first scent of progressive ideology was initially a sweet aroma. Society would only lurch forward with an improvement in the lives of all citizens.

Early institutions were rightfully celebrated. For example, in 1817, the American Asylum for the Deaf was founded in Hartford, Connecticut, and the Boston Perkins School for the Blind opened its doors in Massachusetts in 1829. The latter would come to include Helen Keller and Anne Sullivan. Institutional life was viewed as empowering, and many stories, such as Keller's, provided a glimpse of an untapped reality for those who had been previously underestimated or discarded by society. For many, this new life was liberating, and the breakthroughs have been downright breathtaking. However, in time, another unintended consequence occurred as these same institutions became easy dumping grounds for those who were *different*. While some received proper education and stimulation, others did not. Removed from their families and communities and surrounded by others with disabilities, stagnation became all too common. Along the way, as the world stared in a cracked mirror, admiring its perceived perfection, many became forgotten.

Starting in the late 1940s and early 1950s, the sweet aroma of progressive ideology had turned noticeably foul. In fact, mass institutionalization, without consideration for the individual, had resulted in an intellectual stench. However, out of sight was never truly out of mind. Parents were the first to push back, taking children out of institutions, bringing them back home, and forming parents' groups. One such group, the New Jersey Parents Group for Retarded Children, was formed in October 1946 by a New Jersey housewife named Laura Bloomfield. This brave mother, and many like her, faced stiff resistance from physicians, psychologists, facilities, and bureaucrats, who argued such action might be catastrophic to the well-being of the child, thereby making these difficult decisions nearly unbearable. Many of these early parent groups eventually merged to form the National Association for Retarded Children in 1952, and the organization formally changed its name in 1974 to become the National Association for Retarded Citizens.

As a parent of a disabled child, there is one nagging thought you can never get totally out of your head—what will happen to my child when I am gone? Every parent undoubtedly has the same thought or fear, as nobody will ever love your child in the same way you do. On this, we all agree. Most children will grow older and become adults. Their independence is all but assured. However, there are fewer guarantees for the disabled, and sometimes, they must forever remain as children. If there are siblings, will they care for their adult brother or sister? Would that unfairly alter their lives? If there is more than one sibling, would that cause problems between them and create divisions between their future imagined families? These are the questions that haunt us.

In 1950, Pulitzer Prize and Nobel Prize-winning author Pearl Buck published *The Child Who Never Grew* about her daughter Carol. Born in 1920 with a metabolic disorder called phenylketonuria (PKU), which caused cognitive disability, it was not until her daughter was nearly four years old that she discovered Carol's mind had stopped growing. Chasing the world over for a cure, Buck describes the moment a doctor in America told her, "She will never be more than four years old, at best. Prepare yourself, madame!" Faced with the inevitable, the mother turned her thoughts to a day when she could no longer care for her daughter. Like I said, it haunts you. She kept Carol by her side until she was nine years old and then set out to find her daughter's final earthly home. After doing so, Buck describes how "the child clung to my hand and I to hers." Mom was not permitted to visit for at least one month "for new roots to be put down." It is a rough read. It hurts. You have questions. However, the story does not end there. Later, when Buck would visit her daughter, Carol would whisper, "I want to go home." Through the years, her daughter would indeed go back and forth between places, but after a week or so with her mother, she would inevitably decide she missed her friends and *wanted to go home*. The native West Virginian later writes, "When the wakeful hours come in the night, I comfort myself, thinking that if I should die before I wake … her life would go on just the same." Nearly a century later, those scenes and those words still pierce any loving heart. As parents, it represents a story of love and anguish, which we share together.

Boomer Sooner

Still hours from kickoff, with just a smattering of clouds in the sky, we decided to take a lengthy stroll through campus. Unlike students—rushing through the maze of walks between monstrous brick buildings—we had nowhere to go and plenty of time to ramble and in our wandering, we found ourselves at the doors of *Bizzell Memorial Library*. This central building, much like others on campus, is known for being made in a *Cherokee Gothic* style. The term, first coined by Frank Lloyd Wright during a 1946 tour of the school's buildings, represents a distinctive style that combines conventional Gothic and Native American elements. Decorative facades and statues evoke the Gothic collegiate style of schools in the Northeast, but the red brick and white limestone create a new and vibrant variant, successfully fusing diverse cultures. On a beautiful fall Saturday afternoon, there is no better place to see firsthand those young souls who will one day run our country than inside a campus library. Not surprisingly, the old wooden doors were unlocked, and as we drifted through the *Great Reading Room*, we not only caught a glimpse of intricately carved bookcases but also those glory-bound students nestled throughout with open books, laptops, and notepads. We hope you change the world!

Traversing Oklahoma's campus while dressed in our Number 51 jerseys, we had OU fans literally written all over us. As we moseyed up to *Campus Corner*—the historical commercial district founded in 1917 with a nostalgic college atmosphere and directly across the street from campus—a torrent of *"Boomer"* or *"Boomer Sooner"* greeted us practically every other stride we made in our search for snacks and drinks. Now, in Ohio, whether you are in Columbus or at a shopping mall anywhere in the state, if you are wearing *Buckeye* garb and pass somebody else wearing OSU clothing, if one blurts out, "*O-H,*" you are obligated, lest you be considered aloof or an outsider, to respond with, "*I-O.*" This might happen once or twice while shopping or at an airport, but it occurs considerably more often near campus. However, it is hardly a constant thing. In Norman, on the other hand, this greeting was wonderfully relentless and became old hat for the crew. "*Boomer*" is met with *"Sooner,"* whereas *"Boomer Sooner"* is met with, yep, *"Boomer Sooner."* Daniel often led this verbal volley, much to the enjoyment of all OU fans within earshot.

To better understand this popular cheer used by fans of the University of Oklahoma to support their teams, we need to take a quick trip back in time to the frontier days and unassigned lands in the *Oklahoma Territory*. Under the *Homestead Act of 1862*, originally signed into law by President Lincoln, settlers could claim 160 acres of public land for a period of five years, after which they would receive title to the plot. Several decades before, during the 1820s, the U.S. government conceived of a place—an *Indian Territory*—as an alternative to endless wars, and in the 1830s, began negotiating with tribes living in the southern plains to make way for tribes from the Ohio Valley and Appalachia. In the years that followed, many tribes were forcibly relocated into this territory. However, Washington's map drawing and promises of cheap land were just getting started.

The newly conceived *Indian Territory* was made up of lands wedged between Kansas and Texas, and after the Civil War and the *1866 Reconstruction Treaties with the Five Tribes*, federal negotiators set up reservations in the western part of the Territory for southern plains tribes and reserved the central part for tribes in Kansas and other tribes previously designated to be relocated. As the government carved up land and created new arbitrary borders, a vast middle section of territory, largely comprising present-day Oklahoma, remained "unassigned lands" and not designated to any tribe. Despite the *Homestead Act of 1862*, the federal government assumed control of these lands and refused to allow homesteaders in. The result was a vast "no man's land"—albeit arid, largely treeless, and generally considered worthless—held in limbo. In time, these so-called worthless lands became more desirable for ranchers and farmers, and in response, President Benjamin Harrison finally relented by declaring on March 23, 1889, that these unassigned lands would be open for settlement beginning at 12:00 p.m. on April 22, 1889. Since it would be first come, first served, things were about to get crazy.

Given this predetermined start time, federal troops were assigned to patrol the region's borders, hoping to prevent any early incursions by settlers. However, the area was vast, making it nearly impossible for the cavalry to stop all the people who crossed the border prematurely. Many crossed undetected and found spots to hide until April. Others were invited into the territory to explore during an "open house" period, so they could better understand what they wanted to pursue, as water and timber were crucial features for successful development. This invitation was also intended to prevent everyone from grabbing the first thing they saw, hopefully alleviating further chaos and ensuring that better lands did not go unclaimed. Some of these people, looking for an ideal spot, didn't leave, while others left only to sneak back in. Those that crossed too soon, or more bluntly, illegally, are *Sooners* and, in the early days, the term was meant as an insult. It was synonymous with lying, cheating, and criminality.

On April 22, 1889, at high noon, when cannons boomed, pistols fired, and bugles blared, 50,000 settlers bolted from a starting line, eager to claim uninhabited land as their own. These law-abiding seekers, who dashed across the prairie border in a frenzied sprint, are *Boomers.* Women, although they were not eligible to vote, were included in this land grab, and there was no citizenship requirement. As a result, immigrants, mostly from Western Europe, rushed across the grasslands by the thousands as well. This scene of mayhem has been described as "survival of the fastest." Husbands and fathers on horseback rode ahead, hoping to secure an ideal location to call home, while the family followed behind with instructions to somehow find them. Covered wagons, driven at breakneck speed, tossed family and belongings about like an old wooden roller coaster in a bygone amusement park. Other settlers boarded "iron horses," referred to as "boomer trains," operated by the Santa Fe Railway to be hurled deep into unassigned lands, where they scrambled off to claim their dreams. These scenes, part of a well-written yet almost fantastical script, add another red brick to the *Cherokee Gothic* cathedral called *American folklore.*

So, why is Oklahoma referred to as the *Sooner State*, rather than the *Boomer State,* and why is the University of Oklahoma known as the *Sooners*? These are good questions. The OU football team, which began playing in 1895, was originally nicknamed the "*Rough Riders*" and "*Boomers.*" By the time Oklahoma became the 46th state in 1907, the *Sooner* term had started to shift from insult to a celebrated moniker. The original rascal-like qualities were replaced with a positive, can-do spirit. The following year, in 1908, the University became the *Sooners,* and the rest, as they say, is history.

The newly formed *Sooner State* is also known as the *Panhandle State,* referring to the 166-mile-long strip of land extending west to New Mexico. The 34-mile-wide strip is geographically fascinating as it is the only thing separating Texas from Kansas and Colorado. Previously, this strip was known as *No Man's Land, the Public Land Strip*, and the *Cimarron Territory.* It was also known for being a haven for outlaws. Filled with brothels and moonshiners, it was known as "*the Sodom and Gomorrah of the Plains.*" Often compared to Australia's Outback and, perhaps befittingly, the area has faced a bevy of historical storms and droughts. However, this lawless strip also served as the tip of a spear created on the front line between free and slave states. *The Missouri Compromise of 1820* had forbidden slavery north of the 36½th parallel, so when the United States annexed Texas in 1845, the top portion of the Lone Star State was lopped off. Meanwhile, the *Kansas-Nebraska Act*, enacted in 1854 to create the state of Kansas, employed the 37th parallel to establish a border. The result was a 34-mile gap left between Kansas and Texas, which would finally be given a home when the Indian and Oklahoma territories combined to form the 46th state in the Union.

Two and a half hours before kickoff—on the south plaza of the *Gaylord Family Oklahoma Memorial Stadium*—we gathered with throngs of Oklahoma football fans to await the arrival of Kasey and the *Sooner* football team for the *Walk of Champions*. It was a bright, warm afternoon, and we lined up immediately behind a red rope, securing a front-row spot for both the Oklahoma band and its cheerleaders. With all the noise, I almost missed a text from Kasey telling me the team had left the hotel and was on their way. Dan was geeked, whooping and hollering along with every cheer, and even though I thought he might fade, he never did. Those standing near us recognized our matching number 51 jerseys and, after learning of our story, were nearly as excited to see Kasey as we were and helped ensure newer arrivals did not crowd back Daniel. In fact, they formed a human wall behind us for which nobody dared enter. As previously mentioned, the *Ref!Neks* were also on hand and fired shots as the team inched closer. For some reason, one of the most exciting experiences before a football game is to hear the approach of team buses by way of sirens echoing from a distant police escort. Heard but not yet seen creates heightened anticipation.

Another ping of my phone confirmed the team was literally right around the corner, and sure enough, they were, as I could see the tops of the buses. As the buses approached and then finally came to a stop, time seemed to stand still. And then it happened. The door opened, and Kasey—dressed in a black *Nike* pullover, with khaki pants and carrying a large black Oklahoma bag—made a straight line for Daniel, who was dressed in a crimson-colored jersey. Kasey moved so quickly that a cheerleader—much like a bunny in the clearing of a forest—hopped back to avoid his path. As the two hugged, each had a smile the size of Texas. Given the fierce, century-old rivalry between the *Sooners* and the *Longhorns*, am I allowed to say that? After a few words, he was off again to rejoin his team. It is amazing how 25 seconds can change everything. We call it "the hug felt around the world," and it is a wonderful reminder that we all can use a hug every now and then. Next time you get the urge, forget the handshake and go straight for the embrace. You will be glad you did.

After the much-anticipated reunion, we scurried over to an indoor practice facility to pick up our tickets for the game as guests of Oklahoma's long snapper. This was also a new experience, and it was fun to mingle with the families of the other *Sooner* football players, many of whom wore the jersey numbers of their loved ones. For once, we knew for certain we were the cool guys on campus.

Our Favorite Long Snapper

Peninsula, Ohio, is a village in Northern Summit County, along the Cuyahoga River, and located right smack in the middle of the Cuyahoga Valley National Park. With a population of 536 as of the 2020 census, the village is generally considered part of the Akron, Ohio, metropolitan area. Right up a hill from the village, just outside of the national park, is Woodridge High School. Known as the Woodridge *Bulldogs*, the school district includes the Village of Peninsula, as well as parts of Akron and Cuyahoga Falls, Ohio. At one time, it also included both of my children. One day, when both my kids were still Woodridge *Bulldogs,* and our family still wore plenty of maroon and white, a college coach walked through a hallway in their school and into a weight room primarily used by the football team. Although he may have driven through the national park or grabbed lunch in Peninsula, his main purpose for being in town was to eyeball a potential recruit. What he came to see was a long snapper, and after a half dozen or so snaps of the football, he halted the makeshift practice by stating, "I've seen enough." Pleased by what he saw, Jay Boulware—who is now the running backs coach and special teams coach at the University of Kentucky—knew a great long snapper when he saw one. Right there, and without hesitation, he offered the young man a preferred walk-on spot for the University of Oklahoma *Sooner* football team. Although he had received offers to play at Bowling Green and Toledo, when Kasey Kelleher heard those words, he knew he would be off to Norman, Oklahoma, following graduation.

Some kids seem to have a heart for others who are different. You can see it, and as a parent of a disabled child, you can sense it. Kasey was one of those kids. From an early age, he took an interest in Dan. He was curious. He asked questions. Our son started school later than many of his peers, and we decided early on to hold him back another year. However, with his sister just two years his junior in age, we decided that Daniel would not be held back any longer than one year, as we did not want them to be in the same grade. It seemed unfair to both. We also wanted Daniel to have the same classmates throughout his schooling so that he might develop more meaningful friendships along the way. Kasey, along with a handful of other schoolmates, was exactly what we had hoped for.

The two attended grade school, middle school, and high school together. As for grade school, Daniel split his time between regular classes and separate special education. As such, he and Kasey shared some classes together, and, in time, they developed a bond. One early birthday party involved going to a local bowling alley for bowling and pizza. The party guests gave Dan a signed bowling pin. That pin, signed by Kasey and others, is a reminder of lifelong friendships, as is a photograph of Daniel rumbling down a sideline, with one hand cupping a football and his other grasping his facemask to keep his helmet on straight, en route to scoring a touchdown in a pee-wee football game. Kasey was on this team, and his dad was a coach. It turns out that the kids on both teams rigged a fumble, and Daniel did not hesitate to take the bait, or in this case, the ball. While the other team chased him down the field, they also cheered him, along with his teammates, all the way to the end zone. After the game, Dan was presented with the game ball. Today, it sits atop a shelf in our house, right next to the photograph, with the bowling pin nearby.

Before coach Boulware ever came to town, Kasey, along with many other young men on the Woodridge football team—including my one-day son-in-law, Austin, and Kasey's younger brother, Kyle—had already put in countless hours of practice. Many of those same players had been, at one time, little boys on my son's pee-wee football team. The team had an obvious chemistry, and it showed as the program was clearly on the rise. Multiple post-season runs had the entire area abuzz with excitement. Our daughter was in the high school marching band (she played the Clarinet), and we regularly volunteered to work at the concession stand, selling burgers, hot dogs, and *Chick-fil-A*. Alright, to come clean, my wife regularly volunteered, although I did occasionally help. Daniel was on the sidelines as a waterboy for a season or two and later was known to do a stint or two as a "guest conductor" for the band. He would also help at the concession stand, even if that meant delivering orders without ringing them up. The band director's good nature, my daughter's patience, and my wife's service are all to be commended, along with the honesty of those who were delivered food and had not yet settled the tab. Those Friday nights were a blast and, later, when reminiscing with Kasey, he recalled one of his favorite high school football experiences was running through a blow-up tunnel and out onto the field right alongside Daniel for the opening game of the season. He also recalled the team meals they shared together, especially when he had the chance to sit next to his old friend.

As for those six exquisite snaps of the football under a watchful eye, they were not a fluke. No, they were the result of thousands of previous snaps, great coaching starting from middle school through high school, and a slice of good old heredity, as Kasey's dad had also been a long snapper. However, above all else, his technique had been honed after attending many camps specializing in the craft of long snapping. At 5'10" and 180 lbs., he was originally told he was not big enough to play Division I college football. Not discouraged, between 2014 and 2017, he attended camps in Columbus, Ohio, New Jersey, Pittsburgh, Pennsylvania, Chicago, and Las Vegas. He attended 12 college camps in total and participated in the prestigious *Chris Rubio Long Snapping Camp*. When Oklahoma came calling that day in Ohio, the ball was like a rocket coming from Kasey's hands and his accuracy easily made him one of the best prospects at that position in the country.

Long snapping is a most peculiar art. In football, it is also an absolute necessity—often at the most pivotal moments—in every single game. The long snapper, by all accounts, in football terms, is an odd bird, and their movements on the field are downright unusual. They live in an upside-down world, if you will. Clutching the pigskin with both hands, they set their legs unnaturally apart (greater than shoulder width, to be certain) and look back between their legs at a holder or a punter. With elbows inside their knees, the snapper aims by extending their hands towards the target and their thumbs ultimately turned outward from the body during the release. After rifling the ball back, they immediately assume the stance of the king's guardsman against an incoming wave of castle invaders attempting to go through or over the wall that is now their body. Put another way, it is a moment of precision followed by a backyard brawl. If the play involves a punt, the brawl is followed by prolonged harassment as the long snapper attempts to run down the field.

Having their heads down between their legs, long snappers are in an especially precarious position, and therefore, not surprisingly, certain rules have been established to try to protect them from unnecessary injury. In college football, defensive players are not allowed to initiate contact with the long snapper until 1 second after the ball has been snapped. To help safeguard long snappers, college referees will remind defenders of this rule before the ball is snapped. However, whether they ever really wait is open to debate— just ask any college-long snapper. The NFL, on the other hand, provides no specific time to initiate contact. However, on punt formations, defensive players are prohibited from pushing teammates on the line of scrimmage into the offensive formation, and any defensive player within 1 yard of the line of scrimmage must have their entire body beyond the width of the long snapper's shoulder pads at the snap.

In less than 1 second, a pointy oblong-shaped ball—made of brown pimpled leather and adorned with white stitched lacing—travels 15 yards from the hands of a snapper to the outstretched hands of a punter. Good snaps travel in a spiral with minimal wobble. Great ones travel with tight spirals—right down the middle—requiring little lateral movement from the punter. Great snaps might also be fired with laces up so that the punter does not even need to rotate the ball to get the smooth side of the ball against the punter's foot. Generally, the less the punter needs to do to reel the ball in, the better the boot. As for place kicks, the distance of the snap is roughly half, and with the shorter distance, the ball is fired back low and hard to the waiting hands of the holder. Again, great snaps are those that are not only lightning-quick but are also simultaneously easy to handle. Keep in mind that the holder must catch the ball, stand it upright along the ground, and rotate the ball so that the laces face away from the kicker's foot. The holders, while generally possessing cat-like reflexes reminiscent of a shortstop in baseball, need to get the ball in place with seamless fluidity, and as such, much like the punter, the less the holder needs to do to lasso the snap, the better. With the kicker running up to kick the ball, the ball needs to be there on time. As they say, timing is everything, especially in the kicker's world.

To put this in perspective, during Kasey Kelleher's tenure as a long snapper at the University of Oklahoma, a video was circulated on social media showing him knocking the cap from a plastic water bottle being held by a teammate. Not only is the snap in slow motion, but the player holding the water bottle is facing the camera with the back of his head and hands as equal targets to the incoming football. He never even flinches! My son and I have watched it a hundred times, and although the football is ultimately lost from the camera's eye, the spinning green bottle cap leaves you mesmerized. At the same time, much like a quarterback throwing a pass to a wide receiver, the snap needs to be more than a fastball. It also needs to be an invitation to catch the ball. This is why so few players have mastered the art of long snapping and why Kasey and his ilk are true craftsmen.

With the proliferation of television viewing options, watching Oklahoma football games soon became a weekly occurrence in our household, and when doing so, searching for number 51—on and off the field—became our weekly detective work. It certainly helped that Baker Mayfield had signed with the Cleveland *Browns*, as Oklahoma suddenly became the second game of the week in Northeast Ohio, right behind the Ohio State matchups. Daniel fell hard for the *Sooners* from the moment Kasey showed up in Norman, and he would hoot and holler every time his favorite college football player trotted onto the field for punts, field goals, and extra points.

While Dan went crazy with excitement, my wife and I found ourselves holding our breath as nobody ever acknowledges the long snapper unless something goes horribly wrong. We could only imagine what it must be like for the parents of a long snapper, as, apart from a kicker's parents, it can be downright lonely if things go awry. Most players who step onto the field seek glory. The long snapper, on the other hand, seeks obscurity. By all practical measurements, long snapping is a thankless job. After all, the goal is to literally remain anonymous. In the NFL, punters are hard to name, as are many special team players. However, I'll wager most hardcore fans cannot name more than 1 of the 32 starting long snappers playing in the professional game today. Heck, how many can even name their favorite team's long snapper? The funny thing is, long snappers would have it no other way.

After being redshirted his freshman year, Kelleher served as the snapper on punts and place kicks in all 14 games during the 2018 season. In 2019, he served as a snapper on punts and place kicks in all 14 games, with the place kick unit going 19 of 21 on field goals and a perfect 75 for 75 on extra points. That same year, he was placed on a scholarship. In 2020, he was an Academic All-*Big 12* First Team honoree and played in all 11 games during the Covid-shortened season. In 2021, he was an Academic All-*Big 12* selection and played in all 13 games as the long snapper on punts and place kicks. He was also placed on the *Patrick Mannelly Award* watch list for the nation's best long snapper, and in May of that year, he graduated with a degree in Human Relations. In 2022, while pursuing a master's degree in Adult and Higher Education, he was again an Academic All-*Big 12* First Team Selection. Kelleher played in all 13 games as the long snapper on punts and place kicks. In the end, he played a school-record 64 career games, tying the mark shared with linebacker Bryan Mead (2017-2021). Over time, he grew another inch or two in height and gained another 50 pounds. Turns out he was plenty big enough, and boy, did the *Sooners* get a good one both on and off the field.

During his years as a long snapper, Oklahoma had quite a run. Kasey's four *Big 12* championship rings prove it. In his first three years with the team, the *Sooners* played for a chance to go to the National Championship. Furthermore, Oklahoma beat Florida in the Cotton Bowl and beat Oregon in the Alamo Bowl in two of his other seasons. The *Sooners* went 5-2 against their rival, Texas, including a four-game winning streak. Although technically recruited by Bob Stoops, he never got a chance to play for him, as the legendary coach retired before the start of Kasey's first season. Instead, Kelleher played for Lincoln Riley and Brent Venables. He also played with countless exceptional players, including quarterbacks Baker Mayfield, Kyler Murray, Jalen Hurts, Spencer Rattler, and Caleb Williams. However, unlike these household names, many *Sooner* fans remain oblivious to Kelleher's contribution to the program. In Jeffrey Marx's *The Long Snapper*—the compelling story about Brian Kinchen, who as a 38-year-old teacher came out of retirement to make the winning snap in Super Bowl XXXVIII in the New England Patriots 32-29 win over the Carolina Panthers—Marx beautifully describes this disparity as while Tom Brady was at the Bush White House to discuss steroid use in the NFL,

Kinchen, after visiting his middle school students, was settling down on his couch to watch television. Two teammates, both about to play in the Super Bowl but living very different lives. Of course, almost everyone, including other NFL stars, has a very different life from Tom Brady, as he has more rings than just about anyone, including Kasey.

The truth is many players go largely unnoticed on football teams. For instance, there are plenty of offensive linemen who also go largely unnoticed. Of course, there are plenty of players on special teams—except for the kick returners and punt returners—that join the long snapper in being relatively unrecognized figures as well. However, every player has a role in the drama unfolding on the field and contributes to the game's outcome in some way. As a lawyer, I can attest that newer associates are not treated the same as senior partners in a law firm. Some assignments are downright boring or tedious but remain crucial to the outcome of a case. Dave, a fellow lawyer and good friend of mine, long ago dubbed those assignments as "covering punts." Somebody must run down the field and make a tackle, right? Not every lawyer can make the closing argument in the trial of the century, nor can every player kick a winning field goal as time expires, but somebody better make a tackle on that punt!

On the sidelines, usually near the head coach, are scores of assistants barking out assignments or words of encouragement. Yet, unless one is the latest media darling for an anticipated vacancy for a plum head coaching job, they are usually nameless to any casual observer. Nearby, sometimes seen near a medical tent or running onto the field to attend to an injured player, is a squad of trainers usually dressed in matching khakis and team polos. Again, they remain unknown and most of what they do goes unnoticed by those watching at home or in the stands. Scanning any sideline reveals multitudes of unknown faces and players who will never enter the game. The same can be said for the armies of band members and cheer squads, who belt out fight songs in the heavy heat of an early September day or who dance and cheer seemingly without interruption for hours on end. A human mascot, sweating profusely, runs along the sideline and behind the endzone and, though nameless, is a fellow student and the child of parents somewhere in the stands. At lesser-known schools or in lower divisions, even the usual marquee positions are comprised of names and faces typically unknown by the masses. The list of examples at any given game on any given Saturday afternoon is practically endless. How many have gone unnoticed at the games we have attended? How many have gone unnoticed by you?

The point is that many plays and endeavors throughout one's life require "covering punts." As a father to a son with special needs, I am especially mindful of the many people who have come into our lives and remain otherwise unnoticed. The list includes many friends, family members, teachers, aides, nurses, doctors, coaches, drivers, and parents. It also includes all the other invisible hands that have touched our lives. Thank you from the bottom of our hearts. You not only covered the punt but did so with grace and humility, and your actions have now rippled in a pool of everlasting significance. Simply put, you played a key role in the game. As for our favorite long snapper, you have not gone unnoticed in our family, and most certainly not by our son.

Guests in Norman

On September 29, 2018, wedged between parents and friends of Oklahoma football players, we witnessed the *Sooners* demolish Baylor 66-33. I know it looks like a basketball score, and maybe our uncle's presence had something to do with that, given his history with a bouncing ball. However, it was indeed a football game we witnessed. Second-year head coach Lincoln Riley, fresh off a heart-wrenching defeat to Georgia in the college football playoff in the Rose Bowl the year before, had found a nifty replacement at quarterback from the prior year's Heisman Trophy winner, Baker Mayfield. Coming into the game, the team was undefeated and ranked 6th in the country. However, the team had barely escaped with a victory the week previously, squeaking out a 28-21 win in overtime against Army, and based on team policy, the new quarterback would sit out the first series of our game. What nobody outside the football program knew was that Kyler Murray had not set his alarm clock Thursday night, so he was late to practice on Friday. This small punishment was meant to fit the infraction. Regardless, when he did come into the game, it was clearly something to behold and perhaps the extra sleep was genuinely needed.

Kyler Murray, a Texas kid who was born and raised near the Dallas-Fort Worth metroplex, initially attended Texas A&M to play both football and baseball. However, after the 2015 season, he transferred to Oklahoma and, according to NCAA rules, was ineligible to play in the 2016 season. The following year, he found himself as the backup quarterback behind Baker Mayfield. In 2018, he not only won the starting quarterback job on the football team but also as an outfielder on the *Sooner* baseball team, where he started 50 of 51 games and hit .296 with 10 home runs, 13 doubles, 47 RBIs, 46 runs, and had 10 stolen bases. These feats on the diamond did not go unnoticed as he was the 9th overall pick in the 2018 MLB First-Year Player Draft by the Oakland *A's*.

As for the game at hand, Murray had a day that would go down in the history books as he threw six touchdown passes and ran for another. He chucked the ball downfield and into the end zones, over and over, and with such ease that it almost felt like we were watching a video game. It was the highest point total for Oklahoma since the famous *Mayfield v. Mahomes* shootout against Texas Tech, and Murray's seven-touchdown total tied Mayfield's accomplishment in that same famous duel. Although such fireworks limited the number of Oklahoma punts to a paltry three for the entire game, we got to see plenty of Kasey's snaps on extra points and on one field goal in the fourth quarter. He was flawless, of course. Wearing our number 51 jerseys, we made sure that everyone around us knew that, aside from Murray, he was the best player on the field.

Nine touchdowns and a field goal by the home team made for a raucous afternoon. Before the game, with some concern for Daniel and any sensory issues he might have with unexpected loud noises, Kelleher's family had warned us about the *OU RUF/NEKs* and their guns, which they fire after every kickoff during the game and after every *Sooners* score. Thankfully, my son had no issues and, in fact, loved it. As for the rest of us, it still managed to catch us unaware more than once during the game. These *OU RUF/NEKs*, standing in the back of both end zones during the game, just might be the nation's oldest spirit squad of its kind, dating back to the 1910s, and the name is believed to have been loosely coined during a December 1915 basketball game between Oklahoma and Oklahoma A&M. Several football players, on hand to cheer their fellow *Sooners*, were making such a ruckus that an elderly woman in the crowd reportedly shouted to them, "Sit down and be quiet you roughnecks." Whether her admonishment was deserved or not, it gave birth to a group founded by Charles Leslie High.

In time, the name was formally made *RUF/NEKs*, and the members made certain to wear cowboy attire lest they be confused with oil riggers. The earliest members, much like other college societies and fraternities, had their share of secret rituals and quirky traditions. These early squads, comprising approximately 20 members, were all-male and initially operated outside the University. Slowly, the group came to be embraced by the school, with any harsher types of hazing and blatantly mutinous behaviors being scaled back. In 1921, the famous white and red paddles were introduced, as was the tradition of not shaving their beards following a *Sooner* loss. The first appearance of those ceremonial shotguns we came to dread and/or appreciate is believed to have started in 1955, and with 87,000 fans in attendance at home games, the spirit squad is one of the only groups permitted to use firearms on campus. In fact, firearms safety training is conducted through the OUPD, and the guns are stored and transported by them as well. The weapons—modified 12-gauge shotguns with an extra-large barrel packed with black powder and no lead—are nonetheless "real firearms" and must be treated as such.

Guns aside, the best-known tradition associated with the *RUF/NEKs* is the *Sooner Schooner*—a replica of the Studebaker Conestoga wagon used by settlers in the Oklahoma Territory. Powered by two white ponies named *Boomer* and *Sooner*, the white wagon—with crimson trim and a large "*Sooner Schooner*" spelled out across the bonnet—dashes out onto the field with great speed and in an arcing motion near the 30-line races back off the field before disappearing in a stadium tunnel in the corner of the end zone. This happens every time Oklahoma scores, and the crowd goes nuts. This beloved tradition started in 1964, and *Sooner Schooner* became the University's official mascot in 1980. Two human-costumed mascots dressed as ponies attend most Oklahoma festivities as *Boomer* and *Sooner*. Before this, another official mascot was a dog named *Mex*, who served as the official mascot between 1915 to 1928. After discovering the abandoned pup in Mexico, a U.S. Army Medic brought him to college at OU. *Mex*, who lived at the Kappa Sigma fraternity house, chased off stray animals and, with his red sweater with a big "O," was loved by *Sooner* fans. A tough dog, to be sure, he survived an attempted poisoning by non-Sooner fans and, after 13 years of faithful service, died from natural causes. So loved was *Mex* that the university canceled classes for his funeral and procession. He is reportedly buried in a small casket under the existing stadium.

On a partly sunny afternoon in Norman, Oklahoma, as we sat in the stands, we had no idea that the spirit of *Mex* was so close at hand. However, we were certainly aware of *Sooner Schooner* as we lay witness to the wagon ride for glory nearly a dozen times. Our *RUF/NEKs* had also come a long way from the original lot. Starting in 1973, after a female student sued the *RUF/NEKs* for being denied admission into the group, an all-female sister organization was formed, called *Lil' Sis*. This group, which is also referred to as the *Oklahoma RUF/NEK Lil' Sis program*, works in tandem with the lads. The gals wear crimson dresses and brown cowboy boots, while the guys wear short-sleeved crimson shirts tucked into white pants with brown belts. A few wear baseball caps or cowboy hats, and all wear tennis shoes when things get serious. Together, essentially as one, they run onto the field with flags before the game and sit side by side in the front and back of the wagon as it parades about following *Sooner* scores. Starting the year after the guy trip, in 2019, the *RUF/NEK Lil' Sis* program fired their first shots at a game and, in 2020, a woman from the group, Darby Dean, finally had the honor of driving the Schooner onto the field. Thankfully, Daniel and I were able to see these later inclusions at subsequent games. Last year, in 2023, after Kelleher had graduated, Jadyn

Davis became the first African American woman to lead the *Sooner Schooner*. How awesome!

The *Sooner Schooner* moves at an alarming speed, and the pivot made near the quarter-field is not a slow sweeping arc but more of a pinpoint turn befitting a *Formula 1* racer on the streets of Monte Carlo. It all happens so fast; you promise yourself you will try to catch more of the action next time. In the front of the Conestoga wagon are a gal and a guy driving this train while another hangs *Old Glory* out from the back. Sprinting along both sides while twirling their paddles are other members, followed by another dozen or so people trailing the speeding wagon. This ritual usually goes without a hitch. However, the year after our visit, the wagon tipped over during a sharp turn, violently throwing the drivers to the ground. Considered a fluke, an inside wheel stopped turning and gave way. Thankfully, all participants, both human and equine, escaped without serious injury. Some thirty years prior, in 1993, a similar incident occurred during a home game against Colorado. Although nobody was seriously hurt, the crash managed to rip the artificial turf, which had to be repaired with duct tape during the game. Today, the stadium has grass, allowing for any extra duct tape to be used on the sidelines and addressing uniform issues instead.

Another embarrassing moment occurred in the third quarter of the 1985 Orange Bowl against the Washington *Huskies* when the Sooners had a 22-yard field goal nullified by penalty. Unaware of the infraction, the *Sooner Schooner* crew ventured onto the field to celebrate, resulting in OU being penalized an additional 15 yards. The 22-yard field goal, which became a 42-yard field goal, was blocked. Given this half-century tradition, these are isolated moments and take nothing away from one of college football's most recognizable spectacles. In fact, given Oklahoma's prolific offenses over the years and the resulting celebratory runs onto the field, the record is exemplary. Each year, over 100 students apply to join the *RUF/NEK* and *RUF/NEK Lil' Sis* programs, competing for the 20 spots available. If chosen, their Saturdays, like ours, will never be the same.

Immediately after the final whistle was blown to end the contest, Daniel and I made our way down to the first row of seats, right behind the Oklahoma bench, where other family members gathered to greet players still on the field. Again, much like his beeline off the bus, Kasey made his way over to Dan as if shot from a cannon, and the two old friends warmly embraced. Luckily, I snapped a picture, as it was a remarkable moment. With the help of my brother and uncle, we even managed to squeeze me in for a few shots as well. Kasey then asked Dan if he would wait around and meet him after the game but warned us that it might take a good half an hour or so. We told him not to worry as we were not going anywhere! In the end, it turned out to be rather enjoyable waiting, as we got to meet other players and their parents. It was especially fun seeing the younger kids line up with the hope of nabbing an autograph or two. Eventually, Kasey emerged and shared many stories of the game and college life and although we decided to let our favorite player slip into the night to celebrate with teammates as opposed to hanging out with the old guys, Kasey told us to meet him back at the stadium the following morning as he wanted to show Daniel the Oklahoma locker room. As Dan likes to say, "Oh boy!"

While walking back to the car—located in our dreamy parking spot near the wholly unexpected Art Museum—we decided to grab dinner at a place we had seen when we first arrived. It was called the *Library Bar & Grill*, and even though everyone in the joint was rooting against the *Buckeyes* in their battle against Penn State in another "whiteout" in Happy Valley, we enjoyed the food and atmosphere. We also loved the name and imagined how many students, over the years, had truthfully told their parents, if asked about their whereabouts, perhaps from an unanswered phone call, that they had been at the "library." We also agreed that every campus needs such a place and that most probably has one. Oh, and although the other patrons had the upper hand while we dined, we got to see Dwayne Haskins chuck two touchdown passes in the final minutes of the game to rally the *Buckeyes* to a 27-26 victory over the *Nittany Lions*. This we saw in the lobby at the *Sooner Legends* hotel, where another group of "haters' even managed to tell us that Dwayne Haskins was not playing well and should be benched. Still dressed in our Oklahoma gear, I'm sure it caused great confusion when we enjoyed our "mic drop" moment, and given the five touchdown passes he later threw against our bitter rival, I'm glad they had no idea what they were talking about. *Buckeye Nation* loves you, Dwayne. We always will. Rest in peace, friend.

The following morning, it was our turn to make a beeline—straight to *Gaylord Family Oklahoma Memorial Stadium*. After meeting Kasey outside, he led us through the main entrance of the stadium, where we were immediately greeted by a sleek glass wall containing an abundance of trophies representing Bowl game victories and National Championships. Nearby, as we strolled along another hallway, we came upon a room-length shelf containing several Heisman trophies on display. Dan and Kasey stopped for a photograph in front of quarterback Sam Bradford's 2008 trophy. Oklahoma is tied with Ohio State and Notre Dame, having seven Heisman Trophy winners, and when we were there, the newest belonged to Baker Mayfield, who had won it the previous year. What we did not know at the time of our tour was that we had watched another Heisman trophy winner the previous afternoon, as Kyler Murray would be awarded the trophy in New York several months afterward. When he won the trophy, the year after Mayfield, Oklahoma became the first University to have back-to-back quarterbacks win the Heisman trophy. Interestingly, Yale had the first back-to-back winners in 1936-37, followed by the Army football team in 1945-46. This feat occurred again in 2004-05, when Matt Leinart and Reggie Bush won back-to-back trophies for USC, and was repeated once more after Oklahoma's feat in 2020-21, when Devonte Smith followed Bryce Young to secure back-to-back Heisman wins for Alabama. Of course, I would be remiss, especially as a *Buckeye*, if I did not mention Archie Griffin won back-to-back Heisman trophies in 1974-75, making him the only player to win the award twice. As for Oklahoma, their seven winners are Kyler Murray (2018), Baker

Mayfield (2017), Sam Bradford (2008), Jason white (2003), Billy Sims (1978), Steve Owens (1969), and Billy Vessels (1952). Seeing a Heisman trophy up close was an absolute thrill.

Although the trophy cases were an unexpected treat, the highlight of our tour was seeing the Oklahoma football team's state-of-the-art locker room. More specifically, our greatest highlight was gazing upon our favorite player's locker. First, take any image of a locker room you might have from an old movie or your own school experience, and throw those pictures into the nearest trash bin. Kasey's "locker" was not some old rusty metal shoebox that needed to be slammed shut. No, it was a sleek, modern spread that would make the folks at *California Closet* grin. Each player's image, along with their number, name, and position, was digitally displayed on a white screen above their designated "locker." Each display screen also featured a small, crimson-colored emblem representing the player's home state, and it was cool to see Ohio right next to Kasey's name and photograph, wedged between teammates from Oklahoma and Texas. It was also a reminder that top programs recruit from across the entire country, not just within a state. Tucked behind these displays, which also served as a swinging door, was a comfortable spot for each player's shoulder pads. Below the screens, the player's crimson helmet sat under bright white light in another modest-sized cubbyhole. To the side, set vertically, was a pull-out shelf for storing cleats, and below crimson leather benches were additional pull-out shelves for uniforms and pads. While it is hard to pick a favorite picture from any football trip, the pictures of Daniel and Kasey by his locker, especially those where Daniel and Kasey took turns wearing Kasey's shoulder pads and helmet, are hard to beat.

The trip to the equipment room was equally fascinating, as we got the opportunity to see several helmets being worked on by an equipment manager. Also displayed along the wall behind the worktable were helmets from every team the *Sooners* have played over the years. When I asked Kasey if the scalps were taken from fallen foes, he indicated that it was more of a tribute to the programs of other schools, displayed as a sign of respect for college football. Another room nearby displayed the jerseys of all Oklahoma players currently playing in the NFL. Not surprisingly, there were quite a few, but Kelleher made a point of showing us James Winchester's number 41 for the Kansas City Chiefs, as he was a fellow long-snapper. We also enjoyed a quick trip to the treatment rooms and marveled at the size of the whirlpool, as well as the flat-screen TVs along the walls for those soaking up their recovery. Walking through the complex, Kasey was regularly greeted by fellow players and a smattering of assistant coaches. This was especially cool. Lastly, Kasey walked us toward the field, reenacting what it was like on gameday for the *Sooner* players. As we approached the final gate, he told us to imagine thousands of screaming fans, with the band playing and our brothers by our side. Just inside this final tunnel is a brick wall with the following words inscribed in large silver metal lettering: *"NOW ENTERING THE HEART OF SOONER NATION."* It gave us goosebumps.

Three weeks after we had returned home from Oklahoma—on October 20, 2018—Daniel and I gathered on our family couch to watch the #2-ranked Ohio State *Buckeyes* clash with the Purdue *Boilermakers*. It was a dark autumn day, filled with showers of falling leaves painted yellow and orange. Before the game, we were introduced—like much of the nation—to a Purdue student named Tyler Trent, who was battling terminal bone cancer and was in hospice care. He was also miraculously on hand—in a wheelchair, wrapped in a Purdue blanket and with a Purdue stocking cap—to watch his beloved football team. With tears streaming across my cheeks, I looked up at the ceiling and said, "Oh boy, Dad, we're screwed, and maybe that is all right." Tyler Trent witnessed a complete thumping of our *Buckeyes* and, after the game, joined the *Boilermakers* in the locker room, where he was named one of the team's new captains. Tyler passed away on January 1, 2019, and thousands paid tribute to his remarkable life. Later that same year, on September 7th, 2019—Tyler's 21st birthday—Purdue dedicated the *Tyler Trent Student Gate* before their home opener against Vanderbilt. Tyler would have been doubly pleased, as Purdue won the game. For us, I see another possible guy trip, right, Dad?

Finding Tim

Tim and I were high school friends, albeit not best friends. We ran in the same circles, but we weren't from the same neighborhood. Tim was a transplanted Texan who lived across town, whereas I was a West Akron native through and through, having lived in the same house for nearly all my life. He was big and athletic, whereas I was slight in frame. Still, we shared a great deal, including mutual friends, a love of soccer, many of the same high school crushes, and a knack for avoiding trouble. Both of us took our studies seriously, as college was not an option. It was expected. We were not rich, but certainly not poor. Like many families at our school, we would have been considered moderately affluent. Like many American families, the Reagan 80s had been kind to us. Both of us came from stable homes with parents who remained married, and we each had one sibling. Tim had a sister, while I had a brother. However, in other ways, we remained on separate paths as he was an anchor on the soccer team, while I was, for the most part, except for my senior year, a perennial benchwarmer. Furthermore, although I went to football games on Friday night, he played in them.

Following high school, Tim attended the University of Missouri in Columbia to pursue his studies and try his luck at being a kicker on the *Tigers'* football team. He never came back to Ohio, whereas I, for the most part, never left. My furthest venture from Akron, aside from a semester in Oxford, England, and a summer clerking in Seattle, Washington, was a 120-mile trip to attend *The* Ohio State University in Columbus, Ohio. Later, Tim attended the University of Illinois Urbana-Champaign while I went to Case Western Reserve University in Cleveland, Ohio. We both married Midwestern girls, with his wife being from Indiana and mine from Illinois. We both had two kids, and while he had two boys, I had a boy and then a girl. We both set out to start our families and our careers and, in a world before the advent of the internet, social media, or *Facebook*, we quickly lost contact with each other.

Sadly, this happened to many of our high schoolmates. Looking back through the lens of history, the early 1980s gave rise to a unique post-graduation fragmentation that was peculiar to the time. To further explain, as stated, the internet was still nearly a decade away from being widely available, and cell phones were years away from being commonplace, with landlines being the primary form of communication, aside from writing letters, which people seldom did. However, the world was simultaneously becoming more dynamic, with families moving all about the country for the first time. In the past, postgraduates would either stay home to attend school, return home to start careers, or visit family. This made it much easier to keep in touch. For the first time in our modern life, this was changing. Not only did Tim leave town, but so did his family. When social media and *Facebook* finally took root, there was a literal avalanche of "missing graduates" who were able to reconnect for the first time in years. This is also why so many Gen Xers remain glued to *Facebook*, even at the amusement of their children.

While I ultimately became a lawyer, Tim built a successful business career, first working for Lilly, then Genentech, and after stints in Salt Lake City and Atlanta, he found himself in Greenville, South Carolina, working for a national specialty pharmacy. Even though we still lived hundreds of miles apart, it was around this time we reconnected.

After years of playing football and soccer and walking briskly through airports, sore legs were not uncommon for my friend, especially first thing in the morning or in the evening after a long day. His left leg was especially sore at times, but this was his "plant leg," and, as such, he was surprised it wasn't worse given the thousands of times he had kicked a ball during his playing days on the gridiron and pitch.

One day, while doing a leg press, Tim felt an unusual twinge in his leg and a few months later, when skiing with his sons Ryan and Ben at Beaver Creek, Colorado, he found himself in a hot tub early and often, with Motrin as a constant companion. Keeping up with his two boys was already getting harder, but he seemed especially sore on the runs down the mountain. Upon his return home, he first received an injection, followed ultimately by a scope of his knee. These treatments are all too familiar for an aging athlete, and Tim hoped the worst was behind him. However, later, while attending a business meeting in Charlotte, Tim's foot seemed to get caught on the carpet in the lobby of the Sheraton hotel. The resulting pain was excruciating. After a knee x-ray came back normal, it was decided to perform a hip x-ray, which had never been done up to this point. When the doctor came back to share the results, his dour demeanor hinted that a terrible diagnosis might be forthcoming. My buddy may not have been a doctor, but even he could see the bone looked black.

Tim was instructed to go on bed rest and make an appointment with an oncologist as soon as possible. Unfortunately, his pain was about to get much worse. While at home, his femur fractured, and when being put in an ambulance, the femur completely shattered. Concerned onlookers can still recall the blood-curdling scream that rang out through the neighborhood, and I've been told it was louder than when he missed an open shot on goal.

Osteosarcoma is a type of bone cancer that originates in the cells that form bones, typically affecting the long bones of the body, such as the arms or legs. Tim's osteosarcoma was at the neck of his femur. The femur is the only bone in your thigh and runs from your hip to your knee. Not only is it the longest bone in the body, but it is also the strongest. It supports the body's weight and facilitates movement. The neck of the femur—the spot of my old high school friend's cancer—is the bar-like part of the bone right near the socket of the hip where the leg meets the pelvis. It is the most common location for hip fractures. Snuggled near his hip, the cancer had previously evaded detection, and although it might have shattered his femur, my old chum was determined not to let it shatter his life.

As my gang of cohorts attended the LSU-Florida game in Baton Rouge in 2013, Tim was undergoing treatments that would hopefully not only destroy the cancer but also save his leg from amputation. Crammed into a tiny hospital room with his leg in traction, he underwent eight weeks of chemotherapy to reduce the tumor before surgery. Literally held hostage, he thankfully had family (including his kids, wife, and mom) nearby and a television to watch Clemson football games. On more than one occasion, a nurse or two would stop by to check on him and watch a few plays before moving on to the next room. His ultimate surgery involved removing all the identified cancer and surrounding tissue and replacing the bone affected by the cancer with an internal prosthesis.

Taking aim at any cancer cells that might remain in the shadows of his body, an additional three months of chemotherapy followed surgery. The next phase in his recovery was learning to walk again. First came a wheelchair, followed by months of physical therapy. This was followed by a walker and additional months of physical therapy. Somewhere between the rounds of therapy, he received the news that the tests revealed my one-time teammate was cancer-free. To commemorate the moment, Tim rang a bell in the hospital hallway for the celebratory photo to mark the joyous occasion. His cap hid his loss of hair, and his cane was removed from the shot. By the following year, in 2014, when our gang had ventured to Tim's old childhood state of Texas to see Texas A&M play Ole Miss, he ditched the cane for good. As for his prosthetic device, Tim likes to say his leg is "titanium strong" and he is eternally grateful for the expert care received by his entire treatment team.

At some point along the way, Tim had learned of our "guy trips" and lobbied hard for us to include Clemson as one of our next adventures. Having battled cancer, my friend developed a deep appreciation for living every moment to the fullest, and he wanted to share in any way he could. His love for his family is unmistakable, and he exudes an infectious love for Greenville and all things in the Upstate region of South Carolina. He might not be the local mayor, but he probably should be. As we gathered in his living room, I looked across at my long-lost friend, and it felt like we had never been apart; although he had never met my uncle or my son before, they conversed like long-lost friends. At that moment, I thought to myself, "The magic of our trips just grew exponentially."

One Night in The Upstate

Greenville, South Carolina, is an anomaly. On the one hand, the city, which now tilts towards a larger city over a smaller town, certainly has the stress and drama of any urban center. This includes the typical headaches associated with traffic, crowds, and the hustle and bustle that comes with living in a competitive modern world. These expected, yet nonetheless annoying, headaches have been coupled with breathtaking growing pains as the city has rapidly expanded over the last few decades. This is not unique and is shared by other locales throughout the Southern United States. The fact that the city is split by a river —*The Reedy*—is also not necessarily unusual for a typical city in any region of the country. However, in the heart of downtown, that river, which is a tributary of the Saluda River, not only pumps life into the city but also cascades in white ribbons down 40 feet of large granite rocks in a picturesque park named *Falls Park*. Atop the waterfalls, providing a bird's eye view, is a striking 345-foot curved pedestrian bridge named the *Liberty Bridge.* As the falling water releases negative ions, city dwellers and visitors alike soak up those ions as positive energy. Once they have entered the bloodstream, the production of serotonin increases, thereby making all in proximity a little happier. Besides the natural beauty of a waterfall, in both sight and sound, this is why many scientists believe we humans are so drawn to them. And therein is the anomaly—Greenville is a city full of happy people. I know that almost seems like an oxymoron, but believe me, it is true. Her citizens, who need not take a drive out to the country to view nature's beauty, are physically made happy by the cascading falls, and even when not nearby—*Falls Park*, her transplants are still made happy knowing they no longer need to do battle with the ice, snow and clouds of Cleveland, Buffalo, or Milwaukee. As I said, Greenville is a beautiful anomaly.

As we strolled through this *happy* place and *Falls Park*, we stopped and lingered atop the *Liberty Bridge*—with its impressive string of supporting cables—enjoying views of the falls, river, and array of buildings constructed along the bluffs. One nearby building was the *Hampton Inn & Suites*, a place my parents frequented during their visits to the Upstate in the 1990s and early 2000s. Long before modern travel magazines "discovered" Greenville, my father was singing her praises. He'd come home and tell anyone who would listen that Greenville was a great place to visit or live. Dad had originally come to the Greenville-Spartanburg area for his consulting work at *Michelin* after the French tire manufacturer had made Greenville the North American headquarters in the mid-1980s. He had also made a few visits to the *BMW* facilities, which are also nearby. Soon, he took my mother when he could. Work aside, his favorite part of these business trips was dinners with Mom—when she could manage to sneak away with him—at *Trattoria Giorgio* on South Main Street and, though we briefly discussed having our annual guy trip Friday night dinner there, it was decided to leave this spot untouched and forever frozen in time in our family's collective memory. It would remain their spot, not ours. Inside my wallet, I still carry a card for this restaurant, given to me by my father years ago, "in case I was ever in Greenville with Judi, and I wanted a romantic spot to have dinner." As we stood atop the bridge, gazing out into the horizon, by reflex or intuition, I pulled this tattered card out of my wallet. I imagined my parents walking through this park before or after dinner. It made me feel happy, especially with all those ions floating about. My son, who has seen the card many times, said aloud, "Grandpa sure loved Greenville," and as I carefully tucked the card back inside my wallet, I said, "He sure did, Dan. He sure did."

Wandering the streets of this still manageable—but growing like a beanstalk—spot, it seemed hard to imagine her modest beginnings were centered around a log courthouse built in 1795. With her abundance of natural beauty, logic would dictate her name was derived from the same. However, Greenville is named after Nathaniel Greene, the commander of the Southern forces in the Revolutionary War. This area, which largely escaped much of the destruction inflicted upon South Carolina during the Civil War, slowly emerged as a cotton town. In fact, between 1880 and 1903, utilizing the waters of the *Reedy* and nearby rivers, thirteen mills were opened, and all the mills, in time, had their own baseball teams. Winning baseball games was almost as important as the millwork itself. Joe Jackson worked a twelve-hour shift each day, but on the weekends, he played for the *Brandon Mill* baseball team. At just thirteen years old, he was recruited to play "Mill Ball," and for good reason. Later, Joe would play in the big leagues, finishing with the third-highest batting average of all time (.356), be given a lifetime ban from baseball following the 1919 Black Sox cheating scandal, was given the nickname "Shoeless," and was later portrayed in the beloved movie *Field of Dreams* by *Ray Liotta*.

By our visit, the textile mills, the *Brandon Mill* baseball team, and *"Shoeless" Joe Jackson* were long gone. Although we were unable to visit the *Shoeless Joe Jackson Museum and Baseball Library*, we were able to take a stroll down memory lane, connecting the present with the past, when we paid a visit to *Mast General Store*. Located on North Main Street, the street address boasts a rich retail history dating back to

1898, when it was home to a dry goods store and later served as the *Meyers-Arnold Department Store*. The story behind the *Mast General Store* begins in Sugar Grove, North Carolina and, after multiple stores were opened throughout the *Tar Heel State*, the store we found ourselves in—the first in South Carolina—opened in 2003. Now, if you have never been to a *Mast General Store*, you are in for a treat. Imagine a department store fused together with a grocery, a shoe store, and an outdoor supply shop. Then throw in a *Dick's Sporting Goods* and a *Cracker Barrel* gift shop for good measure. I'm probably forgetting at least a half dozen departments, but you get the idea. It is, after all, a general store. If you can't find what you are looking for, you are probably just overwhelmed. Take a deep breath and ask one of the many friendly staff members to point you in the right direction.

Rick Erwin's was our Friday night dinner choice for the Clemson guy trip. Although we had thought about dining at the original *Rick Erwin's West End Grille* in downtown Greenville, we decided to eat at his newer restaurant, *Rick Erwin's Clemson*, located just outside of campus in *Patrick Square*. With only a later reservation being available at either restaurant, we hoped this would give us more time to locate our Lake House lodging in unfamiliar surroundings and the darkness of night. Located in a newer business district, the light brick building sits at a corner, featuring a black awning and ample, easy parking. Inside the double wooden doors is a modern yet elegant décor, with wood-stained Carolina plantation blinds, matching wood molding, white linens, and ornate carpeting.

The gang ordered calamari and fried green tomatoes for starters and filets for the main course. This was followed by espresso crème brûlée for dessert and, although the restaurant boasts an extensive wine list, we refrained from imbibing, given our upcoming trek near the lake and mountains in the black of night. The service was impeccable, and we were treated to a visit from the big guy himself at our table. Yes, Rick, who happened to be playing host that night, stopped by our table to ensure everything was delicious and even took a moment to pose for a picture with my son. Thanks, Rick! Great place you have there. Oh, and let me know if you want me to forward the picture, as I'm sure it would look great in the restaurant.

Following dinner, Uncle Frank, as our designated driver, managed to artfully navigate around the unseen lake and any red Carolina soil and, to his credit, was able to rest the rental in the driveway of Tim and Carla's Lake House on *Lake Keowee*. Luckily, our hosts had left a few lights on—it sure was dark.

Located in Oconee and Pickens counties in South Carolina's northwest Golden Corner, *Lake Keowee* is a man-made reservoir created in 1971 by Duke Power Company to generate hydroelectric power and to cool the reactors at the Oconee Nuclear Station near Seneca. Long before nuclear energy was ever imagined as a power source, the 26-mile-long-3-mile-wide lake, comprising roughly 18,372 acres, was once home to the Creek and Cherokee Tribes. In fact, *Keowee*, derived from Cherokee, means "place of the mulberries." Prior to the flooding of the valley, an archaeological team from the University of South Carolina conducted an extensive excavation at the former sites of *Keowee Town* and *Fort Prince George.* The former, located on the banks of the Keowee River, was the largest of the seven Cherokee Lower Towns in the colonial period, while the latter was a fort constructed in 1753, named after the Prince of Wales, who later became King George III of American revolution infamy. Thankfully, the team was able to preserve a treasure trove of historical artifacts that would have been forever lost beneath the floor of the 53-foot-deep lake.

For approximately two years, the valley was flooded with 5.3 million gallons of water, but not before two 33-foot-wide, 800-foot-long tunnels were dug for the placement of turbines that would generate electricity from beneath the lake. Remarkably, seven dams, multiple turbines, a handful of tunnels, and a nuclear station were built for

$700 million. This massive civil engineering achievement ultimately created a picturesque lake with shimmering blue waters. It is also a recreational paradise, drawing locals and tourists alike, with ample boating, fishing, waterskiing, camping, and picnicking. Today, multi-million-dollar homes dot the highly desirable playground, making it hard to believe that lots initially sold for $4,000 to $6,000. Glory goes to those with vision or a secret crystal ball.

Clemson, South Carolina

Thin rays of sunlight, poking through the window blinds and reflecting against the wall in my bedroom, served as a personal invitation to be part of a new day. Having arrived later in the evening, we had gone straight to sleep. As such, this was our first good look at Tim and Carla's beautiful house in all her morning glory and, more importantly, our first clear glimpse of *Lake Keowee*. By the time I made my way to the kitchen, I could smell freshly brewed coffee and, after I poured my first cup, I joined the guys who were already on the deck. Typical of many early mornings on a lake, a layer of fog hovered across the water, partially blocking the distant shoreline. This, along with the sounds of birds and wildlife, added to the beauty of our surroundings, making the view even more alluring. We noticed Tim had left some fresh-cut wood in a nearby fire pit, within a circle of chairs, and lamented our late arrival and what might have been. Regardless of missed opportunities and the temptation of lingering longer, we had a full day ahead of us, so we made an early start back to Clemson.

Our first stop was for breakfast at a nearby *Waffle House.* Although this meal might seem ordinary, it was epic! My son's breakfast has become the stuff of legends. It was, quite simply, laughably large. Now, sometimes Daniel is misunderstood when ordering food in a restaurant. To give him as much independence as possible, my wife and I try not to order for him. If the server seems to be following his requests, we go with the flow. On the other hand, if the server appears confused or seems to require our assistance, we will intervene on behalf of all. Our waitress that morning was a sweet, middle-aged woman with a thick Southern accent who seemed to bond with Daniel immediately. After some back and forth with my son, along with a few nods and points at the menu, she turned to the rest of us for our orders. I had no idea what I had for breakfast or what my brother or uncle had to eat. However, I can tell you precisely what my son had. We all can. His first super-sized plate consisted of eggs, hash browns, bacon, and toast. Big, but nothing crazy. However, he got a second smaller plate with sausage and a third with biscuits and gravy. However, the last plate took the gut-busting breakfast order to a whole new level. The final side dish was another super-sized plate that carried a breakfast steak. At this point, there was no more room on our table, so several dishes had to be placed on a nearby ledge.

Usually, I'm the type of guy who pokes fun at anyone who photographs their food, but I just had to snap a few shots for my wife. In fact, we all snapped a few pictures of his feast. Heck, even diners in nearby booths snapped a few photos. Perhaps thinking we had been hoodwinked, my uncle grabbed the check after our meal and insisted on buying breakfast. As he looked at the tab, he started shaking his head and laughed out loud. "How about that? I can't believe that. Wow!" Frank then turned the tab so we could see it. Daniel had simply ordered "*The Breakfast Special.*" If that was the correct order, so be it. If not, I'd like to thank our server and maybe the chef as well for your true Southern hospitality! That *Waffle House* was anything but ordinary.

We arrived in Clemson mid-morning, and after the larger-than-expected breakfast, we decided to take an extra-long stroll through campus. Tim, of course, had set us up with a parking pass. That's just how he operates, as no detail goes unnoticed with him. In any case, the pass really came in handy as the town was already packed. With several hours to go before kick-off, we also made our annual pilgrimage to the campus bookstore for an assortment of *Clemson Tiger* merchandise.

Our first tailgating stop was a visit to the *ClemsonLIFE* tent, as we had been given an informal invitation to stop by and introduce ourselves. Alongside a grassy knoll powdered with fallen leaves from nearby trees, current students, prospective students, and a bunch of eager parents enjoyed burgers, soft drinks, and chips in Clemson folding chairs on a beautiful sunny afternoon. Still unable to walk upright after breakfast, we respectfully declined to partake in lunch offers. Daniel, dressed in a *Clemson Tiger Paw* camouflage visor and an orange *Clemson* pullover gifted to him from Tim the day before, fit right in. In fact, parents were quick to ask us a barrage of questions, thinking he was part of this unique and wonderful program. *ClemsonLIFE*, like other programs nationwide, is designed to provide a collegiate experience that prepares young men and women with intellectual disabilities for competitive employment and independent living through a combination of academic coursework and career exploration. Dan was fortunate enough to participate in a similar program, located near our home in Ohio, as part of the *Campus Transition Project (CTP)* at Kent State University in Kent, Ohio. *"Ay, oh, way to go, Ohio!"* Feel free to sing it in Chrissy Hynde's voice, as I know you want to. Although the list continues to expand, other schools with similar programs include Appalachian State University, Auburn University, California State University (Fresno), California State University (Northridge), Curry College, Lesley University, Marshall University, Missouri State University, New York Institute of Technology, Southern Oregon University, Syracuse University, Texas Tech University, The College of New Jersey, University of Arizona, University of Ozarks, University of

South Carolina, University of West Georgia, and Xavier University. "*Ay, oh, way to go (insert the above names).*" If I have left out any other programs, please accept my sincerest apologies. Hopefully, one day, the list will take pages, and the song can go on forever.

ClemsonLIFE brings an extra "cool" factor to its program, as coach Dabo Swinney is literally "all in." The coach, who has a foundation called *Dabo's ALL-IN TEAM Foundation*, is closely connected with *ClemsonLIFE*, as not only has the foundation donated over $450,000, but Dabo personally enjoys participating in local events for the students of this program. The connection began years before when Swinney played football for coach Gene Stallings at the University of Alabama. This team, which we had seen honored a few years earlier on our trip to Tuscaloosa, had won yet another Alabama National Championship. In any event, not only did Stallings give Dabo his first coaching job, but he also taught him—much like our dad taught my brother and me—important lessons about not sacrificing family for work. The entire Swinney family owes a debt of gratitude to Coach Stallings and was also deeply touched by Stallings' son, John Mark Stallings, previously mentioned as well, who was born with Down syndrome. The Swinney's Foundation, which also focuses on breast cancer research, family issues surrounding drug and alcohol addiction, and elementary school-aged children in economically disadvantaged communities, honors the memory of John Mark by supporting Clemson University's *ClemsonLIFE* program. Who says good guys can't finish first?

These programs ultimately create healthy soil to plant and nurture innovative ideas surrounding inclusion. Several years after our first visit to Clemson, my wife, my son, and I returned to the Upstate and saw firsthand a world of exciting possibilities taking root in what will hopefully one day be a world where everyone has a seat at the table. Right in downtown Clemson, and literally right next door to where the guys purchased much of our *Tiger* merchandise, sits *The Shepherd Hotel.* Inspired by his daughter Jamison, who has Down syndrome, Rick Hayduk—a seasoned hotel leader—had long aspired to operate a hotel and employ individuals with disabilities. With a bit of help from Rich Davies, a third-generation real estate developer and Clemson alum, he did just that. The boutique hotel, featuring a stunning spiral staircase, serves as a sanctuary for travelers and locals alike. The name refers to a good shepherd who positively impacts the flock by caring for them, loving them, and tending to their needs. Staff and guests are warmly welcomed. Our stay was marvelous—including a wonderful dinner—and we would wholeheartedly recommend you plan a visit even if football is not your thing. You'll love this gem, we promise, and perhaps it'll spark an idea you have to help others. Rich-healthy soil does just that. It makes things grow.

Switching gears and back to the Clemson guy trip, our next tailgating stop on game day was at a house right near Memorial Stadium, affectionately known by locals as *Ole Yeller* (post- Covid and now across the street, it is now known as *New Yeller*). Yes, in case you are wondering, the house is painted yellow. There, we met Tim, Carla, and their son—Ben—, along with future friends, enjoyed a few adult beverages, grabbed a snack, and used the much-needed facilities. Operating as off-campus housing for much of the year, the place is converted by its owners (parents) into a Saturday hot spot several times a year. It is also a great place for locals to park on game day. When chatting with fellow tailgaters, we quickly learned all roads lead back to Akron High School soccer; as improbable as it might seem, Tim, my brother, and I went to school with the wife of one of the masterminds behind this tailgating mecca. However, although she was friends with several players on our former soccer team, she was an upperclassman, so we dared not approach her at the time. Thankfully, we finally got the chance to do so decades later, and it was fun to catch up and realize what a small world it really is. Together, we toasted our former school, classmates, and another Clemson win.

Howard's Rock

Have you ever seen a big rock, roped off, usually under glass—like a big piece of chocolate cake—sitting on a black marble pedestal three feet high? I doubt it. Have you ever seen, right near a big rock on a pedestal, a grassy ramp leading into a stadium? Yes, a rock, a hill, and a stadium. Have you ever seen that combo? I seriously doubt it. All right, one more for you. Have you ever seen an entire football team gather behind that same—now fully exposed with the glass removed—rock, then pet the rock like a newborn baby, rush past it, and bound down that hill like kids who just heard the final bell of the school year and are out for summer? If you're familiar with it, you're already aware; if not, welcome to *Death Valley*, *Howard's Rock*, *The Hill*, and what has been described by many as *The Most Exciting 25 Seconds in College Football.*

To dissect this wild scene and all its moving parts, a good starting point is the early 1940s, when *Clemson Memorial Stadium* was first opened. On September 19, 1942, in the first full year of World War II for the United States, forty Clemson players dressed in the basement of the nearby field house, as there were no dressing facilities inside the West end zone of the new 20,000-seat stadium. The team then made a short walk down Williamson Road, entered the stadium at a gate at the top of a hill behind the East end zone, and ran diagonally across the hill to the Clemson sideline. When the team was seen running down the hill, the fans in attendance stood up and cheered. The first entrance was, for all practical purposes, done out of necessity. As for the fans, they have been cheering this entrance ever since then.

A quarter century later, amid the dawn of the Vietnam War, legendary football coach Frank Howard was doing a little spring cleaning in his Clemson office when he came across a large rock he had been using primarily as a doorstop. The rock was a gift from a close friend and a 1919 Clemson alumnus, Samuel C. Jones, who had "borrowed" the rock from Death Valley, California. It had been three years since, and the coach decided he was tired of looking at it, so he told a Clemson booster, Gene Willimon, "Take this rock out there and throw it over in the Valley." Instead of pitching the rock over a fence, Willimon went to the stadium's east side, where he fashioned a stand and fixed the rock atop it.

Now, for further context, Samuel Jones, who "borrowed" the rock from Death Valley and gave it to Coach Howard as a gift, had an ulterior motive. He thought it would be cool to have something from the real Death Valley in Clemson's *Death Valley. Clemson Memorial Stadium* became known as *Death Valley* in 1948 after the football coach from Presbyterian College told sports writers that his team had to play Clemson in Death Valley, where his team seemed to always lose and rarely, if ever, score a point. Throughout the 1950s, the name gained popularity as coach Howard also began referring to the stadium as "Death Valley." (As you may recall, during our earlier visit to LSU, their stadium is also referred to as "Deaf/Death Valley.") The rock, which had traveled nearly three thousand miles, officially made its first appearance on September 24, 1966, during a game against Virginia. Down by 18 points with seventeen minutes left in the game, the *Tigers* roared back and won the game 40-35. Everyone—players, coaches, and fans alike—knew exactly why their luck had changed during the game and why the team had won all the other home games that season. It had to be the rock and the run down that hill.

The following season, coach Howard is said to have told his players before the first game, "If you're going to give me 110%, you can rub that rock. If you're not, keep your filthy hands off my rock." The coach told this legendary story on a local television broadcast after the *Tigers* had beaten Wake Forest 23-6, and most fans appreciated the idea of doing just about anything to help win a game, even if it meant rubbing a rock. However, a few days later, the coach received a letter from one fan who was not impressed, writing, "Dear coach, if you'd believe more in God and less in that rock, you'd be a lot better football coach."

When coach Hootie Ingram succeeded Howard as coach of the Clemson football team in 1970, he inherited a new dressing room in the West end zone and logically concluded the team should make its final entrance from there. Between 1970 and 1972, the team did not run down the hill nor rub the rock, and the result was a dismal 6-9 record. God might not take an interest in football outcomes, but the rock was a completely different jewel. It liked attention. It needed rubbing. Senior Ben Anderson understood this and before his last game at the stadium, he approached coach Ingram about running down the hill again before the South Carolina game. Ingram liked the idea and arranged a bus to pick up the team at the West end of the stadium and drive them to the top of the hill at the East end. On a rainy afternoon on November 25, 1972, Clemson edged out South Carolina 7-6. The team has been making the same entrance ever since. The rock is now known as *Howard's Rock*. As to what makes a "better football coach," only God really knows.

Several years before we visited Clemson, my family enjoyed a wonderful dinner while vacationing in Beaufort, South Carolina. Our waiter was a fine young man who took terrific care of us, and by the end of the evening, we had managed to swap several stories with him. However, one specific story left us dumbfounded. It turns out he was a Clemson student who was home for break and a member of Clemson's Army ROTC. When he learned of our love for college football, he told us as *Guardians of the Rock,* he had been one of many to stand guard over *Howard's Rock* in the 24 hours leading up to a home game against South Carolina and that while doing this they bang on a "beat USC drum" the entire time. In 1992, leading up to this rivalry, a group attempted to remove the rock from the pedestal, although they were unable to do so, they still managed to chip off a piece of the rock. In any event, he told us they take shifts, go through plenty of drums and drumsticks, and wear the resulting blisters as a badge of honor. Unfortunately, this ritual was not extended initially beyond the South Carolina game, as the rock was vandalized in 2013 when the glass case was shattered, resulting in a large portion of the rock being broken off. The culprit, Micah Rogers, was later found guilty by a jury of malicious damage. Then, in 2015, the glass case was broken again, but with no visible damage to the rock. Today, the rock, like nearly everything else in our modern society, is heavily guarded and kept mainly under lock and key.

On November 17, 2019, Daniel, my brother, my uncle, and I witnessed *The Most Exciting 25 Seconds in College Football* before the Clemson-Wake Forest game. Seated near the East end zone, we got an up-close look at it all. Having heard a great deal about this grand entrance, we got inside the stadium early and were able to watch a group of guys in Khakis and *Tiger* baseball caps walk backward in sync while unfurling a narrow orange carpet stretching nearly 70 feet from the base of the rock pedal to almost the bottom of the hill. The area was roped off and tightly guarded. About this time, the Clemson team—dressed in orange jerseys, white pants, and their orange tiger paw helmets—finished their final warm-ups and departed the stadium through the opposite end zone. We looked at each other and said, "Ok, here we go."

About 10 minutes before kickoff, the team boarded three purple and orange buses, rode behind the north stands to the east stands with a full police motorcade, and disembarked at the top of the hill behind *Howard's Rock.* This entire scene, much to the delight of the nearly

81,000 fans, played out on both big screens with thumping music, including *Queen's "We Will Rock You."* At one point, when recordings of coach Howard were played, nearly every fan, speaking in unison with the legendary coach, shouted out, "If you're not going to give 110%, keep your hand off my rock." The crowd was further stoked when a live camera from inside one of the buses showed the players, seated side by side, as they approached. Shortly thereafter, we caught a glimpse of the tops of the buses as they pulled up and came to a stop. In that moment of anticipation, I looked at my son and was thankful to be with him and to share another beautiful Saturday afternoon with the guys. I also smiled, thinking about what my dad had started all those years ago. Here we were, at a Clemson football game near Greenville—a city he so dearly loved.

In 1985, when my brother was still in high school and I was still in college, legendary college football announcer Brent Musburger described the *Tigers'* run down the hill before a game against Georgia as "the most exciting 25 seconds in college football." No doubt a wordsmith who is also loved by Ohio State fans for his "*Holy Buckeye*" call in 2002, capping off an improbable win on fourth and two against Purdue by the team that would become the National Champions, I'd say Musburger's description of the Clemson entrance is a bullseye for all college football fans as well. We watched as the players amassed behind Head Football Coach Dabo Swinney at the top of the hill behind the rock, while on the field, divided into two sections, the Clemson band feverishly played fight songs. And then, initiated by some unseen cannon shot, the players ran, skipped, and leaped down the hill, all while the band cranked out *Tiger Rag*. The father in me was worried about a player twisting an ankle, as the hill is steeper than it looks on television, and the players leaping in the air, much like downhill skiers, were getting some serious air. Thankfully, all appeared to escape unscathed.

As for the game, Clemson whooped Wake Forest 52-3. Coach Dabo, in his 11th season as head coach and coming off his second

National Championship in three years with a 44-16 thrashing of Alabama the year before, had another dominant team. Quarterback Trevor Lawrence, with his trademark long hair pushed back under a white elastic headband, was dazzling, going 21-27 and throwing for four touchdowns. Three of these touchdowns were thrown to future NFL wide receiver T. Higgins. In the backfield was Travis Etienne, who carried the ball for 121 yards on just 16 carries and scored a touchdown. He would later join Lawrence in the NFL on the Jacksonville Jaguars. As for the Clemson defense, much like a brick wall, it was impregnable for quarterback Jamie Newman and the *Demon Deacons'* offense all afternoon.

Since it was the final home game of the season, we joined *Tiger* fans on the field after the band played the school's alma mater, and although we never got close to *Gathering at the Paw* in the center spot, it was fun to swim in the sea of Orange and Purple. We also got to walk down the same hill the players had run down just hours before. As for the Clemson team, loaded with undeniable talent, they would go undefeated and ultimately gain a berth in the National Championship after a bruising affair against our own Ohio State *Buckeyes.* This is the only time this has ever happened following a guy's trip and, to be honest, it was still a bitter pill to swallow. We tried to enjoy the Clemson win, knowing how many wonderful people were happy about it, but to say we were truly joyful would be disingenuous. In the end, it really didn't matter, as no team, not even Clemson, was ever going to beat LSU and Joe Burrow in the National Championship. That crawfish script had already been written and, although much of the country would have enjoyed watching him beat his former team, *Buckeye* fans were spared at least that specific storyline.

Following the game, we drove back to the Lakehouse in *Keowee* and, to our great surprise, not only did Tim make plans to stay with us for the night but had also put a lasagna in the oven for us. Only later did I learn that Tim's wife—Carla—was responsible for our wonderful dinner, which, besides the lasagna, also included salad and garlic bread. Seriously, what a wonderful gesture. It really hit the spot as we were finally famished. With a beer in hand and our bellies full, we settled in front of the television to watch Oklahoma and our favorite long snapper. Unfortunately, Baylor, the team we had seen the *Sooners* whip the year before, took a 28-3 lead early in the second quarter and a 31-10 lead into halftime. The guys agreed. Things did not look good, but Daniel—our true believer—told us Oklahoma was going to come back and win the game. I'd be darned if he weren't right. Oklahoma, behind Jaylin Hurts (whom we had seen play at Alabama before he transferred), stormed back with 24 unanswered points and won the game 34-31. As we watched Oklahoma, just hours after watching Clemson, little did we know that the schools and their coaches would soon intersect. Coach Brent Venables, who had paced the sideline as the assistant head coach and defensive coordinator for the *Tigers*, would later be named the head football coach of the *Sooners* in 2022. As was the case when discovering high school connections while tailgating, it never ceases to amaze me just how connected we all are, especially in the world of college football.

We are all Survivors

At some point, after we had first arrived in Greenville, Tim asked us what we wanted to do before driving out to Clemson for the evening. Although we wanted to take a stroll downtown and see the *Liberty Bridge* and *Falls Park*, we all knew exactly where we wanted to go first. Our journey to the *Upstate*, and most certainly our collective guy trip journey through the years, would seem hollow without a visit to *Cancer Survivors Park*, and we were greatly honored when my friend—our friend—agreed to drive over to the park with us and serve as our personal guide. Of course, Tim knew a thing or two about this park, as he had started on the campaign committee, raising funds, and often volunteered with his family as a further sign of appreciation for the care he received and to give back to the cancer community.

Snuggled tightly in a ravine just off the *Reedy River* and along the *Swamp Rabbit Trail*, and literally just a hop, skip, and jump from both downtown and Tim and Carla's house, sits this very special place. At the entrance is a loosely formed, stainless-steel arch shaped like a heart, painted blue, and adorned with butterflies. The sculpture, called *Butterfly Journey*, is one of many pieces created by local artist Yuri Tsuzuki as part of her *Butterfly Project*. Tsuzuki, utilizing the butterfly as a symbol of transformation, approached this former textile town with the idea of using the entire city as her canvas by placing steel butterflies on light posts and buildings throughout the city. Spotting butterflies atop a post or along the side of a building while meandering through downtown streets is fun for children and adults alike, serving as a reminder of how the city, greatly transformed, has become a beautiful place to call home or visit. Initially conceived by a local high school student, the project took nearly five years to complete and continues to be enhanced annually. As for the park entrance, it serves not only as a reminder of transformation and rebirth but also as a symbol of hope, beauty, and the fragility of life.

The park, which opened just the year before our visit, is a unique blend of gathering spaces and natural walkways created as a place of inspiration for all those who have been touched by cancer. Passing through the arch on a gusty, cloud-covered afternoon, we entered an ample green space with benches and a *Wall of Gratitude*. Although it was downright chilly outside, with the sudden rush of emotions running over us, we hardly noticed. It also helped that Tim had let Daniel permanently borrow his Clemson jacket for this greatly anticipated afternoon stroll in mid-November.

This sacred spot immediately spoke to us, as at the outset, and somewhere near the entrance, we happened upon an inscription from *Psalm 23*: *"The Lord is my shepherd, I shall not be in want. He makes me lie down in green pastures; he leads me beside quiet waters..."* Dad was fond of this verse. In his final days, while he could, he repeated it often. It gave him great comfort, and now, as I recalled him reciting the verse with our pastor from his bed, it did the same for all of us.

I was also moved by another nearby inscription from *A.A. Milne (author of Winnie the Pooh)*: *"You are braver than you believe, stronger than you seem, smarter than you think, and loved more than you'll ever know."* Although placed here for those, particularly children, who are suffering through the tribulations of cancer, I immediately thought about our son. I thought about his marching alongside my daughter, with *Winnie the Pooh, Piglet, Tigger,* and *Eeyore* at Disney World, and it brought a smile to my face. However, I also thought about his scooting along the ground before he learned to walk, about his taking speech lessons, about the hours of physical therapy and occupational therapy, about the hearing aids and glasses he usually refuses to wear, about the passing of some of his closest schoolmates, and about the days he spent in the hospital following his birth. Yes, he is braver than he believes, stronger than he seems, smarter than he (or anyone else) thinks, and most certainly loved more than he will ever know. Our son, whom we named Daniel, has literally been in a lion's den since the day he was born. Although she has walked a very different path, often with her own unique challenges, and as she pursues a career in the male-dominated world of mechanical engineering, this is also true for our daughter.

Near the bosom of the park is the *Center for Hope & Healing*. The glass and stone building hosts educational programs and related activities, serving as a resource center for survivors, patients, and caregivers. A sweeping white steel spire, with a circular terrace just underneath, designated as the Celebration Pavilion, sits atop the Center and is designed to provide a view of the entire park, serving as a beacon of hope. Each night, the spire is warmly bathed in the many designated colors of cancer, serving as encouragement for those fighting cancer and for those who've been affected by it. Running alongside the Center and serving as the primary artery through the park is the *Spirit of Survivorship Bridge,* which spans the Reedy River and offers equally stunning views. As it turns out, this bridge ultimately leads to a connecting walkway via the *Swamp Rabbit Trail,* which in turn connects to downtown and *Falls Park*.

On the other side of the park, we came upon an area designated as *the Children's Garden,* featuring a large bronze statue of a child nuzzling against a lion. The statue, named "*Fear Not,*" was created by Charles Pate, Jr., who was inspired by the courage and faith shown by every child and parent who faces cancer. The child is at peace, as if sleeping or snuggling, while the lion looks straight ahead, serving as a protector and savior. It was then that we were reminded that during Dad's battle, he seldom mentioned his own hardship but instead spoke of children suffering from cancer. It was something that had always moved him, so much so that when he passed away, we asked that donations be made in his honor to *St. Jude Children's Research Hospital* in Memphis, Tennessee (near *The Rendezvous* and our wonderful meal years before). It was there, on this spot, that we all gave a silent prayer for the protection and healing of all children and parents impacted by cancer. As we fought back tears, Tim, noticing our current state, asked us if we would like to walk further up a wooden boardwalk to an area called *Leap of Faith*. It was steep, but it was not the incline that spurred his inquiry.

The *Boardwalk* is a long and winding path made of wooden planks that snakes from the bottom of the ravine area to the top and a second park entrance off Church Street. Along the way, there are scattered benches dedicated in loving memory to those affected by this dreaded disease. Many of the wooden planks have inscriptions from family and friends as dedications to loved ones who laid down their battle with cancer, and for those who still journey on. As we climbed each curve, we stopped to read the many stories discovered literally at our feet until, at last, we found ourselves on a wooden platform with two benches and a small bronze statue known as *Leap of Faith*. As Tim gathered us together to tell us where we were, we instinctively knew we were in another special spot filled with unparalleled beauty and unwavering love.

On April 8, 2013, Lindsey Bates Motley was diagnosed with colorectal cancer. She was 26 years old and 17 weeks pregnant. Later, she gave birth to her daughter Lilla, becoming both a mother and a survivor. Speaking about her journey, Lindsey said, "As a first-time mother with a cancer diagnosis, (it) certainly isn't the pretty picture I dreamed it would be. In a lot of ways, it's been so much better. It's forced me to cherish many, many moments that I probably would've zoomed right past. It's encouraged me to be more present…It's a path that I would choose for no one to have to endure. For me, however, it gave me such strength-strength that I don't think I would have otherwise without Lilla inside me. I felt such excitement and responsibility…" On February 23, 2016, not quite three years later, and after exhausting all standard treatments and several rounds of immunotherapy, Lindsey sadly passed away, leaving behind her precious daughter and a grieving husband.

Lindsey's dad, Tom Bates, along with family and friends, dedicated this portion of the park to her memory. A bronze sculpture created by local artist Doug Young sits along the railing's edge and depicts a cardinal on a branch, looking down on a nest with a baby cardinal as it readies itself to make a first flight. The cardinal, often considered a sighting of someone from heaven, was created as a symbol to represent Lindsey, with a message to her daughter and the world that "a leap of faith" is how we must live each day. Additionally, on a nearby plaque, there are two scriptures. The first, from *2 Corinthians 5:7*, reads, *"For we walk by faith, not by sight,"* while the second, from *Hebrews 11:1*, reads, *"Now faith is the substance of things hoped for, the evidence of things not seen."* The artist of this beautiful sculpture, when asked about this project, has said, "We are surrounded by a great cloud of witnesses, and it is encouraging to know that this is not the end. This is not the end." As Tim told these stories, his voice cracked, and more than once, he became choked up. Our eyes, if not already wet from the brisk November wind slapping against our faces, were only made more so by hearing these stories throughout the park. Lindsey's story felt like an unusually cruel punch to the gut, but we were moved by what we heard.

As we walked back down the wooden boardwalk, no longer even trying to fight back our tears, we had a certain revelation. It was simple and true. I suppose you could call it a paradigm shift. Lindsey's story of cancer was not hers alone. It *is* also Lilla's, and her family, like so many others in *Cancer Survivors Park,* has graciously shared it with us all. Tim's battle with cancer is not his alone; it is also shared with his wife and his two sons. My dad did not walk alone but with my family. Likewise, my mother-in-law's journey was shared with my wife as a teenage daughter and continues with her now as a grown woman. For whatever reason, we never understood this truth. For some reason, we never acknowledged that we are also cancer survivors. These stories we share in perpetuity. What happens to one of us happens to us all. And even if one day it is eradicated from this earth and from our vocabulary, humanity itself will now and forever be a cancer survivor. It is our story in perpetuity. In the meantime, much like a baby cardinal at the edge of a nest, we each must take our own leap of faith. As survivors, it is how we all must live each day.

On our walk back to the car, we stopped near the entrance to take one final look back into the park. By coincidence or subconscious design, I found myself searching for the *A.A. Milne (from Winnie the Pooh)* inscription again. It had been years since I had seen the movie and even longer since I had read the book, but I could still recall the scene vividly. As *Pooh* and *Christopher Robin* chat on the branches of a tree at dusk, all while *Pooh* tries to capture fireflies, *Christopher*, with obvious hesitation, tells *Pooh, "If ever there is a tomorrow when we're not together, there's something you must remember."* As the young lad tries to continue with this most earnest discussion, *Pooh* responds, at one point, by stating, *"(he) would be quite lost without (Christopher)."* Finally, the bear, who has worn himself out from a full day, including climbing branches and trying to capture fireflies, begins to yawn and takes a seat on a larger branch against the trunk of the tree. *Christopher* assures *Pooh* that he is *braver* than he *believes*, *stronger* than he *seems*, and *smarter* than he *thinks*. In other words, he could go on without his friend. As *Pooh Bear* finally begins to fall asleep, *Christopher* leans forward and tells him, starting in a normal voice and then ending in a whisper, "*The thing is, even if we are apart, I will always be with you. I'll always be with you. Always be with you."* As I replayed that beautiful scene, I was reminded that my father would always be with us, and I hoped my children knew that one day, when we were no longer together, I would always be with them.

How can we stop cancer? Theories abound, and much like opinions surrounding weight loss, libraries and bookstores are filled with writings espousing clear or easy answers. But much like dieting, if the answers were straightforward, there would be no need for all those pages on all those shelves. In the late 20th century, the environment took center stage in this investigation, given the dropping of two atomic bombs near the end of World War II, the Love Canal in the late 1970s, and the Chernobyl disaster in 1986, which made perfect sense. This was followed by a river of investigative reports potentially linking cancer to pollution, pesticides, and industrial waste. The stories tugged at our heartstrings and provided us with ready-made villains to aid in our desperate need for resolution.

These events were no doubt terrifying, and needless environmental destruction is always alarming, but they do little to move the enlightenment needle when it comes to stopping cancer. For example, the nuclear bombs dropped on Hiroshima and Nagasaki killed nearly 200,000 instantly or from immediate radiation poisoning. However, any cancer linked to long-term radiation exposure is inexplicably low, as some estimates are as low as fewer than 1,000 cases. Simply put, as horrific as the entire event was, it never produced a *Godzilla* as initially imagined in the justifiably fragile Japanese psyche. Chernobyl creates additional curiosity, as although 600,000 people received high exposure, only 4,000 deaths have been reported. Both are head-scratchers. If these stark events do not produce obvious results, where does that leave us? Have we really moved the needle?

Healthy living—pursued through diet and exercise—is the latest craze, and for good reason. Currently, physicians, researchers, nutritionists, and fitness experts attribute healthy eating and exercise to improved heart health, lower levels of diabetes, enhanced gut health, stronger bones and teeth, a better mood and memory, increased energy levels, and, yes, weight loss. Who doesn't want to look good and feel great? Pass those veggies, please, and sign me up for that gym membership! Many also believe it might reduce the risk of cancer. However, and most disappointing, the link in this regard is fainter than expected. Even worse, like most everything, marketing claims—especially on grocery store packaging—far outweigh the actual science. Leafy vegetables, foods rich in antioxidants, and diets high in fiber do appear to reduce the risk of certain cancers, but the evidence is by no means conclusive and, as a result, we are left to scratch our heads yet again.

Diet and exercise intersect nicely with obesity, and if we know anything, obesity is a major cause of cancer, right? Again, when examining the actual numbers, you may find yourself underwhelmed. My scalp is getting red, but like most people, I'm still hedging my bets. Despite the thin correlation, I know I feel better when I eat healthier and exercise regularly. Pass more veggies, please!

Despite these weaker-than-expected links, several patterns have emerged in the better understanding of cancer. First, cancer is clearly related to age. In fact, age is the biggest risk factor of all. More than nine out of ten cancers are diagnosed in people over 45, and the chances of getting cancer rise sharply from age 50 to 70. Although the exact reasons remain unclear, it might be as simple as a matter of chance. As we roll the dice, repeatedly, and as those 30 trillion cells in our bodies cycle on, mutations—like snake eyes—are bound to happen eventually. Another explanation is that, over time, the body is repeatedly damaged, leading to inflammation and other cell-related issues. Both theories make a good deal of sense and, although depressing at first glance, thank goodness fewer young people—especially children—must face this disease.

Heredity is another factor, and while cancer is not passed down from parents to children, genetic patterns that increase the risk of cancer can be passed down from one generation to the next. Given our father's cancer diagnosis, my brother and I are potentially at greater risk for prostate cancer, and given my mother-in-law's diagnosis, my wife is at a greater risk for developing lung cancer. As they say, "It is all in the genes." However, we have no idea just how much is in the genes when it comes to cancer.

So, is there more cancer than ever before? Maybe. First, as stated, cancer is related to age, and as life expectancy has grown, one would expect a corresponding rise in cancer. Secondly, better technologies have allowed doctors to diagnose the disease, whereas, in the past, many with cancer did not know it.

Here is one final thought on the matter. Caring for cancer, for the time being at least, is on firmer footing than curing cancer. As we maneuver through the maze of incomplete and inconsistent information about the causes of cancer, no clear path has been forged through the forest we traverse. Although we have not yet come upon an opening in the trees or an eagerly anticipated ledge where we can rest and take in a fuller view of the horizon, we can do more than ponder as we plod onward. Prevention and early detection are the greatest tools in our backpack, and by getting regular check-ups and age-appropriate cancer screenings, we can try to catch the rogue devil before it trashes our rations. Oh, and one more thing, make sure to wear sunscreen on your journey.

The following season, as the world was largely bound and gagged during the Covid-19 pandemic, we opted out of our annual "guy trip." That same season, Ohio State managed to win all five games played, and despite Michigan, Illinois, and Maryland canceling their contests with the *Buckeyes*, Ohio State finished 6-0 after beating Northwestern in the *Big 10* Championship and earned a much-anticipated rematch against Clemson. On January 1, 2021, the *Buckeyes* defeated the *Tigers* 49-28 and earned a spot in the National Championship in Miami against Alabama. Remembering Dad's words—"they go; we go"—John, Daniel, and I flew to Florida, where we met Aunt Jill and Uncle Frank for dinner at an outside table the night before the game. When packing for our flight, we made sure to pack our "lucky *buckeyes*," and in the process, we discovered that we had five in total. Since Dad,

John, Dan, and I each had our own, we presented Uncle Frank with the final nut. Initially unable to find words, his eyes welled up with tears, and then he finally managed to utter, "Thank you, guys. Jill and I loved your father, and you're including me on the 'guy trips' has been one of the greatest honors in my life. A 'lucky *buckeye*' is just icing on the cake."

The ensuing evening, we watched Alabama dismantle Ohio State in a total rout reminiscent of Custer's last stand. Mac Jones chucked five touchdown passes, and DeVonta Smith proved he was worthy of the Heisman trophy as he had 215 yards receiving, with three touchdowns. The *Crimson Tide* was truly a well-oiled machine and, at one point or another, we all reached into our pockets to make sure we had not left the "lucky *buckeyes*" back at the hotel or in the rental car. However, as ugly as the game was, we all knew just how lucky we were to be together and to have weathered—along with the world—a once-in-a-lifetime pandemic. Football, along with our guy trips, would soon be back, bigger and better than ever before. Lucky, indeed! Yep, the nuts still work, and we pledged to take them with us if we ever got back to the big show. After all, as Dad said, "they go; we go."

On Being Men

As the years pass, and as I grow older, I find myself increasingly reminiscing about our college football trips and the time spent with my dad, my son, my brother, my uncle, my son-in-law, and our many friends. The towns, the places, and the faces of those we met fade with time, as do the contests seen. Still, in my mind, I return, usually in the quiet of an early morning or when I drift off to sleep and dream as another day turns to night. Now, pen and paper, at least partially, preserve a further wane, as do the pile of caps and stack of t-shirts in my bedroom closet, and the latest trip, as well as the trip not yet taken, help to soothe any creeping melancholy.

While memories dissolve, reflections remain. As I replay each trip, I inevitably return to Oxford, Mississippi, and Ole Miss, and I inevitably find myself in William Faulkner's den at *Rowan Oak*—on a chilly morning—staring at the outline of a story etched on the corner walls. However, now, as previously imagined years before, the days of the week have been replaced with each football trip, mapped through time, starting with Arkansas on one wall and ending with a freshly drawn Kansas State sketch on another. Each with its own tale, but part of a larger narrative, but unlike Faulkner's *A Fable*, this story continues, as it is potentially never-ending, and I am reminded of the feeling

I had all those years ago that we had embarked on something uniquely special, and if properly nurtured, it would only grow with time. Indeed, it has. Even so, I could not have imagined the lessons learned and the insights gained into football, family, community, masculinity, humanity and, ultimately, life itself.

Walking across the creaky wooden floors—with a soft chill in the air—I'm brought back to Faulkner's tales of boys and men and the long shadows cast by fathers on their sons. But now I better understand the importance of teaching boys to be men, and I am especially grateful for the lessons provided by my own father. These lessons, at first blush, seem contradictory to college football itself, as does my own son's adoration—and our encouragement to fully engage—in a sport he would never play and at institutions of higher learning that he could never attend. However, college football, like sports, is about relationships and community. It is also about acceptance and serving others, and these are lessons to hold onto regardless of individual prowess.

Joe Ehrmann, a former NFL player and captain of the Baltimore *Colts*, turned high school coach and creator of the *Building Men for Others* program, writes about masculinity and false masculinity in *InsideOut Coaching- How Sports Can Transform Lives*. His story, along with the story of the Gilman High School football team, is further chronicled by Jeffrey Marx in *Season of Life: A Football Star, a Boy, a Journey to Manhood*. Both are wonderful reads. Ehrmann contends that as fathers and as a society, we do not do a good job of teaching boys to be men, as there is general confusion about the definition of masculinity and what he calls "false masculinity." Ehrmann defines false masculinity as athletic ability, sexual conquest, and economic success. He then pivots and defines masculinity in terms of relationships and our capacity to love and be loved. Next, he rightfully contends we serve a larger purpose than ourselves. Both authors further ponder end-of-life questions, such as, "What kind of father were you? What kind of husband were you? What kind of son were you? What kind of brother were you? What kind of teammate were you? What kind of friend were you? Seeking answers to these questions inevitably helps define true masculinity. I would add a few other questions to the mix: "What kind of neighbor were you? What kind of boss or employee were you? What kind of citizen were you? What kind of person were you?" These further define humanity itself.

Ehrmann believes that manhood carries a unique code that requires accepting responsibility, maintaining integrity, showing empathy for others, and living for the greater good through service. My dad was a man. He lived by a code, and he gladly served others. He taught us true masculinity, and he shredded notions of false masculinity. The same is true of my son. He is courageous and has empathy for others. In my life, I have found myself sandwiched between two real men. These are my thoughts as I jump back and forth through time, coming and going between Rowan Oak, Ole Miss, and all the other wonderful places we have been. In these reflections, it also occurs to me that the same is true of my brother, my uncle, my son-in-law, my friends, and the many others we have met and come to know. Now, I wonder if I was always more of a student than a teacher along this ride.

Losing Dad to cancer has left a crater in our lives and has forever detoured our story. We march on up a hill, but without our captain and, as such, the guy trips can never be the same. However, Daniel's grandpa not only gave us lessons when he was healthy but also when he was ill. He gave us lessons in life and even in death. The latter are tougher lessons, often filled with tears, and we are nonetheless grateful for them. For in loss also comes gain. We have forged a closer relationship with our uncle, and I have rekindled friendships that might have otherwise been lost, like sand on a beach. In the years since Dad passed away, we have gained a son-in-law who has joined us on our adventures and may one day bring his own son, if we are so lucky. This makes me smile, and it is why we boarded that flight to Oklahoma City all those years ago.

I wish Dad had never gotten cancer, and once he had it, I certainly wish he had beaten the sucker. Sometimes, I wonder what our trips would be like if he were still with us. We regularly find ourselves saying, "Gosh, Dad would have loved this." Along those same lines, when Daniel was first born, I would find myself thinking about what he might have been like had he not been born with Down syndrome. In other words, my mind drifted off to our carefully planned trip to Italy instead of our unexpected arrival in Holland. Would he have been a star athlete? Would he have been an honor student? Where would he have gone to college? What career would he have pursued? However, those thoughts were vanquished a long time ago. Science and logic dictated I do so as Daniel is real, and the other a figment of my imagination. Daniel without Down syndrome would not be Daniel at all, and what I am about to say is in no way meant to sound political, preachy, or provocative. It is simply the truth. Genetically, as a fertilized egg, he was a fully coded human being—ultimately engineered as a boy (thanks to the Y chromosome), with dirty blond hair, blue eyes, and, yes, Down syndrome. There are no later steps in this coding. It is, as they say, a one-step process.

Today, I am reminded of the promise made at the *Turf Tavern* all those years ago to carry my son through and, literally over, a crowd so that he might experience everything we did. However, when I made that promise to myself, I had no idea that it was I who would often be carried—much like the story described in the Gospel of *Mark,* of friends cutting a hole in a roof to bring a paralytic to Jesus—by my son and others.

As for college football, it has not only extended a welcome mat to my family but has also figuratively rolled out the red carpet on our visits. We have been treated like royalty, even when we were foreigners in faraway lands, and even when we were loud and silly. Simply put, we have always felt at home. Better yet, we have always been surrounded by an extended family. My son and I have never been followed by security guards like we have been while visiting museums or art galleries in Washington, D.C., and other big cities. Furthermore, nobody has ever spoken down to my son or family, unlike a prior visit to a musical on Broadway when my wife and I were asked by a woman sitting behind us after the show if we thought "our son got anything out of the performance." Such folly dares not enter these shared Saturdays.

It has been said that the quality of a civilization is measured by the respect that it has for its weakest members. There are no other criteria for judgment, and our personal experience has shown that college football towns and their fans represent the highest echelon, offering a glimpse of what once was and what might yet be. It turns out that by traveling to different college towns and into enormous concrete structures, we have unexpectedly wandered through a cathedral of God's love and light.

Our Story

Those who are *different* have long been marginalized in society, whether they have been rounded up, dispersed, hidden out of plain sight in obscure-unnamed institutions, or amassed together in carnivals, museums, and "freak shows" for all the world to point and gawk upon. Their individual stories and their stories recited together as a group are not theirs alone. Their stories are intertwined with all stories of history and society. From the beginning, certain people have been *different* or *atypical.* From the beginning, this has been *our story.*

This story—*our story*—is not always an easy read. It's got plenty of bleak chapters. Many born disabled did not survive, while others were cast aside. Words of ignorance populate nearly every page. Archaic views, including the racist ideology of slavery, held that Africans brought to the Americas were, by definition, "disabled." Indigenous people, who had no word for disability in their native language or concept of it in their society, soon joined them. Innumerable bad guys appear throughout the story, often when least expected. Sadly, our heroes often turn into villains throughout. The church, which had initially welcomed the disabled, turned and became mutated, casting blame for the disabled at the feet of their parents. The child's disability, they lectured, could be traced to parental sin. Civil War was replaced with civil rights for some, but not all. Idiots became known as retarded, and lunatics became known as insane. This was considered progress. Genetics took away blame but created killing fields, and modernity, which originally helped extend life, was turned inward as a weapon against it.

However, the story—*our story*—is also a wonderful read. It's got plenty of chapters filled with beauty, love, and grace. Those deemed disabled are often our most compelling characters with amazing and improbable plotlines. As readers, we rejoice in their triumphs and are saddened by their setbacks. Regardless, we are always left inspired. Although we mourn for the hero lost, we also take delight in the villain redeemed and smile when ignorance is crushed under the weight of enlightenment. Lastly, we are left heartened with the knowledge that *our story* is not yet over, and we are free to help write the next chapters.

A Fine Young Man

Throughout the years, Dan has been heavily involved with music. Not only was he a member of the school choir and served as a self-appointed guest conductor for the high school marching band, but he has also taken drum lessons and piano lessons. In fact, at one point or another, he has also played or tried to play the guitar, the violin, and the trombone. More recently, he has set his sights on the bagpipes, and, thanks to his grandmother, he has a brand-new set that he uses to belt out his interpretation of *Amazing Grace.* Daniel is also no stranger to the stage, as he not only enjoys performing impromptu Disney musicals for family and friends but has also performed in a formal production of *Shrek* in a nearby theatre, where he played an unusually silent wolf. We are still unsure if the wolf was supposed to have any lines, but the costume was certainly adorable. He has certainly gotten over any of his stage fright as he recently performed improv before a packed audience at Weathervane Playhouse as part of a group called *The Improvaneers*—an all-Down syndrome improvisation troupe and believe me, he, along with everyone else on stage, had plenty to say that night.

Currently, Daniel attends *EchoingU,* where he participates in studies focusing on money management, nutrition and wellness, communication and social skills, emergency preparedness, time management, and job market preparation. Through this program, he also volunteers one day a week, usually at a food bank or a nursing home. Unfortunately, Dan has few friends outside of class and a limited social life. The same is true of many of his peers, as most do not drive, and most live at home with their parents or in group homes. Every summer, he attends a one-week camp with his classmates, and twice a year, he participates in a Jesus Prom, popularized by Tim Tebow, or a similarly themed activity. Let me tell you, they are something else. Imagine hundreds of young adults—dressed to the nines—entering a beautifully decorated venue with throngs of cheering people. As they are announced and applauded in, the energy is contagious and reminiscent of the treatment received by Hollywood stars at the red-carpet arrivals before the Oscars. Once inside, dinner is typically served, followed by hours of dancing and karaoke. It's hardcore stuff, and after you have attended one of these events, you couldn't care less about Tim Tebow's throwing mechanics. In our house, Tebow wears a cape, as do the many volunteers. You all deserve the red-carpet treatment as well. In the meantime, take a bow.

Following the passing of his grandfather, Dan has finally returned to his duties as an usher at our church. This was a job the two held together, and it was a wonderful development to have him back with the flock. Although he still lives at home with his parents and his cat, he wants to learn to drive, buy a house, and get married. Sound familiar? The American dream is alive and well!

For the most part, his health has been good, except for a heart scare following the Covid-19 pandemic. Like many young men, he was inexplicably diagnosed with myocarditis, and we are doing our best to avoid conspiracy theories, but the timing sure makes it hard. Thankfully, he has not had any recent episodes. One misnomer about people with Down syndrome is that they are always happy. Nothing could be farther from the truth. They display the same range of emotions as the rest of us, and depending on the day or moment, Daniel can experience a variety of emotions, including sadness, frustration, fear, excitement, anger, or happiness. Like I said, he is just like the rest of us. However, we have noticed he can take stubbornness to a whole new level, and we now have a better understanding of the saying "stubborn as a mule."

Like almost everyone nowadays, Dan is attached to his cell phone and laptop. He receives and sends multiple texts each day and is part of a group text with Uncle John, Uncle Frank, Austin, and me. On Saturday nights, especially during college football season, our phones sound like slot machines in Vegas. Daniel also repeatedly calls and facetimes his grandmother—Gee—along with Uncle Frank and Aunt Jill. He has also been known to add Uncle Ed, Aunt Sue, and Aunt Carol when he is feeling extra chatty. When not on his phone, he enjoys working on his computer, compiling schedules and lists for upcoming events. The young man is quite the planner. While many curse the modern world with its newfangled technologies and never-ending social connections, technology has greatly assisted those with disabilities by allowing further access and integration. Lastly, Daniel daily reminisces about his grandpa and is apt to say, "Ah buddy, I sure do miss you." We all do, Dan, we all do.

Why was my son born with Down syndrome? Why did Dad get cancer? More selfishly, why did this happen to me? How could a loving God devise such a scheme? Ultimately, there are no earthly answers to these questions. However, I take comfort in knowing there is indeed a loving God. I also take comfort in knowing there have always been those who are *different* among us and that cancer has always been with us as well. My son was not the first and only person born with Down syndrome, nor was my dad the only person to succumb to cancer. It has always been *our story*. My wife and I share no more blame than my father. It was not our fault. It just happens and answers to our questions must wait until we cross our bridge. Sometimes you plan a trip to Italy, but you find yourself in Holland, and as Ms. Kingsley beautifully states, "If you spend your whole life mourning the fact you didn't get to Italy, you may never fully enjoy the very special, the very lovely things … about Holland." Faith requires an acknowledgment that we do not pilot all of life's flights, even when we foolheartedly wish we did. Today, I am reminded of my crying in a hospital chapel all those years ago and again when my dad fought and finally put down his battle with cancer. However, now I rejoice in knowing the special gifts that have been given to me. Yes, God, I hear you, and I am pleased. I hope you are as well.

As Ohio State football fans, if things had been different, we may have never wandered from the *Buckeyes* and the *Horseshoe* on a fateful afternoon while dining on Bay Street in Beaufort, South Carolina. We may have never known that "the old that is strong does not wither" and that "deep roots are not reached by the frost," even in those hostile lands outside of Columbus. We still bleed scarlet and grey, but inside, we are a rainbow of color. No, we are not lost. Our wanders have brought us home to an even bigger family.

Another Football Weekend

Daniel's phone rings and vibrates across the kitchen counter. His mother, sensing he may have lost track of time, or at least his phone, calls out for him, "Daniel, Daniel, come quick; Uncle Frank is calling you." It's a typical Saturday morning in the fall, during college football season, and Uncle Frank has called our son about their weekly *Gameday* ritual. The two of them, along with Rece Davis, Kirk Herbstreit, and the rest of the ESPN crew, will soon make their picks for the featured matchups. For the longest time, the two hopelessly tried to sync these calls by each having their television set on *Gameday*, but since we are in Ohio and Uncle Frank is in Florida, one of them was inevitably on a slight delay, causing confusion and frustration. Now, my uncle Facetimes Daniel so they can do the picks together at the exact same time. My son picks fi rst, followed by the ESPN crew, and then my uncle. However, like much of the country, Daniel eagerly awaits Lee Corso's fi nal pick, and if he agrees, he loves it, and a good deal of hollering ensues. However, if he disagrees, he shakes his head in disbelief and gives an exaggerated thumbs-down to the coach.

Regardless of his reaction, my wife and I always love hearing my uncle's laughter on the other side of the call.

Earlier in the morning, about halfway through our first cup of morning brew, Daniel had begun his other Saturday gameday rituals. After playing an assortment of songs from *Beauty and the Beast* and the *Lion King*, he segways into *The Best Damn Band in the Land*, playing stirring renditions of *Buckeye Battle Cry* and *Hang on Sloopy*. From there, he skillfully pivots to pieces from other marching bands across the country, including The Oklahoma Marching Band, The Texas A&M Marching Band, and The Clemson Marching Band. Along the way, he will manage to play a piece or two of every band we have seen. If another guy's trip is planned but has not yet taken place, the band for the upcoming destination is most definitely on his playlist, and both before and after those visits, one might describe those bands as being in "heavy rotation." Even though Saturday mornings are designated as "no alarm clock" days, my wife and I still get up a little earlier for that first cup of coffee, as we know things are about to get raucous.

The night before, on a screened porch off the back of our house, Daniel and I, when not listening to the prattle of nearby owls, discussed our plans for the weekend. When the weather permits, these Friday night chats are also a family tradition. The porch, made almost entirely of cedar, faces into the dark of the woods, and "my chair" sits in the furthest corner. It really is my designated spot, as I've never seen anyone else sit in it except Daniel's cat. When not in my chair, the white and black feline also enjoys the ledge above it and listening to the prattle of those nearby owls with us. Next to my chair is a small wooden table, just large enough for a small lamp and a glass partially filled with a piece of ice and my latest Kentucky bourbon crush. On more than one occasion, while taking a sip, I've been reminded of my father's love of Friday nights. He was fond of saying, "Aren't Friday nights the best?" They really are, Dad, they really are. Followed only by Saturdays and college football. Right, Dad?

Daniel, who, although of legal age, is no fan of alcohol, especially bourbon. He sat in his designated spot alongside my wife on a nearby loveseat with a glass of juice or ginger ale. He brought his phone out with him, although he has also been known to bring his laptop as well. Since it was a fall night, our discussions inevitably turned to whether his sister and brother-in-law were coming over the next day. The three of us, quite frankly, had our fingers crossed as we love being together with the entire family, and when Claire is home, the sun shines a little brighter. Regardless of her plans, Daniel, my wife, and I will nonetheless consume our fair share of Saturday football. Flushing out the plans, if any, we inevitably began discussing the football games scheduled for the following day.

This is where his phone came in handy, and this is also when my wife, who had been enjoying a glass of wine, made her exit. Her eventual departure was not unexpected, as what we were about to do would tire just about anybody, including hardcore football fanatics. This is when she usually leaves, or on some nights when she retreats only to return with yarn and knitting needles. The cat, who discovered a bug crawling near the ceiling, didn't seem to mind the football talk at all, but then I wondered about the real reason my wife had left. In any case, we will methodically go through every major college football game scheduled for the next day. We do this *every* Friday night, without exception. Starting with Ohio State, we make our way through the *Big 10* games, followed by every team we have seen play on the guy trips. We conclude our investigation with teams not yet seen and conferences not yet visited. Regardless of who is playing, Daniel is fond of saying, "Wow, that's a great game," or even if the game looks lopsided to the pundit world, he will describe it as "Ooh, that's a tough game." I'm struck by how he views the world. There is an unmistakable innocence in it. To him, the games all seem competitive, or at least worthy. Now, thanks to him and *the guys*, they all seem great to me as well. Every single one of them. Further, thanks to him and *the guys*, the season itself is yearned for most, and not the final confetti and the championship ring.

On a nearby round glass table, thankfully covered by an outdoor tablecloth as the nearby patch of pines and clean glass have never been well acquainted, there sits a small lamp, along with a small white metal sign that reads, "Welcome to Our Porch." Yes, I need to get that dude up on one of the porch walls one of these days. In the meantime, it has found a home propped up against the base of the lamp. Also on the table, right below the sign, are three slightly weathered pieces of legal-sized yellow notebook paper, filled with scribbled names and dates for an upcoming—now current—season. This ritual, with these scribblings, started in the early spring when bleak winds filled our Ohio skies, and the porch was not yet open for Friday nights. Somewhere in those scribbles, circled and starred, is the next/latest guy trip. Or, as my brother is fond of saying, somewhere in those scribbles is the "*best guy trip ever*." Those notes, past and present, are probably our greatest manuscript. Surely, they are mine. The culmination of a long and timely process, they reveal beauty in a tradition started by my father. They also reveal the beauty of the time spent with my children and serve as a reminder to a dad of what is sublime.

The last bits of Friday had slowly slipped through our fingers. The chorus of owls had been replaced by a symphony of crickets. The lamps had been shuttered, and now all that had remained was the flickering of the last few candles lit earlier in the evening by my wife. My glass sat empty, and Daniel's phone had been turned off and tucked into the bed that is his pocket. His cat was cuddled next to him on the loveseat, eyes shut, with her front paws tucked under her body. Moment by moment, the unseen forest anxiously awaited our final curtain call, so it might return to the moon and stars and a more familiar light. As I watched him yawn, my son looked over at me and said, "Grandpa sure did love the guy trips, didn't he?" "He sure did, Dan, he sure did," I responded. This was a conversation we had before. It is another ritual. I continued further, "Dan, do you love the guy trips?" Dan responded affirmatively with a "Yep, I sure do." We then had a similar and well-rehearsed dialogue involving Uncle John, Uncle Frank, and Austin. This was followed by a period of silence and contemplation. I could barely see my son now as the porch had grown mostly dark, and then I heard him ask, "Dad, do you love the guy trips?" My response had been waiting on the tip of my tongue, "I sure do, son, I sure do."

Another Season

Since our visit to Clemson, we have continued our wonderful college football adventures. We have journeyed to Knoxville, where we watched the Tennessee *Volunteers* battle the eventual National Champion Georgia *Bulldogs* along with another 100,000 rabid *Vol* fans. Not only did we witness the team running through the T, but, as I previously mentioned, we also sang *Rocky Top* until we were completely hoarse. A completely unexpected joy was the hospitality shown to us on our visit, as we were accompanied by another good friend, Todd, who, as a native of Knoxville and a Tennessee graduate, served as designated driver to the game and local tour guide. I'm still not sure how he managed to park his truck in a tiny lot along an improbably steep hill. At our Friday night dinner at the *Lonesome Dove* in downtown Knoxville, we were joined by Uncle Frank's good friend and another Tennessean— "*TR*." It was a joy to see them laugh and otherwise reminisce, and it was another reminder of what makes the guy trips so much fun. Finally, we were also treated to unmatched hospitality on this trip, as we were the guests of the Ferguson family, who welcomed us into their home as if we were long-lost friends or family. Heck, not only did we have our own private bedrooms in their home, but we were also served endless cups of steaming hot coffee, along with amazing, handmade breakfasts that were fit for a king. You are truly kind, and we appreciate you for allowing us to be part of your lives.

That same year, Daniel and I were invited to a Kentucky *Wildcat* game and, although not technically a guy trip as the other usual suspects did not attend, the Bates family—longtime family friends—deserve special mention. Thank you for showing us Lexington and the University of Kentucky. Not only did we enjoy the meals, the tailgating, the bourbon, and hearing thousands sing Stephen Foster's *My Old Kentucky Home*, but we also enjoyed watching the *Wildcats* double up on LSU. It was also our first introduction to coach Mark Stoops and quarterback Will Levis, and based on the rumblings of the LSU fans seated behind us, it was not surprising LSU's head coach—Ed Orgeron—was let go after the season.

The following year, after Dan got the itch to see TCU, the guys traveled to Fort Worth, Texas, to watch the *Horned Frogs* battle it out with Kansas State, and for the first time, we were joined by my son-in-law—Austin. What a great addition to the guy trips! And what a game it was—and what a team we saw. Although the *Horned Frogs* were down early, they came back and won the game 38-28. The ragtag team, with first-year coach Sonny Dykes, made improbable wins a weekly occurrence. A few weeks after we visited the *Lone Star* State, the magic of quarterback Max Duggan, whose personal comeback story is as improbable as the team itself, was on full display as he rallied his team in the fourth quarter against Baylor. The frantic sprint by the field goal unit onto the field, along with the winning field goal as time expired, was a harbinger that the team had a date with destiny.

This trip also introduced us to a player who would ultimately have a date with destiny for the entire *Buckeye Nation.* The starting quarterback for Kansas State—Adrian Martinez—was banged up on the second drive of the game and was replaced by the backup quarterback—Will Howard. The backup—a third-year quarterback who had not played since Martinez transferred from Nebraska—threw for two touchdowns and ran for another in the losing cause. We all commented at the time, "That kid looks pretty darn good." Turns out, we were right! He's pretty darn good!

While in Texas, we not only enjoyed the Fort Worth Stockyards—where we managed to watch a little bull riding—but also savored steaks at *H3 Ranch* and pre-game burgers, fries, and shakes at *Dutch's*. Later, during the Christmas break, together with our TCU PJs, Daniel, Austin, Uncle Frank, and I watched the *Horned Frogs* one last Houdini act as they managed to beat our bitter rivals up North and earned a place in the National Championship game. Unfortunately, our Ohio State PJs did not have the same allure later that same evening and, although Georgia absolutely punished the *Horned Frogs* in the final game, we still believed in TCU. Simply put, we "*All Hail Hypnotoad*."

In 2023, the gang traveled to Tallahassee, Florida, to watch the Florida State *Seminoles* go to war with the Duke *Blue Devils*. Our second venture into the *ACC* was a matchup between two top 20 teams, with Duke ranked 16th in the country and the undefeated *Seminoles* ranked 4th. Duke, behind quarterback Riley Leonard, took a 20-17 lead into halftime. However, after Leonard was knocked out of the game, Florida State ultimately pulled away in the fourth quarter behind quarterback Jordan Travis. Leonard was one tough competitor, and, at the time, little did we know we would see him play again on an even bigger stage. Before the game, Daniel had his picture taken with Chief Osceola, the Florida State Marching Band, and the Florida State Cheerleaders, creating our newest classic shots for the photo album. We were all mesmerized when the Chief, high atop his white spotted Appaloosa horse named *Renegade*, rode to midfield with a burning spear and planted it into the turf. Of course, a trip to watch the *Seminoles* would not be complete without the Florida State war chant, best known as the "Tomahawk Chop." Surprisingly, our elbows never tired as it is performed relentlessly, and watching nearly 80,000 fans chant in unison never grew old. The trip was also our first venture into the world of Airbnb and Vrbo, which proved to be another great addition to our trips. Friday night dinner found us at *Savour,* on E.

Park Avenue, for another excellent meal, and on our walk to dinner, at a hotel right next door to our destination, we happened upon the *Blue Devils* football team, who, much like us, were in the process of their Friday night pre-game rituals.

In the end, things turned sideways for Florida State a few weeks after we visited *Doak S. Campbell Stadium* when Jordan Travis suffered a season-ending knee injury in a game against North Alabama. Things then became downright controversial as the 4th-ranked and undefeated Seminoles, who managed to eke out a 16-6 win over Louisville in the ACC Championship game, were left out of the College Football Playoffs. A few weeks later, Georgia obliterated Florida State 63-3 in the Orange Bowl. It was the biggest blowout in bowl game history, seemingly validating the decision to leave Florida State out of the playoffs. However, it also opened a Pandora's box as many players for the *Seminoles* had opted out of the game, thereby leaving fans on both sides and throughout the nation with a dud of a contest in Miami.

Indeed, many questions now linger about the need for traditional Bowl games, especially in the world of an expanded playoff and around players opting out of their final games. Furthermore, the NIL rule changes that allow college athletes to profit from their name, image, or likeness have already resulted in money being thrown around like a millionaire's convention in Monte Carlo. As for the transfer portal, buckle up, as we are all about to take a ride with *Hahn Solo* and *Chewbacca* on the *Millennium Falcon*, and when the celebrated starship finally hits hyperdrive, there is no telling what universe we might find ourselves in.

Our next planned trip (as of this writing) has us packing our bags and heading off to Manhattan—Manhattan, Kansas, that is. We can't wait to see the Kansas State *Wildcats* battle the Oklahoma State *Cowboys* in "The Little Apple," especially since we will be joined by our favorite long snapper—Kasey Kelleher—for our annual pre-game dinner.

Speaking about our favorite long snapper, recently, when I caught up with Kasey, I asked him if any games stood out to him and, of course, he had many vivid memories about the *Red River Rivalry* games against Texas at the Cotton Bowl in Dallas, and many other *Big 12* games for that matter. Clearly, he had a great deal of respect for these teams, their programs, and their fans. Kansas State, he said, was an especially tough place to play as the fans brought a great deal of energy, and he always loved looking up at Baylor's stadium from field level. Of course, he left his greatest praise for the Oklahoma program and its fans. He also has great respect for his fellow long-snappers, including the young men he battled with to become the starter for the *Sooners*. Much like a fraternity, regardless of campus, these players share a common craft and are brethren for life. Kelleher also enjoyed the three games (Baylor, West Virginia, and Kent State) that Dan attended. Good answer, Kasey. However, one game really stood out to him, and it was coming back home to his home state during his freshman year, when he beat the *Buckeyes* in *The Horseshoe*. Somehow, I'm not surprised.

So, where to go next? Only the notebooks know. As for Notre Dame, Texas, Florida, Mississippi State, Vanderbilt, Missouri, Oregon, Iowa, Nebraska, Wisconsin, Washington, Minnesota, USC, Purdue, Indiana, Illinois, Maryland, Michigan State, Northwestern, Rutgers, UCLA, California, Duke, Georgia Tech, Louisville, Pittsburgh, SMU, Stanford, Syracuse, Virginia, Virginia Tech, Wake Forest, North Carolina, North Carolina State, Miami, Boston College, Utah, Oklahoma State, Baylor, Iowa State, West Virginia, Arizona, Arizona State, BYU, Cincinnati, Houston, Colorado, Kansas, Texas Tech, UCF, Army, Navy, Airforce, Oregon State, Washington State, Appalachian State (still love y'all, and you know why), James Madison, or any of the other 100+ Division I football programs, we hope to see you soon. Given these numbers, it might be tough, and I'm reminded of one of Dad's favorite lines: "Hey, I've been doing the math, and we might need to start doubling up the guy trips." Regardless, we intend to do our best and if we do manage to pull it off, we will move on to all the outstanding programs in Division II. Lastly, although Penn State and

Michigan are tough sells, especially for my brother and me, give us your best shot. We are all ears, as even if we are not crazy about your team, we don't doubt the beauty and significance of your traditions, as true rivalry, in the end, is built on mutual respect.

Not surprisingly, over the years, I've been asked about our favorite game. A common refrain goes something like this: "Jim, if you could pick just one trip and see one game, where would it be?" This is difficult to answer, as each place was charming and each game enthralling in its own way. This is not an excuse for this legitimate and expected query, promise. We loved them all. We really have. The moments shared are all equally cherished, but I do obviously long for the days spent with my father. However, without hesitation, I can share my favorite part of our trips, and I also have a clear second choice. So here goes.

My favorite part of our trips was—and still is — our Friday night dinners. Although it's difficult to articulate, let me try. First, the dinners represent the first part of our trips, so, of course, they are on Friday nights. In other words, the whole weekend is still ahead of us. Not surprisingly, for the exact opposite reason, my least favorite part of our trips is inevitably our flight home. I am willing to bet I am not alone, as hardly anyone enjoys the end of a much-anticipated and well-deserved vacation. The Monday blues that follow are real and can be devastating! Another thing I appreciate is the anticipation of the upcoming game and the unknown experiences that await the gang. Put another way, I've always enjoyed Christmas Eve a little more than Christmas Day. Does that make sense? If you prefer tearing into the wrapping, you might find this odd. However, if you are still unsure, I'd like to offer you this visual to see if it might sway you. Imagine the tree with gifts wrapped below. Now, picture what it looks like the moment you've finished opening all the gifts. The first picture, in my mind, is an image untouched. Have I made my point?

Another reason our dinners are easy to love is that we pick top-notch places to eat, drink, and be merry. Quality food and service, paired with great company, make for a remarkable time. It's simple math. Try it. You get the same answer every time.

Lastly, and I believe, most importantly, the Friday night dinner experience is not alone. We share it with countless others. A typical Friday night dinner in a college town before a home game is truly something to behold. Imagine a wedding—without line dancing and that awkward speech from the Best Man—or an airport reunion for those old enough to remember when you were allowed to wait by the gates. For the younger crowd, you really missed out but try to picture an airport reunion near the baggage conveyor. Every table is filled with friends and family. Many are long-time acquaintances, with some reunited for the first time in years. Hugs, laughter, and gigantic smiles abound. The jubilation is contagious. Tears of joy flow like drink orders, and alumni groups are more prevalent than appetizers. Families, dressed head to toe in the local team's apparel, fill large tables, sometimes with multiple generations represented. It is Christmas Eve for everyone. Regardless of what game, they are all an informal Homecoming. Some tables find parents seated with their college-aged children. Eager to hear stories about campus life, they are also more than happy to pick up another college tab. Sometimes I find myself gawking and realize others are doing the same with us. Catching eyes, you simply smile and nod. They know how good it is. To quote one of my favorite Queen songs, *"It's a kind of magic,"* and it is meant to be shared.

My second favorite part of the trip is the pre-game festivities. Take everything, as I have said before, but throw in a little more alcohol and a healthy dose of adrenaline. Now blend it with a helping of nervous energy. Unlike a fancy restaurant, you can use your "outdoor voice here." Yelling is common and nobody is mad—at least not yet. The music is also louder, with the marching band taking center stage as it should be. The excitement grows as the game draws near. It's still

Christmas Eve, but Santa's sleigh has been spotted by a pilot outside of LaGuardia. The stories here and the upcoming battle on the field are the source of legends. This is what tradition is made of.

For me, sharing Friday night dinners and pre-game festivities with the guys, especially my son, echoes an eternity. Thank you, Mom and Dad, for starting a football tradition that lives on to this day. It is now forever another small part of college football lore. As Dad would say, "That's way cool." I would also like to thank my brother John, Uncle Frank, Austin, and all the others who have joined us along the way for enriching Daniel's life. I am eternally grateful.

Epilogue

On January 20, 2025—an especially cold and blustery evening in Atlanta, Georgia—we were on hand to watch the Ohio State *Buckeyes* defeat the Notre Dame *Fighting Irish* 34-23, winning the College Football National Championship. It was an improbable run through a gauntlet of mighty opponents in the first-ever 12-team playoff. Equally unlikely, was watching two quarterbacks—Will Howard and Riley Leonard—whom we had seen play on different teams on previous guy trips—battle it out. Buried in our pockets were our lucky *buckeyes*, side by side, with poker chips, inscribed with: *"Do Right-The Stallings Standard,"* in honor of the legendary coach and recently released documentary. These were given to us as a gift by the filmmakers during our visit to the University of Alabama in Tuscaloosa earlier that day. This gesture would not only ensure that we would continue to carry these charms in our pockets, but the guy trips, and our Ohio State *Buckeyes*, would now be forever bound together.

When the final whistle blew, Daniel looked up at the dome ceiling towards the sky and said, "Grandpa, I sure do love you." As for my brother and me, we looked at each other and said in unison, "They go; we go."

Afterword

Wandering through *The Grove* at Ole Miss, much like children gazing at a Christmas display, I can recall our wonder and amazement. I can also remember something our father seemingly said in jest. Dad turned to Daniel, my brother, and me and said, "When you get to Heaven, if you can't find me right away, come look for me here in *The Grove*." Dad, we will. We promise. However, we know full well that when we step off that plane, like in the days of old, you will be waiting for us at the gate. For my friends, family, and those who read these words, if it's a Friday night during the college football season—or any other time—please stop by our table and say hello. We would love to chat with you. It will only add to the magic and if you don't meet us at our Friday night dinner or in this season of life, you know where to find us on a Saturday afternoon. Come look for us in *Our Grove*.

Glossary of Terms

One of the reasons I wrote this book was to share my family's love of college football. While some readers might be entirely immersed in football, I understand that others may not be. This list is a quick reference for anyone new to or unfamiliar with this world. I've also thrown in a few words or terminology that I've used in this writing, including a few soccer (the other "football") terms. If you were previously a "newbie," welcome aboard. We are glad to have you! Also, if you ever find yourself in England, check out a *Premier League* football match. You will be happy you did, even if some of the language you hear might be a bit colorful.

Anfield. A stadium in Liverpool, England, for Liverpool Football Club (F.C.).

Arsenal. The Arsenal Football Club—commonly known as simply Arsenal. The team is based in North London, England. Their nickname is *The Gunners.*

Avengers. A team of superheroes originally appearing in American comic books published by *Marvel Comics.* Besides comics, the *Avengers* have appeared in multiple movies.

Backfield. This is the area behind the offensive line, where the quarterback and the running backs (sometimes called halfbacks, fullbacks, or just backs) are located.

Big 10. A collegiate athletic conference that was historically based in the Midwestern region. Today, the conference is comprised of 18 teams, spans from coast to coast, and is referred to as the *B1G.*

Big 12. A collegiate athletic conference that consists of 16 full-member universities (3 private and 13 public universities).

Bitter (Bitters). A traditional British style of Ale, known for its hoppy and bitter flavor.

Both feet down. In college football, a receiver must have at least one foot in bounds for a valid catch. In the NFL, a receiver must have both feet in bounds for it to be a valid catch.

Buckeye Nation. The collective identity and spirit of The Ohio State University and its fans encompass the traditions, pride, and community associated with being a "Buckeye."

Dotting the i. The Ohio State University Marching Band's tradition in Script Ohio, where a sousaphone player or, in rare cases, a non-band member, stands as the dot in the "i" in "Ohio." This is considered a great honor.

Dungeons & Dragons (D&D). A fantasy role-playing game created by Gary Gygax and Dave Arneson.

Dutch Orange Clockwork. Also known as "Clockwork Orange," this nickname refers to the fluid style of play employed by the 1974 Netherlands national football team. More recently, this term was featured in an episode of *Ted Lasso*, where Coach *Beard* became obsessed with unlocking the mystery of "total football."

Gridiron. A football field. Not to be confused with a pitch.

Horseshoe. It is a nickname for Ohio Stadium and the home of the Ohio State Football team. Another nickname is "The Shoe."

Iron Bowl. The annual college football rivalry game between the University of Alabama and Auburn University.

Marvel. *Marvel Comics* is a comic book publisher located in New York City and is now a property of the Walt Disney Company.

Mary Coyle. A candy and ice cream shop located in Akron, Ohio.

Michigan. See That Team Up North.

Old Ebbitt Grill. A restaurant in Washington, DC.

Pick. An interception.

Pitch. A soccer field. Not to be confused with the gridiron.

Premier League. A professional football (soccer) league in England, and the highest level of the English football league system. It consists of 20 clubs, which operate on a system of promotion and relegation with the English Football League (EFL)—England's second-highest league.

Receiver. Players tasked with catching passes from the quarterback.

Red River Rivalry. The rivalry football game between the University of Texas and the University of Oklahoma. The name originates from the Red River, which forms the border between the two states.

Redshirted. A delay in an athlete's participation to prolong their period of eligibility. Typically, a student's eligibility in a given sport is four years.

Safety. A defensive score resulting in two points.

SEC. The Southeastern Conference (SEC) is a collegiate athletic conference located primarily in the South Central and Southeastern United States.

Shotgun. In football, this refers to an offensive alignment where the quarterback stands a few yards behind the center, receiving the snap through the air rather than directly from the center at the line of scrimmage.

Special Teams. The players on the field during kicking plays, like kickoffs, punts, and field goals. This would include kick returners and punt returners.

That Team Up North. Michigan. More specifically, the University of Michigan. Ohio State Coach Woody Hayes first used this term to acknowledge the intense rivalry between the schools. Interestingly, Bo Schembechler, another significant part of this rivalry as the head coach of the Michigan football team, was from Barberton, Ohio, and played football at Miami University of Ohio under Woody Hayes. He was also an assistant coach for several Ohio teams, including Bowling Green and Miami University of Ohio, and under Woody Hayes at Ohio State. Despite their bitter rivalry on the football field, the two men remained close friends.

The Big House. It is a nickname for Michigan Stadium and the home of the University of Michigan football team.

Touchback. Typically, if the ball is kicked out of bounds in the end zone, then the ball is placed at the 25-yard line in college football.

Turnover. When the team in possession of the ball loses it to the opposing team, typically through a fumble or interception.

Walk-on. A player who joins the team without a scholarship. This is usually through an open tryout.

Whiteout in Happy Valley. The Penn State football tradition involves fans wearing white to the game in Happy Valley, Pennsylvania.

You'll Never Walk Alone. A song played before home games at Anfield, for Liverpool Football Club (F.C.). The version played was released in 1963 by *Gerry and the Pacemakers*.

Acknowledgements

First and foremost, I would like to tip my hat to those who have a tender heart for those who are different and those who are hurting. He sees you, even if you are invisible to others. As for me, on behalf of my family, I would like to thank the many teachers, aides, specialists, administrators, therapists, physicians, nurses, neonatologists, oncologists, researchers, inventors, and hospice professionals. You were by our side when we needed you most. The same is true for our many incredible friends. Specifically mentioned in these pages or not—Thank you all!

One day, while chatting with my son-in-law—Austin—about our next potential guy trip, he told me, "You really should write a book about these trips." So, there you have it. That's how it all started. A few months later, I called my marvelous publishing partner—Libby Jordan—and asked if she would return to the fray with me again. Thankfully, she said "yes," even if it ultimately meant her having to contemplate my exact placement of thousands of commas. Also joining the team again is Danna Steele from d*early creative,* who, much like her first go around with *A Chance to Breathe,* has given me another aesthetically beautiful creation. Hopefully, the words within do it justice.

As always, a huge thanks to my immediate family. Just so you know, I might be done, but probably not. I'd also like to thank two friends—John York and Rich. Before other souls, you dared to look at my scribbles and hear my thoughts. Additional thanks to my daughter—Claire—for her technical support. Her father went a little crazy on the space bar. Or so he's been told.

To Leza and Jen, I owe you a great deal of gratitude. You regularly held down the fort while I banged out words from my porch. One day, when my eyes were hurting, my "little sisters" let me borrow theirs. Thank you for all your help both on and off the field. I would also like to thank my colleagues in the legal world. My juggling act was made easier by your courtesy and professionalism.

A special thanks to *The Beer Club for Men*. Your weekly encouragement to write (and have a second beer) was much needed, especially when I was thirsty. As for Doc and Harry, we miss your beautiful minds. We are forever survivors. I would also thank my "*Monday Night Friends.*" Your love of God is contagious. "Be the yeast!" Of course, I would be remiss if I did not also thank *The Capstone Business Alliance* and my Thursday morning breakfast crew. We will get Russ and Tony on the next cover, pinky promise. Along these same lines, I'd like to thank my business network in South Carolina. You have welcomed this Yankee like one of your own. It has not gone unnoticed. Furthermore, I'd like to thank my soccer mates, past and present. We may not have won them all, but we had fun trying to win a few.

In order of our trips, I would like to thank: the University of South Carolina, the University of Arkansas, the University of Mississippi, Louisiana State University, Texas A&M University, the University of Georgia, Auburn University, the University of Alabama, the University of Oklahoma, Clemson University, the University of Tennessee, Texas Christian University, Florida State University (our thoughts and prayers are with you), Kansas State University, the University of Kentucky, and the University of West Virginia. The same is true for all your fans. Y'all are the best! Along these lines, a note of appreciation goes to Columbia, South Carolina; Fayetteville, Arkansas; Oxford, Mississippi; Baton Rouge, Louisiana; College Station, Texas; Athens, Georgia; Auburn, Alabama; Tuscaloosa, Alabama; Oklahoma City, Oklahoma; Norman, Oklahoma; Greenville, South Carolina; Clemson, South Carolina; Knoxville, Tennessee; Fort Worth, Texas; Tallahassee, Florida; Manhattan, Kansas; Lexington, Kentucky, and Morgantown, West Virginia. I hope I have properly shared your stories.

Dr. Chandra Clark and Dr. Michael Bruce (creators of the documentary *Do Right-The Stallings Standard*) also deserve praise, not only for their movie—which captures the legacy of Coach Gene Stallings—but also for their delightful welcome on a brisk morning in Tuscaloosa. Your impromptu tour of the University of Alabama shows that Southern hospitality is more than a slogan, and helping me out on a separate, more personal mission will always be cherished.

One specific teacher from my high school deserves my belated acknowledgement. Mrs. Smith, I'm sorry I didn't listen to you more carefully, especially during your grammar lessons! Also, I finally understand why you had us read William Faulkner. I hope to chat with you about him again one day, but until then, rest in peace.

Lastly, many thanks to college football. Yes, you are flawed, but aren't we all?

Further Reading

Adams, John A. Jr. *Standing Ready: The Golden Era of Texas Aggie Football and the Beginning of the 12th Man Tradition.* College Station: Texas A&M University Press, 2022.

Anderson, Lars. *Chasing the Bear: How Bear Bryant and Nick Saban made Alabama the Greatest College Football Program of all Time.* New York: Grand Central Publishing, 2019.

Bain-Selbo, Eric. *Game Day and God: Football, Faith, and Politics in the American South.* Macon, Georgia: Mercer University Press, 2009.

Bevere, John. *The Bait of Satan: Living Free from the Deadly Trap of Offense.* Lake Mary, Florida: Charisma House, 1994, 1997, 2014.

Brown, Steven E. *Ed Roberts: Wheelchair Genius.* 2006; revised, the Institute on Disability Culture, 2015.

Brown, Timothy P. *How Football Became Football: 150 Years of the Game's Evolution.* West Bloomfield, Michigan: Brown House Publishing, 2020.

Buck, Pearl S. *The Child Who Never Grew: A Memoir.* New York: *Ladies' Home Journal.* 1950; reprint, Open Road Integrated Media, Inc., 2017.

Dugast, Aude. *Jérôme Lejeune: A Man of Science and Conscience.* 2019; Original French edition, San Francisco: Ignatius Press, 2021.

Dunnavant, Keith. *The 50 Year Seduction: How Television Manipulated College Football, from the Birth of the Modern NCAA to the Creation of the BCS.* New York: Thomas Dunne Books, 2004.

Dwyer, John J. *The Oklahomans: The Story of Oklahoma and Its People.* Norman, Oklahoma: Red River Press, 2016.

Eagles, Charles W. *The Price of Defiance: James Meredith and the Integration of Ole Miss.* Chapel Hill, North Carolina: The University of North Carolina Press, 2009.

Ehrmann, Joe. *InSideOut Coaching: How Sports Can Transform Lives.* New York: Simon & Schuster, 2011.

Evans-Rogers, Dale. *Angel Unaware: A Touching Story of Love and Loss.* Originally published 1953, 1981: Revell, 2004.

Evans, Suzanne E. *Forgotten Crimes: The Holocaust and People with Disabilities.* Chicago: Disability Rights Advocates, 2004.

Finebaum, Paul. *My Conference Can Beat Your Conference.* New York: HarperCollins Publishers, 2014.

Friedlander, Henry. *The Origins of Nazi Genocide: From Euthanasia to the Final Solution.* Chapel Hill, North Carolina: The University of North Carolina Press, 1995.

Fung, Jason Dr. *The Cancer Code: A Revolutionary Understanding of a Medical Mystery.* London: HarperCollins Publishers, 2020.

Gannon, Megan C. *Special Saints for Special People: Stories of Saints with Disabilities.* New London, CT.: Twenty-Third Publication, 2019.

Gubar, Justine. *Fanaticus: Mischief and Madness in the Modern Sports Fan.* Lanham, Maryland: Rowman & Littlefield, 2015.

Johnson, George. *The Cancer Chronicles: Unlocking Medicine's Deepest Mystery.* New York: Vintage Books, 2014.

Lang, Ron. *A Season of Homecomings: Living, Learning & Loving Every School in the SEC.* Ron Lang, 2020.

Lawrence, John & Hise, Dan. *Faulkner's Rowan Oak.* University Press of Mississippi, 1993.

Lejeune-Gaymard, Clara. *Life is a Blessing: A Biography of Jérôme Lejeune-Geneticist, Doctor, Father.* 1997; Original Publication; English Translation by Ignatius Press, San Francisco, 2000: Jérôme Lejeune Foundation, Paris, 2010.

Lesy, Michael. *Rescues: The Lives of Heroes.* New York: HarperCollins, 1991.

Marx, Jeffrey. *Season of Life: A Football Star, A Boy, a Journey to Manhood.* New York: Simon & Schuster, 2003.

—, Jeffrey. *The Long Snapper: A Second Chance, A Super Bowl, A Lesson for Life.* New York: HarperCollins, 2009.

McMahon, Sean & Valerie. *This Year's Game: One Couple's Annual Pursuit of College Football Rivalry & Revelry.* St. Helens, Oregon: Slip of Paper Publishing, LLC., 2019.

Millard, Candice. *Destiny of the Republic: A Tale of Madness, Medicine and the Murder of a President.* New York: Doubleday, 2011.

Mukherjee, Siddhartha. *The Emperor of All Maladies: A Biography of Cancer.* New York: Simon & Schuster, 2010.

Nelson, Jon. *A History of College Football in Georgia: Glory on the Gridiron.* Charleston, South Carolina: The History Press, 2012.

Nielson, Kim E. *A Disability History of the United States.* Boston: Beacon Press, 2012.

Oriard, Michael. *Reading Football: How the Popular Press Created an American Spectacle.* Chapel Hill, North Carolina: The University of North Carolina Press, 1993.

Parini, Jay. *One Matchless Time: A Life of William Faulkner.* New York: HarperCollins, 2004.

Simons, Eric. *The Secret Lives of Sports Fans: The Science of Sports Obsession.* New York: The Overlook Press, 2013.

Stallings, Gene. *Another Season: A Coach's Story of Raising an Exceptional Son.* Boston: Little, Brown & Company, 1997.

Wann, Daniel L.; Melick, Merrill J.; Russell, Gordon W.; Pease, Dale G. *Sport Fans: The Psychology and Social Impact of Spectators.* New York: Routledge, 2001.

Weinreb, Michael. *Season Saturdays: A History of College Football in 14 Games.* New York: Simon & Schuster, 2014.

Wright, David. *Downs: A History of a Disability.* Oxford: Oxford University Press, 2011.

Wright, Steve. *Aggressively Human: Discovering Humanity in the NFL, Reality TV, and Life.* Virginia Beach, Virginia: Koehler Books, 2023.

About the Author

James Gardner received his B.A. from *The* Ohio State University and his J.D. from Case Western Reserve University. As a practicing lawyer for more than thirty years, Jim is a passionate advocate for the disabled and those who have been injured. Penned as a love letter to his family and to the "guy trips," *Finding Our Grove* is his second book. When not watching college football, he and his son are planning their next adventure and can't wait to see you soon!

www.ingramcontent.com/pod-product-compliance
Lightning Source LLC
LaVergne TN
LVHW100507110826
845146LV00002B/549

* 9 7 9 8 9 8 8 4 9 5 7 2 7 *